Jeweled Splendors of the Art Deco Era

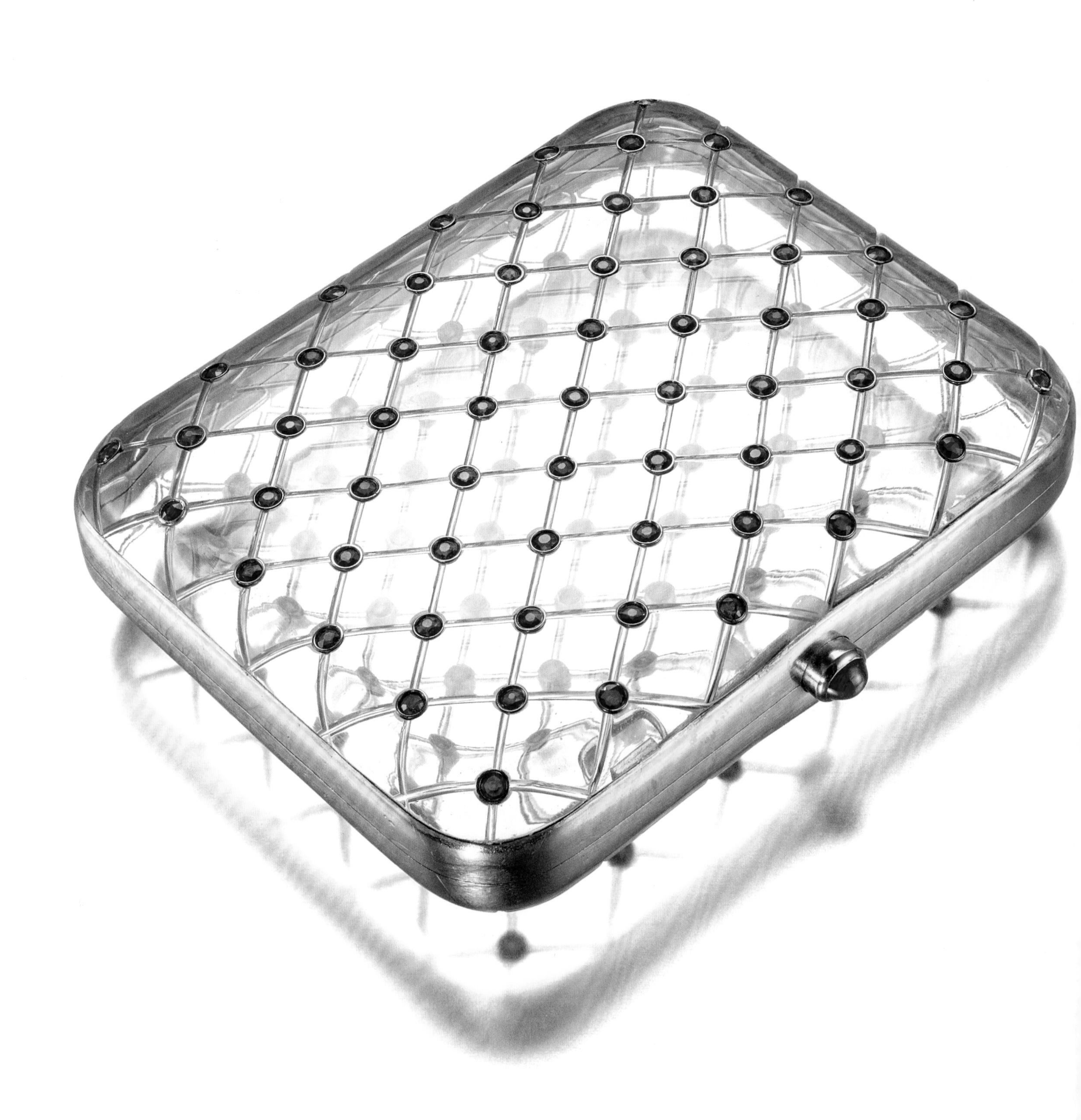

Jeweled Splendors of the Art Deco Era

The Prince and Princess Sadruddin Aga Khan Collection

Foreword by **Princess Catherine Aga Khan**

Introduction by **Pierre Rainero**

Essays by **Evelyne Possémé, Stephen Harrison, and Sarah D. Coffin**

Catalogue and Afterword by **Sarah Davis**

Cartier Paris

Contents

When I was a young girl in Alexandria, I collected photographs of American movie stars, which I stored in old biscuit tins. I never dreamed that one day I would be the owner of a seriously important collection of something quite different and that collecting would become such a passion of mine.

Early on, I developed an interest in rare books and their beautiful bindings. And then, one Christmas Eve, my husband Sadruddin gave me a magnificent jeweled box made by Cartier in the 1930s.

Thereafter, for Sadruddin it seemed that any occasion was an opportunity for him to present me with a new piece for the collection. I imagined him viewing them all, admiring them, and picking them out just for me. Each had a personality of its own and each was more richly colored and imaginative than the last. They were created by the greatest French jewelers of the high period between 1925 and 1935: Cartier, Van Cleef & Arpels, Bulgari, Boucheron, Lacloche, and many others. With the boxes came exquisite clocks that were equally varied and magical, even though they were seldom used to record the passing hours.

Those passing hours were the happiest of my life. So, when at last I decided to part with the collection, it was with the certainty that it could make others as happy as I had been and that the magic contained in these works of art would go with them wherever they went. With a long, last look of love and gratitude, I imagined them ending their stay at Bellerive entirely happy, ready to carry their beauty to people who would love and treasure them, just as I had done.

Catherine Aga Khan

Princess Catherine and Prince Sadruddin Aga Khan in a photograph announcing their marriage, 1972.

A Van Cleef & Arpel's "Aubergine Motif" cigarette case from 1927, an anniversary gift engraved with an inscription from Prince Sadruddin to Princess Catherine: "Kate happy 25th, dearest love – S. 25.11.97." [50]

Introduction

Pierre Rainero

A man of extraordinary taste and culture, Prince Sadruddin Aga Khan, with his wife, Catherine, assembled a collection of 116 works created by the greatest jewelers in Paris. In this exceptional collection, gathered over many years, Cartier holds a special place. The majority of *nécessaires*, cigarette cases, and timepieces, including two rare *pendules mystérieuses*, which constitute this princely collection, came from the Cartier Paris workshops, founded in 1847. Prince Sadruddin Aga Khan is an emblematic figure in the meeting of East and West, and as a collector was aware of the aesthetic dialogue between the two cultures given new form by Cartier in the 1920s and 1930s. A careful look at the Cartier pieces in the collection reveals the great sources of inspirations that marked the creations of the time.

For the three grandsons of the founder—Louis (1875–1942), Pierre (1878–1964), and Jacques (1884–1941)—Chinese, Indian, and Persian worlds were fertile terrain to draw inspiration from. The designers were told to explore the library of rare illustrated books assembled by Louis Cartier and familiarize themselves with the original iconography of these distant lands. Compared with the small surfaces available on traditional jewelry, the broad surfaces presented by *nécessaires* and cigarette cases offered ideal presentation for new interpretations of these distant motifs. The Cartier pieces in the collection of Prince Sadruddin display eloquent examples of *botehs*, leafy arabesques, floral patterns, dragons, and carp; each of these creations has its own language and was carefully chosen by the collector.

Louis Cartier's library was supplemented by a collection of objects, purchased from Parisian dealers that gave material form to these countries. The objects include Egyptian faience, carved jade from the Qing dynasty, Japanese inro, and Persian miniatures. This last group was well known to Prince Sadruddin because some of the Persian miniatures in his own collection came from Louis Cartier's collection. (The 1998 book and exhibition from the British Museum, *Princes, Poets and Paladins: Islamic and Indian Paintings from the Collection of Prince and Princess Sadruddin Aga Khan*, display some of his extraordinary art collection.) The motifs of Persian bookbindings were thus taken as models by the jewelers, who transcribed in colored enamel the gilded motifs they saw pressed into the leather.

Louis Cartier opened his collection of objects to his designers, encouraging them to use motifs and sometimes embedding objects from it within modern compositions. These unique pieces constitute an original facet of the history of jewelry. One very rare 1929 *pendule mystérieuse* features two carved nephrite lions, originally Chinese; these serve as a base for a citrine dial [100]. This masterpiece of the clockmaker's craft belongs to a series of fourteen timepieces, made by Cartier between 1922 and 1930, featuring antique animals or figurines.

The original design drawings for the Imperial Guardian Lion mystery clock, Cartier Paris Archives, 1929. Cartier Paris Archives

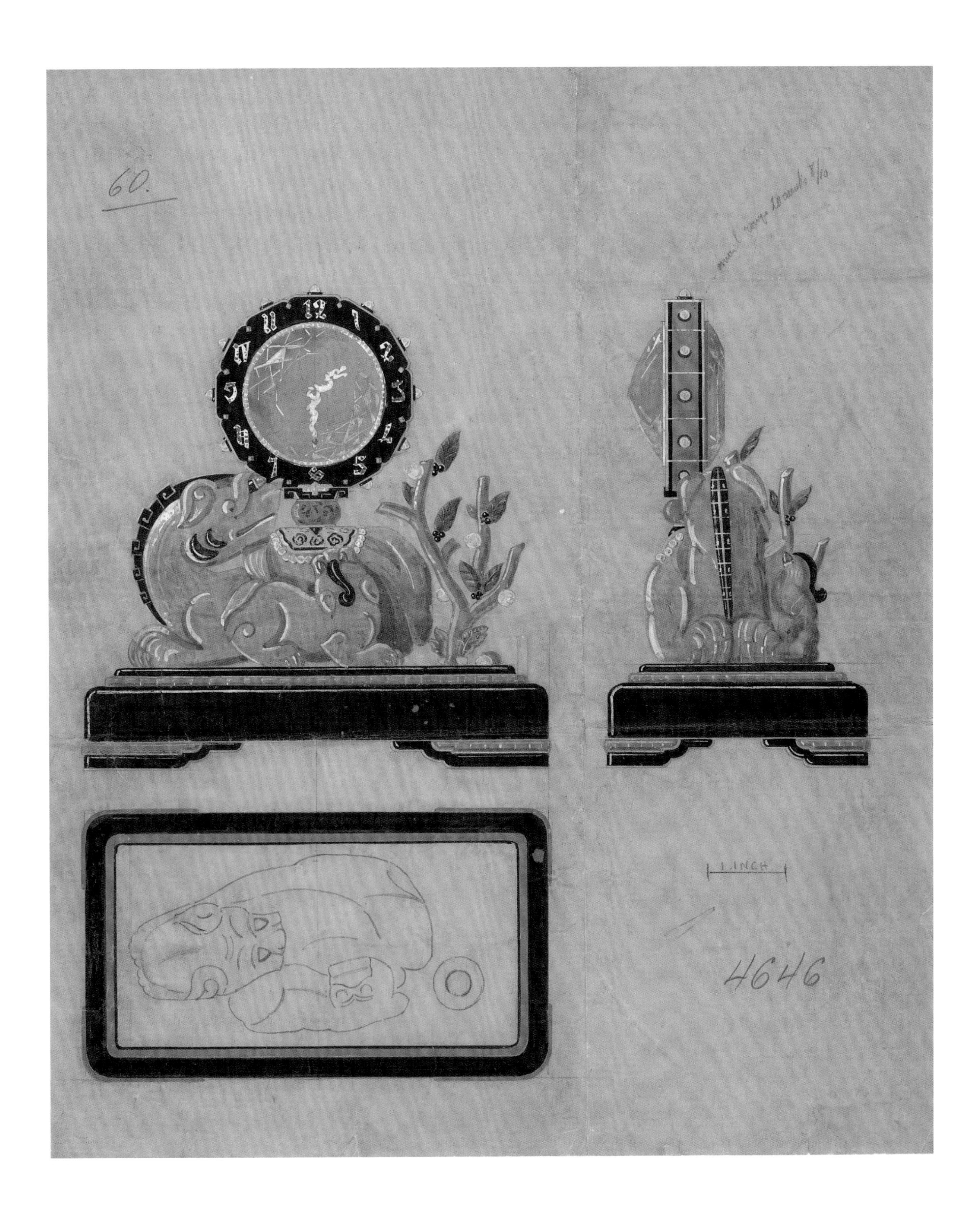
60.
1 INCH
4646

Sir Sultan Mahomed Shah Aga Khan III, Prince Sadruddin's father. Photograph by Elliott & Fry

Opposite:
Princess Andrée, the Begum Aga Khan, Prince Sadruddin Aga Khan's mother, wearing the Halo Tiara, a diadem of Egyptian inspiration in platinum and diamonds, created by Cartier in 1934.

The curiosity of the Cartier brothers led them to travel widely. Jacques, who headed the London branch from 1906, visited the Persian Gulf and India in 1911, meeting many of the Indian princes, including His Highness Mahomed Shah Aga Khan III, the father of Prince Sadruddin. On his Indian travels, Jacques Cartier bought a number of magnificent emeralds, sapphires, and carved rubies from local merchants. From his encounter with the East stemmed a new aesthetic, as exemplified in the pieces selected by Prince Sadruddin. On a 1925 onyx *nécessaire*, engraved rubies and emeralds outline the foliage of a cypress tree, a cherished motif in Islamic art [80]. The same tree appears on another *nécessaire* made in the same year, which depicts an enameled panther in a garden of cypresses and blossoming fruit trees. In 1914, the first panther jewel, a watch, evoked the coat of the animal with onyx and diamonds; by the 1920s, the Cartier panther took a two-dimensional form on *nécessaires*. This piece is a fine example: beyond the panther, in the background, a ruby cabochon evokes the sun, discarding any pretense of realism in favor of the gem's rich hue [6]. In the twenties, Cartier took daring liberties with color codes. For instance, they unhesitatingly matched blue, green, and orange (in duos and trios) for another very beautiful *nécessaire* in the collection, one that blends lapis lazuli marquetry and carved jade outlined with a fillet of coral and diamonds, the whole depicting an undulating cloud motif [99]. The prince, an enlightened connoisseur, with an understanding of this dimension in Cartier's history, has clearly identified the importance of these pieces.

The relationship between Cartier and the prince's family is a rich one that goes back a long way. In Cartier's Paris archives, which have been kept at their rue de la Paix premises since 1899, there is mention in 1902 of Mahomed Shah Aga Khan III's first purchase. This was a diamond corsage, in the Garland Style popular at the turn of the century, with a central gem cut in the shape of a heart. Orders followed for other important pieces in a similar vein, such as tiaras and necklaces. In the 1920s and 1930s, the Art Deco creations attracted the Aga Khan's attention, as did pieces inspired by India. A shared aesthetic thread runs between father and son. The imprint of the Aga Khan is visible on several of the great stylistic creations in Cartier's history. One of these was a superb Art Deco collar exhibited at the International Exhibition in Barcelona in 1929, composed of diamonds provided by the Aga Khan. In 1931, one of these diamonds, a forty-carat gem, was recorded in Cartier's London archives, as part of a collar made for Prince Ali Khan, again demonstrating the link between the jeweler and the family in both London and Paris. In 1934, the Aga Khan acquired an original head ornament—known as a Halo Tiara—made by the London atelier for his wife HH Begum Andrée Aga Khan, the mother of Prince Sadruddin. The tiara, inspired by ancient Egypt, is composed of a band adorned with zigzags and decorated with stylized lotus flowers and buds. Today, this is one of the iconic pieces in the Cartier Collection, which includes over fifteen hundred pieces of historic jewelry, watches, clocks, and precious objects assembled by Cartier since 1983.

It is no surprise that Prince Sadruddin has sought out great works of art, given that the same is true of his family. To contemplate the Cartier pieces side by side with the work of other contemporary jewelers in the collection enriches our reading of them all. It demonstrates to even greater effect the preeminence of a style that was unique to Cartier, in which a sense of proportion, line, and volume; an immaculate balance between decorative elements and their stylization; and a perfect mastery of the jeweler's craft combine to identify the definitive Cartier object. The Cartier object, in fact, is something exquisitely fashioned in the true line of *objets de vertu*, the memory of which is revived here by this extraordinary collection.

East and West:
Oriental Exoticism in the Decorative Arts

Evelyne Possémé

The term "exoticism" describes a multitude of outside influences, with which the arts in general—and the European decorative arts in particular—have been familiar since ancient times. It is known as "oriental" (from the Latin *orientalis,* eastern) because the lure of distant countries and civilizations had from antiquity been eastwards from Europe, as the west remained bounded by the Atlantic Ocean, until the discovery of the American continent by Christopher Columbus in 1492.

An idealized fantasy of the Orient fed the collective imagination of European artists for many centuries, despite the political, military, and commercial vagaries of history. In geographic terms, this instinctive, almost unwitting discovery of a different world was first made by way of the land routes from the Middle and Far East. The Eastern civilizations revealed themselves only gradually, according to their antiquity, their emergence as powers, or their isolation. China and the creations of China were the first and most lasting revelation; the more recent Islamic civilization of the Near East emerged in the seventh century CE and was effectively discovered for Europe by the eleventh-century Christian crusades. Japan, much more distant and impenetrable, took until the nineteenth century to make an impression, even though Japanese lacquers and porcelains had been brought to Europe by the various East India companies, often by way of China, as early as the seventeenth century.

The Western artistic imagination continued to be piqued by the East, despite the irregularity of commercial and political relations between the two. All these elements combined to fashion the personality of Prince Sadruddin Aga Khan, brought up between France and the Middle East, who over a lifetime assembled an extraordinary collection of boxes and clocks that testifies to the aesthetic and artistic wonder generated by this age-old cultural collision.

Original stock card, Van Cleef & Arpels, Paris, 1930.

Europe and the East

The spell cast by the Orient over Westerners began with the conquests of Alexander the Great, whose armies advanced to the steppes of Central Asia and the banks of the Indus, to arrive at the outer limits of East Asia. Alexander's military conquests were ephemeral, but the cultural and commercial links they engendered remained in place. In the first century BCE, the Greeks and Chinese were in contact by land and sea; most notably through the silk trade, the Chinese being the sole contemporary masters of silkworm cultivation and silk manufacture. The subsequent barbarian invasions, followed by the Arab conquest, closed the traditional land and sea routes for over a thousand years, but indirect exchanges continued by way of Persia and Syria. Emperor Justinian in Constantinople was concerned about this imbalance and attempted—without

1
Noble Hunt Vanity and Cigarette Case by Van Cleef & Arpels, Paris, 1930

success—to introduce silkworm culture in the Peloponnese. Nevertheless Byzantine art, with its motifs of dragons, phoenixes, and Chinese clouds, shows the survival of the Silk Road, even though the West remained ignorant of the Chinese golden age then under way. The period of the crusades brought Westerners back into direct physical contact with oriental luxury, and after that textiles and objects began to flow back to Europe, along with the plundered relics and treasures of Palestine.

The opening of the southern sea route around the Cape of Good Hope by the Portuguese explorer Vasco da Gama, followed by the halting of Ottoman expansion at Vienna in 1529 and 1683, led to a revival of East-West commercial relations. In the seventeenth century, Jesuit missions and a proliferation of East India companies—Dutch, British, and French—created a regular flow of the finest goods from India, China, and Japan. The appetite for such things was fed by numerous publications, including the late thirteenth-century *Travels of Marco Polo*. The earliest travelers' tales were text only until 1665, when Dutchman Johan Nieuhof published the story of his journey to the court of the Manchu emperor, illustrated with more than one hundred prints, most notably of the pagoda in Nanking and Peking's imperial palace. Nieuhof's book was a huge success and was reprinted again and again into the nineteenth century.

The term "chinoiserie," as applied to the decorative arts, dates from the nineteenth century, but it covers an array of motifs that were very widely utilized in the seventeenth and eighteenth centuries. Without any precise knowledge of the Asiatic countries, their inhabitants, or their products, the creators of chinoiseries made no distinction between Turkey, India, China, or Japan, muddling them together under the catchall title of the Indies. The same went for Ottoman Turkish, Persian, Indian, or Chinese motifs. In fact chinoiserie, as manifested during these two centuries, was a purely Western invention. The goods being imported at that time—porcelain, lacquer, gemstones, textiles, embroideries, and painted or printed fabrics—were hopelessly unequal to the demand and as a result were so expensive that only princes and aristocrats could afford them. This shortage of fine Eastern merchandise, coupled with the huge demand for it, caught the attention of European industrialists. The first Western-manufactured porcelain made its appearance in Germany (Meissen) and France (Limoges) at the beginning of the eighteenth century. Likewise the craze for Chinese and Japanese lacquered furniture led European cabinetmakers to research its manufacture, resulting in the invention of new

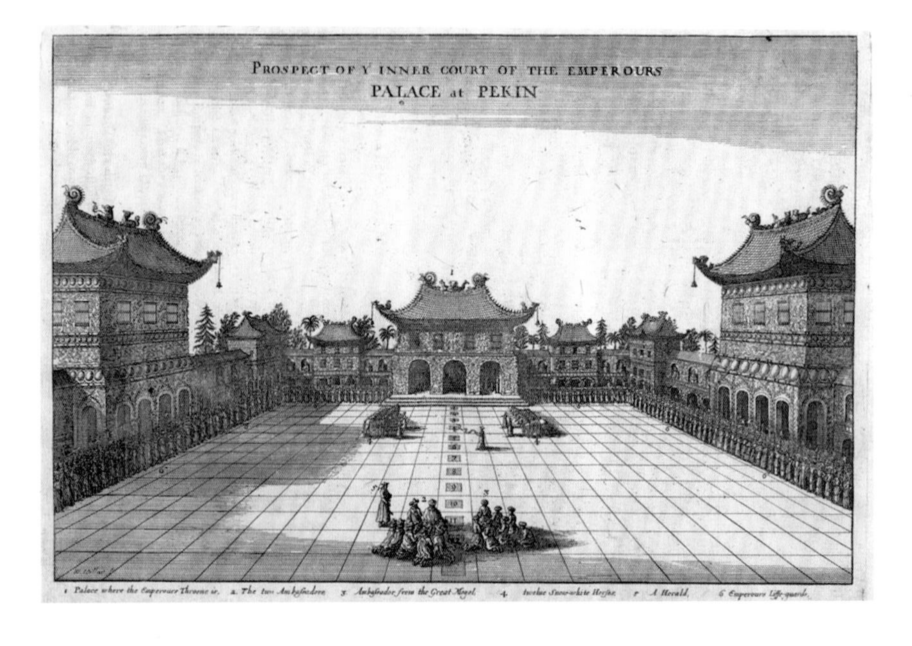

Johan Nieuhof, "Prospect of the Inner Court of the Emperor's Palace at Peking," 1665.

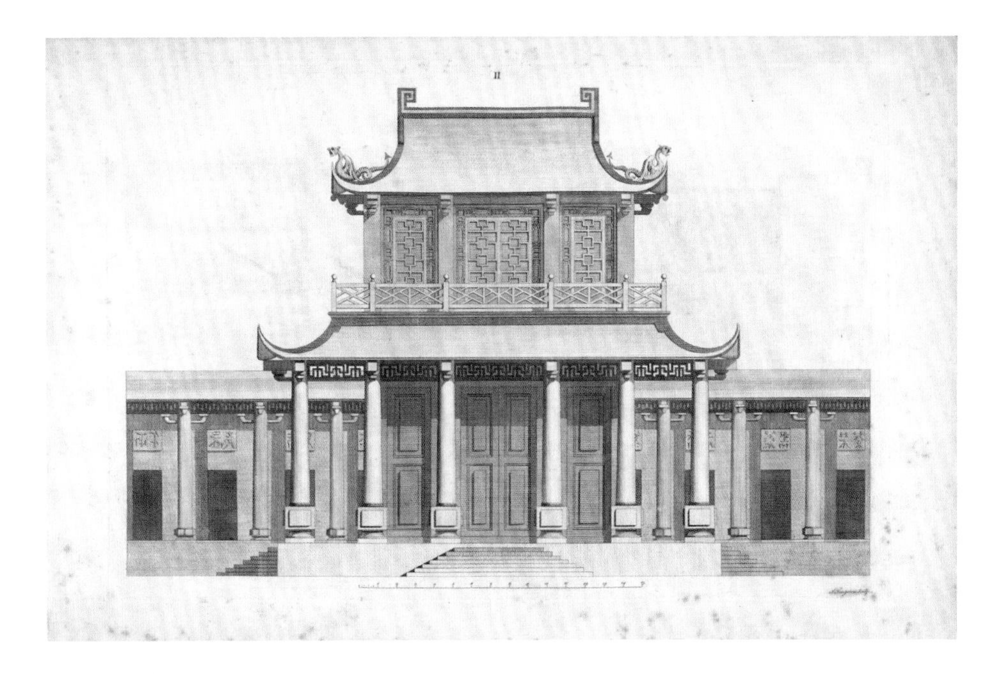

Plates from William Chambers's *Designs of Chinese Buildings, Furniture, Dresses, Machines, and Utensils,* 1757.

varnishes by pioneers like the Martin brothers in Paris. Japanese lacquer was a feature of the French collection of Cardinal Mazarin, which was later inherited by Louis XIV. The collection of Queen Marie Antoinette, for the most part passed on to her by her mother, the Archduchess Maria Theresa of Austria, is still famous. The imitation of oriental silks—the originals, known for their lightness and durability, had been carried to Europe in steadily growing quantities since the Middle Ages—suddenly blossomed into a brand new European industry. Italy had been inspired by oriental motifs such as mountains, dragons, phoenixes, vases, stars, and clouds since the late thirteenth century, and as early as the mid-fourteenth century, Lucca and Venice had been celebrated for textiles marrying the designs of Islamic and Far Eastern art with those of the West. The famous *indiennes,* printed cloths, were first imported in bulk by the British; later they were made at the Oberkampf factory at Jouy-en-Josas, near Paris, from designs by Jean Bérain and Jean Pillement. Chinese wallpapers were likewise much appreciated from the sixteenth century and a number of antique examples may still be seen in European museums. The curved line of furniture legs so distinctive of the French Regency and Louis XV styles originated with Chinese furniture of the Ming period that was imported by the Compagnie des Indes françaises starting in the early eighteenth century.

In 1755, William Chambers, a Scottish architect, published an account of his voyages to China with reproductions of Chinese buildings and furniture; this marked the beginning of a new era with more documentation and fewer flights of fancy. Chambers's models were widely copied in the second half of the eighteenth century by European craftsmen—hence the small cabinet in the Chinese style made by Pierre Garnier, recently acquired by the Musée des Arts décoratifs in Paris.

In the nineteenth century, oriental exoticism became one of the constituent elements of a new trend dubbed in France "*historicisme,*" with clearer and better-informed distinctions between the different countries and civilizations. For this, China was only one reference among a host of others and, from the start of the century, the importance of Middle Eastern and Islamic art began to grow more evident. The discovery of the Muslim aesthetic came through the recognition and subsequent study of the Alhambra in Granada and the Mezquita in Córdoba, which were the most magnificent surviving remains of the Muslim presence in Spain.

Romantic painters and writers discovered North Africa, focusing on its special light with thrilling scenes of hammams and seraglios. The steadily broadening scope of contemporary travel and the stories published by travelers, together with books about ornamentation, allowed artists to learn about a beauty different from that of classical antiquity. Their discovery spread around the Mediterranean basin from Spain to the Maghreb, from Egypt to the Middle East, and thence to the Ottoman Empire and finally Iran and Mughal India. By the turn of the twentieth century, museum exhibitions and publications provided a scientific approach to this art, and its close study, by which time artifacts in ceramic, glass, brass, carpets, textiles, and leather had already made their mark on the imagination of European artists. In 1907, the Iranian revolution brought Persian manuscripts and their miniatures to Europe, revealing the principal forms of art in countries where fresco and easel painting were completely unknown.

In 1855, the opening of Japan to international commerce led to the discovery of a highly original approach to art. Japanese prints and their special perspectives had a decisive influence, not only on the work of Impressionist painters but also in other domains of the decorative arts. Japanese porcelain was already familiar, but the 1867 Exposition universelle in Paris revealed to an astonished public the stoneware used in Japanese tea ceremonies, known as *cabossé* (dented) ceramic. Stoneware, sword hilts, inro, lacquers, and block printing were especially influential on European and especially French artists, including ceramicists, such as Ernest Chaplet, Paul Jeanneney,

Vitrine cabinet by Pierre Garnier, 1761.

Georges Hoentschel; brassworkers, such as Jean Dunand; jewelers, such as René Lalique, Henri Vever, Lucien Gaillard; and many others. Far from the inventions of chinoiserie and a few forlorn attempts at japonaiserie, this was decorative art that did not just set out to imitate; it actually succeeded in grasping the true spirit of Japanese art. It was known as *japonisme* in France.

In the 1920s, these different influences began to be fully assimilated in Europe. Oriental exoticism manifested at that time through motifs, as well as by the use of special materials and techniques whose oriental origins were enough to give the artwork an entirely new character. Prince Sadruddin Aga Khan, ever a strong advocate of dialogue between cultures, was not mistaken when in the 1950s he began collecting oriental miniatures, and in the 1970s began buying boxes with his wife, Princess Catherine. These were cigarette cases and vanity cases made by the greatest Parisian jewelers of the 1920s, in which an oriental inspiration generated works of great originality and aesthetic quality. In both collections he looked for his own favorite themes: gardens, flowers, hunting, nature, animals (especially big cats), and humans.

Persian miniatures collected by Prince Sadruddin Aga Khan. Top: "The munificence of Ja'far al-Baramaki to 'Abd al-Malek," from *Akbar-i Barmakiyan* (Traditions of the Barmecids), Mughal India, circa 1595. Below: "Rustam pursues Akvan, the onager-div," from the *Shahnama* of Shah Tahmasp, attributable to Muzaffar 'Ali, Tabriz, Iran, circa 1530–35.

Islam and the Decorative Arts

In the domain of decorative arts, and especially jewelry, these diverse sources of inspiration manifested throughout the twentieth century, often as a result of political events. In the Middle East, which the French and other Westerners had first encountered through the Egypt of the pharaohs, General Bonaparte's Egyptian campaign in 1798 marked a first revelation by way of the books it generated, and this was confirmed in 1836 by the placement of the Luxor obelisk on the Place de la Concorde, given to France by Muhammad 'Ali, Viceroy of Egypt. This interest was subsequently heightened by Jean-François Champollion deciphering hieroglyphs via the Rosetta Stone, and the opening of the Suez Canal during the reign of Napoleon III in 1869. All these events made pharaonic Egypt fashionable; hieroglyphic characters and Egyptian bas-reliefs decorated necklaces and bracelets from the Restoration onwards, until the 1878 Exposition universelle—hence the Egyptian jewelry of Émile Philippe and the lotus flowers and scarabs of René Lalique. In the 1920s, the discovery of Tutankhamun's tomb revived the interest of jewelers such as Cartier, Van Cleef & Arpels, and others, and pharaonic designs even appeared on watch casings, as illustrated by the fob watch in the collection [111], with its bust of a pharaoh wearing the traditional striped headcloth known as a *nemes*.

The art of Muslim countries appeared in Europe following the colonial conquest of Algeria by France in 1830. The geometric motifs of Algerian passementerie adorned ladies' hairpins made by Édouard Marchand. Petiteau of Paris created brooches in silver, black enamel, and coral, with Moorish decoration made up of black leafy scrolls inspired by the motifs of the basins and ewers of the Middle East, with niello work set against backgrounds of etched copper. Other designs were rich in coral and lapis lazuli, which were revisited by the designer Eugène Julienne and the jeweler Eugène Crouzet under Napoleon III. The motif of the turbaned Indian also had considerable success during the Romantic era and can often be found in bracelets and brooches, where Morel et Duponchel used the theme of birds defending their nests, plus a snake and a bare-torsoed turbaned man. Similarly, Boucheron created a tiepin featuring a turbaned man, which can be seen in the Nissim de Camondo Collection of the Musée des Arts décoratifs in Paris. There was also the odalisque or sultana, reclining in front of a backdrop of oriental arches and smoking a nargileh, in a brooch by Charles Rudolphi.

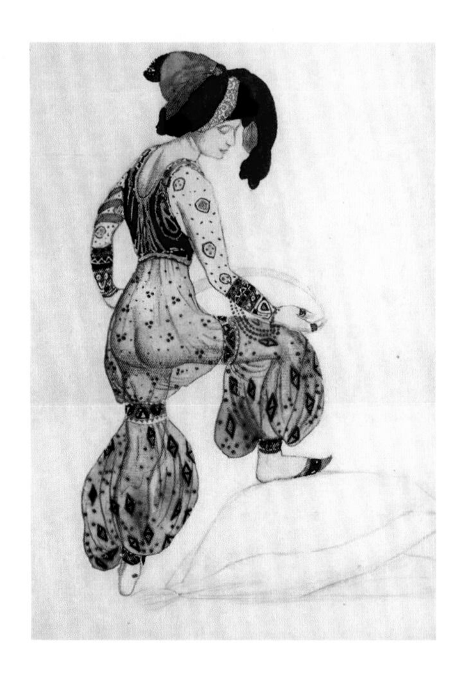

Léon Bakst, costume design for the Ballets Russes production *Schéhérazade*, 1910.

An important Persian miniature collected by Prince Sadruddin Aga Khan, "A noble hunt," attributable to Muhammad 'Ali, Mughal India, circa 1610.

Between 1910 and 1920, the Middle East returned to the forefront of public interest with the advent of the Ballets Russes, and especially *Schéhérezade*, a ballet based on *One Thousand and One Nights,* which Jean-Charles Mardrus had recently translated into French (1898–1904). This introduced the plumed turbans, gathered coats, and dresses of Paul Poiret. The first Persian miniatures were presented at the Musée des Arts décoratifs in 1912, thanks to the generosity of great French collectors; among these was the jeweler Henri Vever, who created brooches in enamel or colored gemstones representing Persian musicians, horsemen, or courtiers against a diamond-encrusted background. These were directly inspired by the miniatures he collected, whose quality can be admired today in the collection of the Freer Gallery at the Smithsonian Institution in Washington. In 1913 in New York, Cartier accompanied an exhibition with a publication entitled *Catalogue of a collection of jewels . . . created by Messieurs Cartier . . . from the Hindoo, Persian, Arab, Russian and Chinese.* The cover reproduced the design of a Persian or Ottoman bookbinding; the exhibition featured twenty pieces from Louis Cartier's personal collection, twenty jewels of Indian inspiration, and ten of Persian inspiration, a feathered headband, a brooch with a motif of vases of flowers, and pearl bracelets with old enamel clasps.

At that time, the terms "Hindu" or "Indian" were used somewhat imprecisely for antique Mughal jewelry, as well as for more recent Indian enamel jewelry. Mughal and Persian art influenced each other and at the time were associated under the single title of "Indo-Persian" art. In 1901, Cartier received an order from Queen Alexandra of Great Britain for a necklace of pearls, emeralds, rubies, and two square-cut emeralds, gems originating from antique Indian jewelry in the royal treasury. Louis Cartier's collection of antique Mughal jewelry was frequently exhibited and the pieces were also for sale to Cartier's clients; some elements of them were reused to create brand new pieces in the Indian style. The company regularly sought out and ordered antique cut and sculpted gems. The work on some stones, notably leaves cut from rubies, emeralds, and sapphires, was carried out in India, even though this type of cutting was unknown there and was first done for Cartier and, after that, for other Western jewelers. Cartier also bought numerous Mughal emeralds that were carved with flowered branches, figurative scenes, or sacred script, which turned up again in jewelry made for maharajas or rich European and American clients. French jewelers were equally enthusiastic about emeralds cut in ribbed melon shapes and they regularly dismantled the plaques of multicolored enamel they found on old Indian jewelry to remount them on clasps or as central motifs for Indian-style necklaces and bracelets. Sometimes stones that were hardly cut at all, or irregular in shape, were reused to give a "barbarian" aspect to certain pieces of jewelry. Of course, the commercial relations of the Cartier brothers and the other Parisian jewelers with Indian princes fed exchanges of this kind and nourished the production of antique Indian jewelry, whether remounted or fitted into creations to suit contemporary tastes.

This Indo-Persian and, more broadly, Arab and Middle Eastern influence yielded certain basic elements such as Indian precious stones, but it also yielded minerals like rock crystal. This had been used in Egypt and Syria from Fatimid times for court tableware, especially ewers, a practice that also prevailed at the Mughal court. At the 1889 Exposition universelle in Paris, Vever presented little boxes of rock crystal encrusted with Ottoman colored gems, some in arabesque forms. This successful combination of materials was still current in the 1920s, in a cigarette case and its box of matches [45].

2
Noble Hunt Vanity Case by Lacloche Frères, Paris, circa 1930

A Persian miniature collected by Prince Sadruddin Aga Khan, depicting the poet Hatefi, Iran, circa 1511.

A photograph from the Boucheron archive, 1926, shows the case was originally designed with a lipstick case attached, but it was modified by Boucheron before it was sold in 1929.

3
Persian Scene Vanity Case by Boucheron, Paris, 1926,
Manufactured by A. Frey

The landscapes, scenes of hunting, or images of court life in Persian miniatures are the most easily identifiable subjects in the iconography inspired by Muslim art. Jewelers had a rich set of Persian samples to copy, by way of the numerous exhibitions in the early twentieth century, and copy they did. Cartier, Van Cleef & Arpels, and Boucheron reproduced scenes of this type, most frequently in mother-of-pearl marquetry, in collaboration with the Russian-born artist Vladimir Makovsky (also Makowsky). Today, the same motifs can be related to certain miniatures in the collection of Prince Sadruddin Aga Khan. A horseman hunting deer (Van Cleef & Arpels, [1]) parallels the miniature of "Rustam pursues Akvan, the onager-div."[1] The inspiration for a horseman hunting with a falcon made for Lacloche [2] may well have come from a Mughal miniature depicting a nobleman on horseback.[2] The court scene in polychrome enamel on a Boucheron vanity case, with two figures surrounded by courtesans seated on a carpet at the foot of a flowering tree [3], is freely inspired by similar scenes from the *Shahnama* of Shah Tahmasp, such as "Firdausi and the three court poets of Ghazna" and "Haftvad and the worm."[3] The theme of another box is particularly interesting and intimate: amid a landscape of mother-of-pearl, a Persian mosque stands in an oasis surrounded by mountains that have a curious resemblance to the tomb of Prince Sadruddin's father, Sultan Mahomed Shah Aga Khan III, which is built on a hill overlooking the Nile in Egypt and has the same bulb-like dome [4].

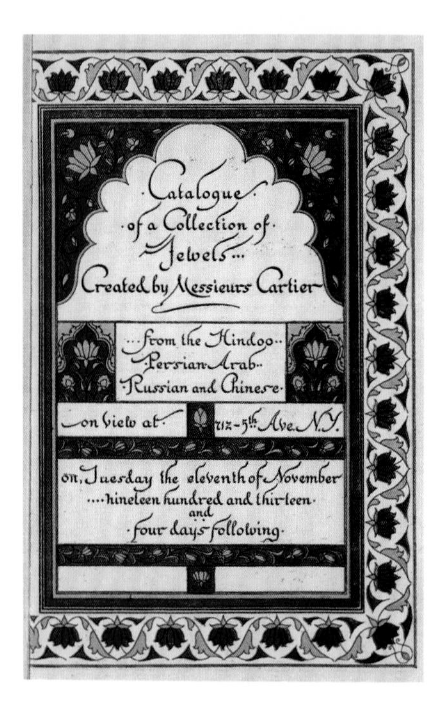

The mausoleum of Sir Sultan Mahomed Shah Aga Khan III, overlooking the Nile in Aswan, Egypt.

Catalogue cover based on Persian book design for a Cartier (New York) show in 1913, featuring jewels of "Hindoo, Persian, Arab, Russian and Chinese" inspiration. Cartier Paris Archives

4
Persian Mosque Vanity Case by Black, Starr & Frost, New York, circa 1929, with Mosaic by Vladimir Makovsky

A Persian prayer cloth, Iran, Qajar period, late nineteenth century. The cloth depicts a mihrab, cypress trees, and a garden, in a type of composition that inspired the use of two trees on some Cartier panther boxes.

In Iranian landscapes and Persian miniatures, the cypress is the predominant tree; its elongated, elegant outline is invariably present in oasis or garden scenes.[4] The sculptural quality of the cypress made it a favorite exotic motif, repeated by jewelers on the lids of boxes and cigarette cases. Van Cleef & Arpels used ivory enamel highlighted with gold leaf and flowering foliage against a black background [83]. Cartier's cypress tree is associated with the panther: depicted in diamonds and onyx on a terrace framed by two emerald cypresses, on a round Cartier powder compact [5], and later, a majestic black one, modeled in dark blue enamel, in a garden of mother-of-pearl mosaic, with a tree flowered with turquoises and flanked by three cypresses of decreasing size [6]. Other themes are the palm frond, lanceolate leaf, and cypress of sculpted emerald, from which Cartier hung a matching watch [115]; the same motif adorns the lower parts of a rock crystal desk clock, also by Cartier [110].

A theme that is common in Persian miniatures, the Middle Eastern garden, is even more present in the designs of Persian carpets, where it is shown as if from above; often at the center there is a pool of water, an indispensable element in gardens in this culture. This particular motif, rectangular and blue in color, was ideal for the flat surfaces of cigarette boxes and vanity cases: hence the broad rectangular plaque of lapis lazuli, with cut-off corners, surrounded by multicolored flowers and foliage, on boxes by Van Cleef & Arpels [95] and by Ostertag [7]. The design of Cartier's enameled cigarette case with foliage [8] may represent a pool of water or mihrab, a prayer niche.

Lady with Panther by George Barbier, 1914, commissioned by Cartier and used for advertisements. Cartier Paris Archives

5
Panther Compact by Cartier, Paris, circa 1928

6
Panther Vanity Case by Cartier, Paris, 1925

Opposite:
The original design drawings for the box from the Cartier Paris Archives, 1925. Cartier Paris Archives

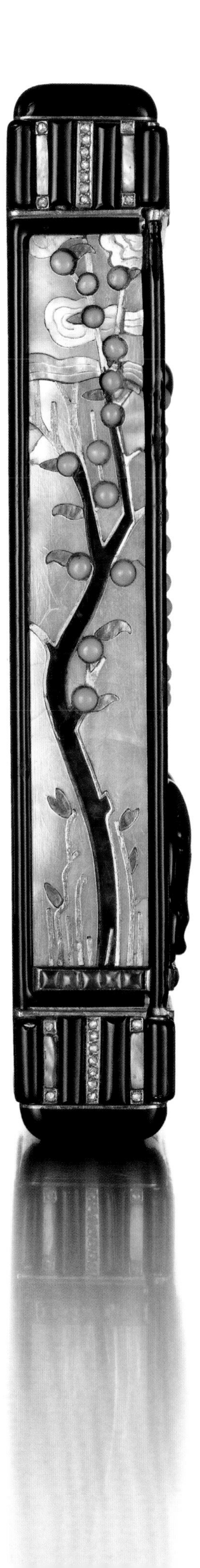

7
Persian-style Cigarette Case by Ostertag, Paris, circa 1929, Manufactured by Alfred Langlois

Opposite:
8
Envelope Cigarette Case by Cartier, Paris, circa 1930

9
Vanity Case by Cartier, Paris, circa 1930, Manufactured by Henri Lavabre

Opposite:
10
Persian-style Vanity Case by Lacloche Frères, Paris, circa 1925, Manufactured by Alfred Langlois

Illuminated Persian manuscripts illustrate scenes from court life as well as stories and legends. One sixteenth-century myth often depicted relates how the god Ohrmazd created a tree and two immortal birds on the shores of the Vourukasha Sea. Every year, hundreds of new branches sprout from the tree and hundreds of its seeds ripen. One of the birds, Amrosh, shakes the branches and the seeds fall to the ground. The other bird, Chamrosh, gathers them up and drops them into the sea. After this the seeds are carried into the sky by a rain cloud and fall again to earth, making it fruitful. This legend is pictured on a vanity case by Cartier made of gold trimmed with black enamel; in the center of the main surface is a small bas-relief of enamel and precious gems, which represents the flowering tree and the two birds [9]. The same story is surely represented in a more allusive form on an onyx Cartier box showing a tree with a trunk of diamonds and leaves of cut emerald. Two ruby birds are perched in it, and at its foot the ground is littered with tiny diamond seeds [80].

After the figurative scenes come all the themes and ornamentation that recur in every decorative art that draws on the designs of Indo-Persian textiles and carpets, such as flowering arabesques with free, supple coils, sometimes with flowers at their tips and even the heads of animals, as seen in the vanity case with watch by Janesich [116], and by Lacloche Frères [10], or the more symmetrical carpet motifs of a Strauss, Allard & Meyer vanity case [11], all three made of gold against an ivory-colored enamel background. Carpet motifs were also reproduced in some of

Qur'an, India, 1681. The floral designs and color choice of illuminated manuscripts is reflected in many of the boxes.

the Mughal miniatures in the collection of Prince Sadruddin and Princess Catherine Aga Khan, showing scenes of interiors. One example is a miniature of the *Akbar-i Barmakiyan*, "The munificence of Ja'far al-Baramaki toward 'Abd al-Malek" or two pages of the *Akhlaq-i Nasiri* of Nasir al-Din Tusi.[5] Other motifs, such as the scrolls representing rocks in oriental ceramics, overlapping scales, or blue or turquoise fan shapes, can be seen on many boxes, forming beautiful, carpet-like, geometric patterns, as on the Cartier box [96].

Muslim art influenced the choice of ornamental stones—lapis lazuli, turquoise, and coral—to provide lavish color for boxes of gold and silver. Louis Cartier built up an extensive collection of Persian miniatures, just as Henri Vever had done before him, and Prince Sadruddin Aga Khan would later collect and appreciate. The subjects and colors of the miniatures can be seen throughout the boxes and clocks in this book, drawing a parallel between the Indo-Persian influence of Prince Sadruddin's two great collections.

11
Persian Vanity Case by Strauss, Allard & Meyer, Paris, circa 1930

China and the Decorative Arts

Chinese art has always been a steady source of inspiration for the West. The porcelain and silk imported to Europe from the late seventeenth century onward offered a repertoire of forms and motifs that was appreciated by artists, who freely borrowed recurrent Chinese motifs such as dragons, clouds, landscapes, and mountains. Following the sack of the Summer Palace in Peking in 1860, jade and nephrite were adopted in Europe, tentatively at first—with Eugène Fontenay using jade for brooches in the form of insects in 1860, and again in 1867 for his marvelous amphora-shaped earrings—and then more confidently in the 1920s. Sometimes jewelers, goldsmiths, and silversmiths made use of original sculptures; Cartier, for example, did this with its *pendules mystérieuses*. An example in the Musée des Arts décoratifs incorporates an antique Chinese scholar's screen with dragons sculpted in bas-relief. Painted cloisonné enamel was a Chinese technique rediscovered by the enameler Tard, then applied to gold and silver work in 1867 by Maison Christofle, and used in jewelry in 1869 by Alexis Falize. *Lac burgauté* (lacquer inlaid with shell or mother-of-pearl) was also Chinese in origin. Both techniques were adopted in Europe in the second half of the nineteenth century, and were still utilized in the twentieth.

Chinese jade sculptures were popular in the West because of the beauty and rarity of the material, and, in the 1920s, Western jewelers incorporated them freely in their creations. Statuettes of Buddha were affixed to box lids by Cartier [12]. The jeweler also reused jade seals in pendants or mounted fibulas of Chinese jade as brooches. Symbolic motifs sculpted in jade were similarly recast, as with the future Buddha's sign of illumination placed at the four corners of the same Cartier vanity case. Other motifs were taken from more recent jade sculptures, like the bonsai design on the lid of a round powder compact from Cartier's workshop [13]. The origins of others are more difficult to work out: this is true of the many jade or nephrite bas-reliefs that decorate certain boxes made by Cartier. The technique and subject matter are clearly Chinese in origin, as seen in the sculpted bas-relief of Pekingese dogs [14], melons and flowers [15], Chinese children playing ball in a garden [16], and various small sculpted coral, jade, or nephrite plaques decorating the corners of Cartier boxes [17]. This type of plaque was also used by other jewelers to make up bracelets of alternating jade and coral.

13
Bonsai Tree Compact by Cartier, Paris, 1928, Manufactured by Auguste Peyroula

Opposite:
12
Buddha Vanity Case by Cartier, New York, circa 1930

14
Pekingese Vanity Case by Cartier, Paris, circa 1929

15
Vanity Case by Cartier, Paris, 1926

16
Garden Scene Vanity Case by Cartier, Paris, circa 1924,
Manufactured by Alfred Langlois

17
Cigarette Case by Cartier, Paris, circa 1927

Some of these bas-reliefs represent legends from Chinese mythology and their most popular figures. One such is the legend of the carp or koi and the dragon illustrated on a round Cartier powder compact [18]. This describes the legend of the carp that swims up a rushing river and leaps over the Dragon's Gate above a waterfall on a legendary mountain. Only the bravest and strongest carp could accomplish this exploit and as a result are themselves transformed into dragons, the symbol of power and courage, and hence representative of the emperor.

The dragon was a frequent motif in Art Deco jewelry on account of its highly sculptural image and the colors that could be associated with it, notably red and black. Also its representation could be associated with a number of other Chinese legends. For example, the episode of the Dragon and the Pearl is reproduced in a mother-of-pearl mosaic by Makovsky on a Cartier vanity case [19]. Here the surfaces of the box depict two different moments, one with the dragon swimming among clouds engraved in a plaque of mother-of-pearl, coiling its tail around columns of malachite, the body straining toward an oval ruby representing an eclipse of the sun. On the other side, the dragon lies beneath a sun outlined in gold. The mystical pearl represents the sun itself, which symbolizes wisdom and illumination. On other boxes by Cartier the dragon appears among clouds, wrought in mother-of-pearl against a background of black enamel [20] or in black enamel against a background of red and gold [21]. The dragon appears in legends and in certain Persian miniatures in the collection of the Aga Khan, one of which, "Gushtasp slays a dragon on Mount Saqila" from the *Shahnama,* is a marvelous illustration of the aesthetic proximity between China and Persia and demonstrates the constant reciprocal contact that existed between the two cultures.[6] The same is true of the miniature of "The court of Gayumars," which belongs to the same manuscript, whose quality and historical importance are truly exceptional.[7]

Persian miniature collected by Prince Sadruddin Aga Khan. "Gushtasp slays a dragon on Mount Saqila," from the *Shahnama* of Shah Tahmasp, attributable to Mirza 'Ali, Tabriz, Iran, circa 1530–35.

18
Koi and Dragon Compact by Cartier, Paris, circa 1930

19
The Dragon and the Pearl Vanity Case by Cartier, Paris, circa 1927, with Mosaic by Vladimir Makovsky

20
Dragon Compact by Cartier, Paris, 1924

21
Dragon Vanity Case by Cartier, Paris, circa 1927,
Manufactured by Renault

22
Lac Burgauté Box by Cartier, Paris, circa 1927

23
Lac Burgauté Vanity Case by Cartier, Paris, circa 1928,
Manufactured by Auguste Peyroula

After sculpted jade, another ancient Chinese technique that was rediscovered at the beginning of the twentieth century was *lac burgauté,* which specialists like Jean Dunand used for the decoration of furniture and objects. It involved the insertion of pieces of mother-of-pearl into lacquer backgrounds, usually black. Jewelers were attracted by the technique, often including antique Chinese plaques in their creations. A vanity case executed by the box makers Strauss, Allard & Meyer for Janesich depicts a Chinese landscape with flowers and trees along the banks of a stream that winds through the scene, with a Chinese pagoda in the background [89]. A mirror-like water surface is rendered with tiny leaves of mother-of-pearl, which are also used to depict flowers, trees, and buildings against a background of black lacquer. Other boxes show Chinese figures in landscapes: On one Cartier piece, there is a depiction of two women and a man talking on the bank of a river, while a servant waits beside a wagon full of packages [22]. Another, also by Cartier, shows figures on a terrace or near a bridge on either side [23]. In addition, there is a Cartier desk clock in rock crystal, with a panel showing two figures kneeling in an interior [107]. The *lac burgauté* technique makes all these pieces very special.

They may have the same sources and represent the same subjects in a similar style, but these lacquer panels cannot be confused with mother-of-pearl mosaic landscapes, of which the principal proponent was the Russian-born artist Vladimir Makovsky, who was working at the time for the great jewelers of Paris in several different styles—Chinese, oriental, and medieval. This special technique for creating mosaics with pieces of mother-of-pearl of different shades, sometimes encrusted with ornamental stones such as coral, is usually attributed to Makovsky, whether signed by him or not, and even in the absence of written references. Some of them were inspired by Chinese landscapes found in Chinese drawings or painted paper scrolls; there are also seascapes, of which one of the finest is a box made by the American company Black, Starr & Frost [24], where the mother-of-pearl scene is framed by a network of geometrical lines. Another piece [25] has seascapes on both sides: one in mother-of-pearl with junks and trees in the foreground, and the other in cloisonné enamel with figures and a punt, plus a mountain in the background. Both plaques are surrounded by Chinese cloud motifs in gold against a black background. A box by Boucheron [26] represents a mountain landscape with a stream, waterfalls, and rocks: this is a faithful imitation of Chinese drawings. A jade-green enamel frame decorated with Art Deco geometric motifs surrounds the landscape. A final example is a mother-of-pearl mosaic representation of the Chinese legend of the fox spirit, which draws strength from the moon: the coral-and-gold fox is shown sitting on a rock under a pine tree, his nose pointed to the sky [27]. These few mother-of-pearl mosaic boxes demonstrate an extraordinary syncretism between East and West, for although their themes are taken from Chinese art, their technique and rendering are Western.

24
Landscape Vanity Case by Black, Starr & Frost, New York, circa 1929, with Mosaic by Vladimir Makovsky

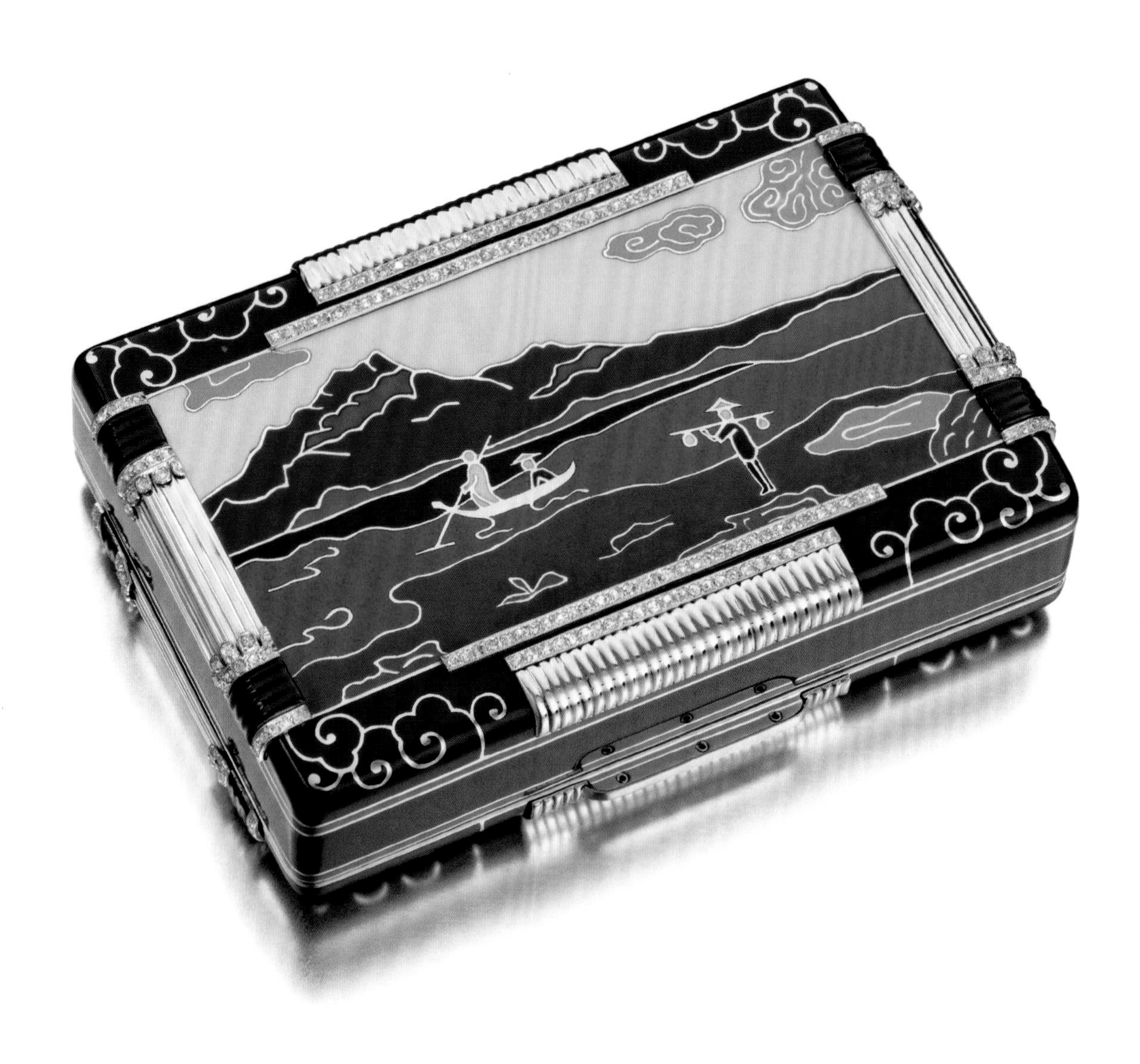

25
Landscape Vanity Case by Black, Starr & Frost, New York, circa 1929, with Mosaic probably by Vladimir Makovsky

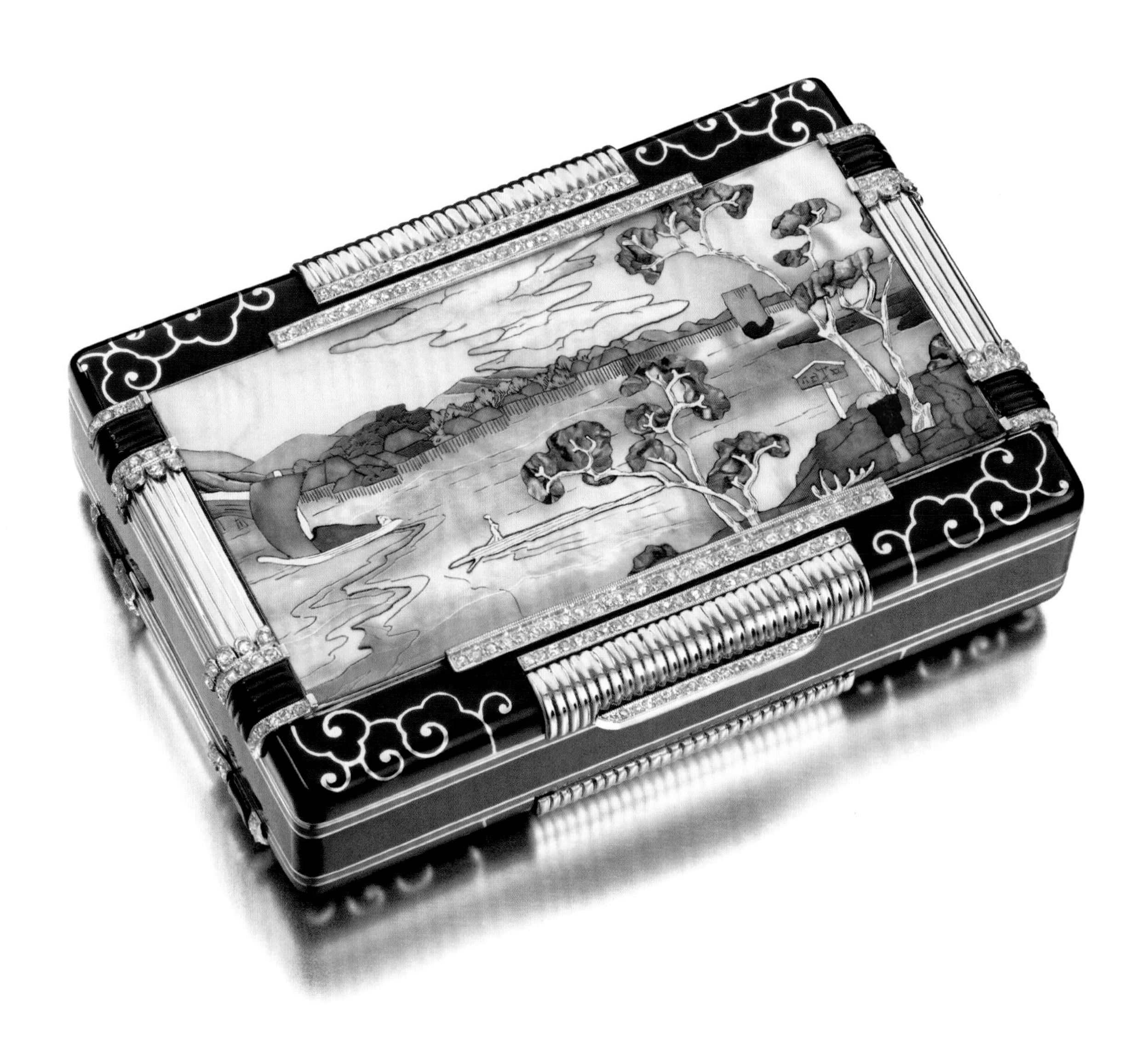

Landscape hanging scroll in the style of Huang Gongwang by Wang Shimin. China, Qing dynasty, 1666.

26
Mountain Landscape Vanity Case by Boucheron, Paris, circa 1928

Some motifs are harder to interpret with certainty, though frequently depicted, even if the more linear and allusive renderings do not always allow them to be identified. Very often these motifs are architecturally structured, such as the motif of red lacquer Chinese imperial doors, which only the emperor's family and princes of the empire were permitted to use. These doors adorn the lid of a vanity case made by Strauss, Allard & Meyer for Lacloche Frères circa 1924 [28]. Another such motif is the Chinese gong, treated in linear fashion with three circles, one suspended and the two others at an angle through which a cord passes with elements like counterweights, outlining a portico [29]. Other subjects are more recognizable, like the Chinese cloud accompanying the dragon, which features, for instance, as a decorative line of separation between plaques of carved jade and a plaque of lapis lazuli, on a Cartier box [99]. The cloud reappears outlined with gold thread against a background of black enamel in an anonymous French box [30], whose clasp is decorated with the very common motif of the *ruyi*, a sort of rounded stylized cloud, which represents the wish "that everything should happen as you desire." This is present on a Cartier box [56] and on a number of others, with the motif executed in diamonds, gemstones, carved jade, or coral. The same design may be found, in round or rectangular form, on two other boxes whose lids are decorated with still lifes of vases or baskets of flowers in bas-relief, inspired by Chinese porcelain. Both pieces are by Cartier [31 and 32]. Another box shows Chinese ideograms symbolizing joy, fashioned in diamonds and set on a Cartier vanity case with other Chinese motifs, including a pagoda roof [33].

27
Fox Vanity Case, France, circa 1928

28
Imperial Door Vanity Case by Lacloche Frères, Paris, circa 1924, Manufactured by Strauss, Allard & Meyer

29
Vanity Case, circa 1925

30
Cloud Vanity Case, France, circa 1925

31
Jardinière Vanity Case by Cartier, Paris, circa 1928,
Manufactured by Ploujavy

32
Cigarette Case by Cartier, Paris, circa 1929

33
Vanity and Cigarette Case by Cartier, Paris, circa 1920

Katsushika Hokusai, "Noboto Bay," from the series *Thirty-six Views of Mount Fuji*, Japan, circa 1830–32. This woodcut shows the form of gates (torii) recreated in the motifs on the vanity case.

Japan and the Decorative Arts

Japan, hitherto a closed society, was opened to the outside world in the 1850s, under pressure from the American navy. After that date, and for over a century, Japanese objects flooded into the West, allowing certain connoisseurs to amass important collections of Japanese prints, tea ceremony stoneware, sword guards, lacquers, and stencils. These objects were to become inexhaustible sources of inspiration for Western artists. To begin with they generated simple, literal representations with minimal artistic input, or japonaiseries, but within a generation Westerners were studying Japan in greater depth and with a more critical eye, and Japanese art became a source of inspiration and revelation to major artists in their search for new forms of expression. This was the case of the Impressionist painters, as well as the decorative artists of Art Nouveau—especially those involved in designing jewelry, like René Lalique and Lucien Gaillard. Japan was crucial to the Art Nouveau period, but becomes less visible in the period of Art Deco, when most of the boxes in Prince Sadruddin and Princess Catherine Aga Khan's collection were made.

The most important, indeed essential contribution of Japanese art was to the shape of the vanity case, which was adapted from that of the Japanese inro, a medicine box with several superimposed compartments linked by a cord; this held them together round the sides and was clasped at the top by a bead, or *ojime*. The inro was hung from the belt by a netsuke button, which acted as a kind of counterweight; it was made in the shape of a rectangle with rounded corners, and was generally made of lacquered wood with the bead and button of ivory or carved wood, and it endowed Western vanity cases with their generally quadrangular or barrel shapes.

Art Deco, like Art Nouveau, constantly revisited the motif of the landscape with pagodas, as in the vanity case made by Strauss, Allard & Meyer for Linzeler & Marchak, which was decorated with a mother-of-pearl mosaic designed by Vladimir Makovsky to show a seated monk meditating on the terrace of a snow-covered house fronting a Zen garden [34]. Other models by the same maker reproduce a Japanese motif, the blossom-laden branch of a plum tree, rendered with diamonds against a background of black enamel, placed against three semicircles on a red enamel box [63]. Another box with rounded corners made by the same atelier for Lacloche Frères [64] has a lid entirely covered by a branch blossoming with diamonds, against a background of black enamel and framed by parallel, irregular lines set with diamonds that look like icicles; together, these two motifs depict the peculiarly Japanese love of blossoms covered with snow. Another box for Lacloche Frères [88] displays on its onyx lid a trellis motif of diamonds, on which appears a branch of red and blue chrysanthemums rendered in buff-top precious stones cut in irregular cabochons, all beautifully rendered in colored relief. In other pieces, the inspiration for more geometrically designed flowers is drawn from the Japanese textiles that were brought to Europe from the early nineteenth century, for example, a vanity case by Strauss, Allard & Meyer, in the form of an envelope decorated in the middle with a band of flowers in turquoise blue enamel against a gold background [87]. Finally, one of the most frequently reproduced motifs in *art japonisant*—like Mount Fuji or Hokusai's *Wave*—is the koi, or carp, which appears in both Chinese and Japanese art, but whose representation is familiar in Japanese prints, sword guards, and stencils. This was already a feature of René Lalique's jewelry in the 1880s and in numerous French pieces of the second half of the nineteenth century, notably Dammouse's porcelain dishes. It is reproduced in a vanity case by Cartier [35]: several carp appear in black enamel, with scales picked out in gold, swimming in waves rendered in Japanese

34
Zen Garden Vanity Case by Linzeler & Marchak, Paris, circa 1925, with Mosaic by Vladimir Makovsky, Manufactured by Strauss, Allard & Meyer

style, with gold whorls, against a background of cream enamel. The composition is free, with carp swimming in all directions, and wavelets covering the entire lid, so there is no single dominant line of view. This attractive piece attests to the complete understanding of the Japanese approach, which is such a feature of the Western work called *japonisant*.

The Japanese influence is also evident in architectural motifs that were much used in clockmaking, such as the torii of Shinto temples, which are typical of certain clocks made by Cartier. Japanese art, on the whole, was therefore more profoundly assimilated in the West than Chinese, whose motifs were so much more readily available. Particular Japanese techniques and materials were regularly used: lacquer, for example, was a constant feature of gold and silver work as well as jewelry, and was used most of all in cigarette cases and vanity cases, on which it is still sometimes mistaken for black enamel.

Oriental exoticism has always nourished European and Western art. In the seventeenth and eighteenth centuries this consisted of chinoiserie, a blend of motifs used in random conjunction, whatever their origin. But in the nineteenth and twentieth centuries, better information and research led to a deeper understanding of distant civilizations; however their fascination remained undimmed, and European artists continued to feast on differences and discoveries, creating an art that was constantly renewed and original. As to all these achievements of French jewelers in the 1920s, when artists were so broadly inspired by the Far East, it is no coincidence that Prince Sadruddin and Princess Catherine Aga Khan chose to include a pendant by Dusausoy, which was presented at the Exposition internationale des Arts décoratifs et industriels modernes, in Paris, in 1925 [75]. This malachite pendant represents a tree, treated in the Western manner but rarely represented in French jewelry, sheltering beneath its canopy a cluster of houses that resemble Chinese or Japanese pagodas; the foreground is occupied by a band of diamonds. The Prince and Princess collected their pieces according to their obvious sources of inspiration, but also liked to possess objects that demonstrated the rich dialogue of civilizations. It was precisely this dialogue that gave birth to original works like this pendant, made by one of the era's greatest and most imaginative jewelers.

Katsushika Hokusai, "Two Carp," Japan, circa 1833.

35
Koi Vanity Case by Cartier, Paris, circa 1930

Catalogue Texts

Sarah Davis

PERSIA AND ISLAM

1

Noble Hunt Vanity and Cigarette Case by Van Cleef & Arpels, Paris, 1930

A vanity and cigarette case decorated on the front with a mother-of-pearl, hardstone, and gold scene flanked by a geometric pattern of black and red enamel and gold that wraps around the back, all accented by rose-cut diamonds, the top and bottom applied with black enamel, with hidden button thumbpiece; interior with fitted mirror and compartment, the other a cigarette case; gold, with French assay marks

Signed Van Cleef & Arpels, no. 33546
Measurements: 8.8 x 5.6 x 2.0 cm, 3½ x 2 3⁄16 x 1 3⁄16 inches

In the style of a Persian miniature, the scene on this case depicts a king on the hunt aided by a greyhound. Hunting as a royal activity has a long history in both Eastern and Western cultures. Iranian tradition regarded the hunt as an essential part of the prince's education, allowing him to travel his lands to assess political situations, keep the army alert, and as a way for a ruler to pass wisdom to his sons. This scene bears a striking similarity to a miniature from Prince Sadruddin's collection known as *A Noble Hunt*. Depicting a scene integral to the mental, physical, and emotional well-being of a Middle Eastern royal, this case undoubtedly appealed to Prince Sadruddin as a collector of Persian miniatures and as a prince of Islamic heritage.

Compared to the fanciful interpretation of a noble hunt miniature by Lacloche Frères [2], this is a more realistic interpretation that cleverly shows depth within flattened perspective, as the horse appears to be climbing the hill in pursuit of the prey. The horse, rider, and hunting hound are shown in dynamic motion, revealing the hand of a skilled mosaic artist. The strong geometric border references the elaborate borders of illuminated manuscripts, but modernizes it through color and pattern choice.

2

Noble Hunt Vanity Case by Lacloche Frères, Paris, circa 1930

A vanity case decorated with a mother-of-pearl and carved hardstone scene with borders of black and red enamel accented with ornate diamond-set foliate motifs; platinum and gold, with French assay marks and British importation marks

Signed Lacloche Frères France
Measurements: 9.0 x 4.7 x 1.3 cm, 3 9⁄16 x 1 7⁄8 x ½ inches

In the form of a Persian miniature, the mosaic on this case depicts an Islamic prince on a steed with his hunting falcon on his outstretched hand within a fanciful floral landscape of oversized pinwheel-like flowers (see also 1).

3

Persian Scene Vanity Case by Boucheron, Paris, 1926, Manufactured by A. Frey

A vanity case decorated in polychrome enamel with a scene of a Persian prince kneeling on a patterned carpet, surrounded by courtiers and attendants within a garden with flowering tree nearby, the sides enameled in blue, the reverse in black, onyx thumbpiece; interior with fitted mirror and two compartments; gold, with French assay marks

Signed Boucheron Paris, with maker's mark for A. Frey
Measurements: 8.0 x 4.7 x 1.0 cm, 3⅛ x 1 13⁄16 x ⅜ inches

This case, described by Boucheron in the stock book as "Persian style," was originally designed with the attached chain and lipstick holder depicted in the archival photograph, but the case was separated and sold alone in 1929. The scene depicted in the enamel work is inspired by, if not copied from, a Persian miniature. The importance of the central figure is denoted by the style and height of his headdress as well as by his location seated on the carpet. Another important figure sits to his left and they are deep in discussion while the other figures stand in the lush garden.

This box was manufactured by A. Frey, an artist who worked for Boucheron making vanity cases and cigarette boxes. His mark is a lozenge containing a butterfly or moth, with the wings stamped A and F.

4

Persian Mosque Vanity Case by Black, Starr & Frost, New York, circa 1929, with Mosaic by Vladimir Makovsky

A vanity case with a central mosaic panel by Vladimir Makovsky depicting a Persian mosque in a lush landscape composed of tinted mother-of-pearl and hardstone, surrounded by a geometric pattern of layered rectangles in black enamel and two shades of blue enamel outlined in gold lines, with diamond accents, the reverse with similar layered enamel rectangles; gold and platinum

Signed Black, Starr & Frost, mosaic signed M for Vladimir Makovsky
Measurements: 8.2 x 5.8 x 1.8 cm, 3¼ x 2⅜ x ¾ inches

The mosaic on this vanity case depicts a Persian mosque in a mountain scene with trees in the foreground. The scene bears a striking resemblance to the tomb of Sir Sultan Mahomed Shah Aga Khan III, Prince Sadruddin's father, with a bulbous tower perched atop desert hills and a verdant oasis in the foreground. Makovsky's use of flattened perspective in his mosaics would also have appealed to Prince Sadruddin as a collector of Persian miniatures that employed the same style (see also 24).

5

Panther Compact by Cartier, Paris, circa 1928

A black enamel compact with the figure of a panther in diamond and black onyx strolling on a line of baguette diamonds flanked by two emerald cypress trees, baguette diamond thumbpiece; interior with fitted mirror; gold and platinum, with French assay marks

Signed Cartier Paris Londres New York, Made in France
Measurements: 4.4 x 4.2 x 2.2 cm, 1¾ x 1⅝ x ⅞ inches

The panther is the single most important icon in Cartier's history. First introduced in a George Barbier drawing in 1914, the dangerous elegance of the creature inspired jewelry and stunning vanity cases. The earliest representations were jewels created with a panther skin. Jeanne Toussaint commissioned a panther vanity case in 1917 that was likely the first full depiction. Later the design director of Cartier, she is inextricably linked with the company's depictions of the panther, and was even known as *La Panthère*. Like this case, hers featured a diamond cat with black onyx spots, pacing between two emerald cypress trees. The panther appears to be a direct reference to Barbier's drawing, with the feline in profile between trees instead of columns. This vanity case features the addition of diamond stars turning the black enamel into the night sky. (See also 6.)

6

Panther Vanity Case by Cartier, Paris, 1925

A vanity case depicting a dark blue enameled panther on a row of buff-top calibré-cut rubies, against a mother-of-pearl garden landscape with a cabochon ruby sun, and a tree with cabochon turquoise blossoms, the borders and reverse decorated with raised onyx bars alternating mother-of-pearl inlay accented with diamonds, the push-piece designed as a gem-set songbird; interior with fitted mirror, perfume vial, lipstick case, and covered compartment for powder; gold and platinum with French assay marks

Signed Cartier, Paris Londres New York, 0389, 2064
Measurements: 10.2 x 4.4 x 1.8 cm, 4⅛ x 1¾ x 11/16 inches

Of all the Art Deco objects created by Cartier, this ranks as one of the most important. Featuring the sleek figure of a panther striding confidently in a verdant jungle landscape, the entire scene is a miniature of an elaborate magical world. The original color sketch for this box is found in Cartier's stock design record book in the Paris archives. Created in 1925, this box was shown at the Exposition internationale des Arts décoratifs.

According to Hans Nadelhoffer, Cartier excelled at integrating the fairytale world of the Orient into their jewelry, objects, and clocks. Of the iconic panther items, the boxes were some of the most spectacular (see also 5). Nadelhoffer goes on to say, "the most significant of these panther vanity cases, a miniature masterpiece of color, appeared in the year of the Exposition des Arts Décoratifs. . . . The vanity case depicts a black enameled panther prowling in a fairy-tale garden beneath a ruby sun." The designers were equally inspired by the colors and stories of the Ballets Russes as they were by the Persian miniatures in Louis Cartier's collection, and a touch of both can be seen here. The design of the panther also seems inspired by the work of Paul Jouve, an artist who specialized in African animals and illustrated Rudyard Kipling's *The Jungle Book* in 1919. The colorful, exotic, and just slightly ominous scene on the vanity case embodies the 1920s aesthetic at its most sublime.

7

Persian-style Cigarette Case by Ostertag, Paris, circa 1929, Manufactured by Alfred Langlois

A cigarette case with hinged lid decorated in Persian style with stylized floral and geometric motifs in hues of blue, red, and green on a cream and gold striped background, two ends with geometric pattern, the push-button clasp a hidden panel at the front, also with a hinged opening on one short side; interior with fitted mirror; gold

Signed Ostertag, Brevete S. G. D. G., with maker's mark for Alfred Langlois
Measurements: 7.7 x 3.4 x 1.5 cm, 3 1/16 x 1 3/8 x 9/16 inches

This cigarette case was created for Ostertag by Alfred Langlois in the Persian style influenced by the decoration found on carpets and bookbindings (see also 10). While beautiful, this box was also technically interesting and had an unusual hidden button opening, as well as an extra hinged section on one end. Alfred Langlois filed a patent for this style of box on May 13, 1929: "We know that it is very difficult to get cigarettes out of full boxes because, for lack of space, we cannot lift them with a finger. The present invention, a new cigarette box, is characterized by an articulated end with a spring hinge that provides a way for the finger to fit in the box and raise the cigarette and it then closes itself when the cigarette is free."

8

Envelope Cigarette Case by Cartier, Paris, circa 1930

A cigarette case of ribbed gold designed as an envelope, the hinged lid embellished with a stylized Persian-style palmette in white and black enamel with cabochon sapphires; interior with a holding bar for cigarettes; gold

Signed Cartier Paris, 864031A, 58629, Brevete S. G. D. G., with maker's mark CAH (unknown)
Measurements: 8.1 x 5.4 x 1.3 cm, 3 3/16 x 2 1/8 x 1/2 inches

The form of the envelope lent itself to the graceful motion of opening the flap and sliding a cigarette out, and it was a theme seen in a small number of Art Deco box examples from makers including Cartier, Van Cleef & Arpels, and Strauss, Allard & Meyer (see also 87).

9

Vanity Case by Cartier, Paris, circa 1930, Manufactured by Henri Lavabre

A vanity case composed of polished gold with white and black enamel trim, the central square motif depicting two birds within a floral scene applied with blue, green, red, white, and yellow enamel, framed by a diamond border, the sides applied with black enamel in the form of meandering vines, with diamond and enamel thumbpiece, suspended from a black enamel, diamond, and gold chain supported by a diamond-set ring; interior with fitted mirror, powder compartment, and two lipstick sections, one with detachable lipstick holder; gold, with French assay marks

Signed Cartier, Paris, Londres, New York, 1006, with maker's mark for Henri Lavabre
Measurements: 8 x 4.5 x 1.2 cm, 3 3/16 x 1 3/4 x 7/16 inches

Cartier created several pieces with a small, framed motif of two birds in a bejeweled tree. The Cartier Collection has a vanity case, makeup box, lighter, and cigarette case dating from 1928–1932. The scene is from Persian mythology and is referenced in the sixteenth-century text *The Persian Rivayats*: "The Creator Ohrmazd has produced on the shores of the sea Vourukasha a tree and two birds who are immortal and without death. Every year a thousand new branches spring up from that tree and all kinds of seeds hang on those branches and all those seeds become ripe. A bird called Amrosh comes and sits on one of the branches and shakes it and scatters down to the ground all the seeds. Another bird called Chamrosh comes and strikes all the seeds with its wings and sides and throws them into the sea. All those seeds go inside a cloud full of rain and that cloud rains on the ground and all the seeds appear on the earth."

The design of this box is also similar to a box from 1913 in the Cartier Collection that was owned by Daisy Fellowes and has the same overall design with a slightly different plaque and chain. The early date is surprising for such a modern piece and variations were made until the 1930s.

10

Persian-style Vanity Case by Lacloche Frères, Paris, circa 1925, Manufactured by Alfred Langlois

A vanity case decorated in Persian style with a pattern of gold flowers and foliage heightened in blue, red, and green enamel against a cream enamel ground, the sides decorated with additional foliate motifs in a black enamel ground, further enhanced with rose-cut diamonds at four corners; interior with beveled mirror, powder compartment, and lipstick holder; with French assay mark

Signed Lacloche Frères France, with maker's mark for Alfred Langlois
Measurements: 7.9 x 5.0 x 1.0 cm, 3⅛ x 2 x ⅜ inches

A variation on the meandering floral vine also incorporating paisley (or *boteh*) forms overlapped to create a central flower. These design motifs were often seen on Persian carpets, illuminated manuscripts, and bookbindings, and were widely adapted to Western use. This vanity case was created by Alfred Langlois, who was known for his beautiful boxes and clocks. While this was made for Lacloche Frères, he is most closely associated with Van Cleef & Arpels [95, 50, 51] as he signed an exclusive agreement to create for them in 1932.

11

Persian Vanity Case by Strauss, Allard & Meyer, Paris, circa 1930

A vanity case with the central motif depicting an elaborate Persian floral and scroll design applied with cream, light and dark mauve, and green enamel, the reverse of similar but simplified design, bordered by a mauve enamel and diamond-set trim, the short sides set with carved jadeite sections of gourd and foliate design studded with rose-cut diamonds, both framed by mauve enamel, with diamond-set thumbpiece; interior with fitted mirror and two compartments; gold and platinum, with French assay marks and British importation marks

Stamped 30460, with maker's mark for Strauss, Allard & Meyer
Measurements: 8.5 x 5.6 x 1.3 cm, 3¼ x 2¼ x ½ inches

The design for this box is based on a modified meandering floral of the type found in Owen Jones's many books on ornamentation, particularly in the Chinese and Persian examples. While the allover floral is a typically Islamic design, it was widely adapted in China during the Tang dynasty, permeating the decorative arts.

CHINA AND JAPAN

12

Buddha Vanity Case by Cartier, New York, circa 1930

A vanity case centering upon blue guilloché enamel, the four corners accented by circular carved jadeite disks with diamond accents over a gold and black enamel background, the center plaque depicting a carved jadeite Buddha within an ornate lozenge frame of diamonds, with a cabochon sapphire thumbpiece, suspended from a black enamel and gold chain; interior section slides out of the case from the top revealing a writing tablet, mirror, compartment, detachable lipstick holder, and removable pencil; gold and platinum

Signed Cartier, NY, 340
Measurements: 8.1 x 4.2 x 1.5 cm, 3 3/16 x 1⅝ x 11/16 inches

Since the seventeenth century, interest in distant trade brought Asian art objects into Europe, including statues of Chinese and Japanese deities. In the 1920s, Cartier made enchanting designs that both reinterpreted Asian design and incorporated original carved pieces. The jadeite figure with an exposed belly on this case appears to be Maitreya, the future Buddha. The diamonds create an ethereal body halo. The carving on the disks at the four corners depict the *dorje*, symbol of enlightenment.

13

Bonsai Tree Compact by Cartier, Paris, 1928, Manufactured by Auguste Peyroula

A compact centering a bonsai tree of carved jadeite greenery with cabochon sapphires and red enamel trunk in a carved jadeite pot, with red enamel feet and rose-cut diamond handles, the compact further applied with a cream-colored enamel geometric pattern within a blue enamel border, the side of ribbed gold with white enamel geometric pattern within diamond-shaped frames; interior with inscription "6 Juillet 1929"; gold, with French assay marks

Signed Cartier Paris, 0780, with maker's mark for Auguste Peyroula
Measurements: 5.5 x 5.4 x 1.5 cm, 2 3/16 x 2 1/8 x 5/8 inches

Japanese bonsai and Chinese *penjing* are ancient arts that depict landscapes in miniature. The ideal is to create a beautiful tree or a scene with the proportions of a life-sized landscape. Creating the landscape and caring for the tree are essential parts of the art form that is based on contemplation and ingenuity. Depicted on this compact is a bonsai tree carved with representations of the celestial bodies the sun and the moon, with sapphire stars. The geometric pattern on the top and side of the compact is a sacred and auspicious symbol in Hinduism, Buddhism, and Jainism.

14

Pekingese Vanity Case by Cartier, Paris, circa 1929

A vanity case set on the front and back with openwork carved jadeite plaques against red enamel, the carvings depicting dogs amongst foliage, studded with small diamond plaques accented by black enamel, within black and red enamel borders, the sides set with jadeite, mother-of-pearl, and coral segments, accented by bands of diamonds and black enamel; interior with fitted mirror, two compartments, and a detachable lipstick holder; gold and platinum, with French assay marks

Signed Cartier Paris Londres New York, Made in France, 01026
Measurements: 9.2 x 6.1 x 2.1 cm, 3 5/8 x 2 7/16 x 13/16 inches

The plaque depicts several Pekingese playing with a ball amidst trees in a garden scene. An ancient Chinese breed resembling guardian lions, the Pekingese (also known as the Lion Dog, Peking Lion Dog, Pelchie Dog, or Peke) was favored by emperors for thousands of years. A long-tailed bird appears at each corner. This type of plaque benefits from being held in the hand and turned to catch the light and reveal the carved images.

15

Vanity Case by Cartier, Paris, 1926

A vanity case composed of nephrite panels carved with flowers and melons (similar to carved panels on the Cigarette Case [17]), diamond-set florette octagons or half-octagons at the corner of each panel, at each end a panel with jade batons and buff-top sapphires, the edges of the case outlined with gold and blue enamel, the clasp button, also a rectangle with inverted corners, set with a jade baton and similarly outlined in gold and blue enamel; interior with fitted mirror, two powder compartments, and a lipstick holder; gold, with French assay marks; engraved "Mrs. Leith, 14A Manchester Square W."

Signed Cartier Paris Londres New York, 0476
Measurements: 9.3 x 4.7 x 1.9 cm, 3 11/16 x 1 7/8 x 3/4 inches

The color combination of bright blue and green was iconic of the bold Cartier Art Deco jewels. These colors were often seen in designs by Louis Cartier and by Charles Jacqueau. In this box, the bright blue of the enamel and sapphires and the green of the jade perfectly match Léon Bakst's most famous costume design for Nijinsky in the Ballets Russes' *L'Après-midi d'un faune*. Although the motifs on this case are Chinese, the same color combination can be found in Cartier Art Deco jewels of various inspirations.

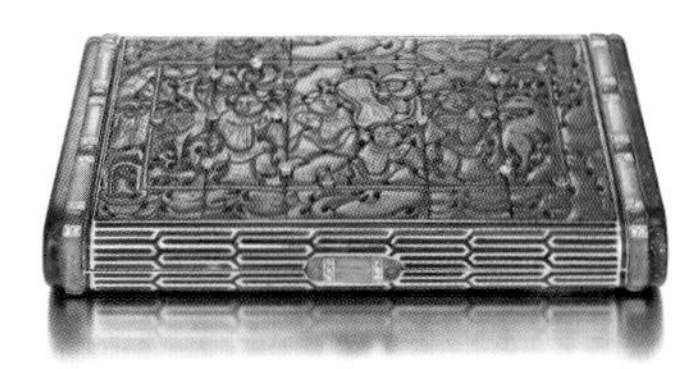

16

Garden Scene Vanity Case by Cartier, Paris, circa 1924, Manufactured by Alfred Langlois

A vanity case composed of a carved jadeite plaque depicting four figures in a garden scene, studded with rose-cut diamonds and cabochon rubies, framed by blue enamel, flanked at each side with bands of carnelian and amethyst segments accented by diamonds, ends of lapis lazuli, long sides and back decorated with a blue enamel and gold geometric pattern, with amethyst, carnelian, and diamond thumbpiece; interior with fitted mirror, two compartments, and a detachable lipstick holder; gold and platinum, with French assay marks and British hallmarks

Signed Cartier, Paris, 1155, with maker's mark for Alfred Langlois
Measurements: 8.6 x 5.5 x 1.3 cm, 3 3/8 x 2 1/8 x 1/2 inches

The carved panel on this vanity case depicts four Chinese boys in a verdant paradise setting suggested by the deer and crane flanking the figures. The figures have their hair in two buns, a traditional style for boys under the age of twelve, before they could wear a headpiece. Their youth is also suggested by the wide-sleeved jackets and wide-legged pants. Each of the boys is holding a treasure in his hand.

17

Cigarette Case by Cartier, Paris, circa 1927

A cigarette case featuring semi-transparent rectangular agate panels on the front and back surrounded by black enamel, accented on the corners and sides by carved coral segments with cabochon emeralds, the back applied with black enamel stripes around an agate panel, two sides composed of carved onyx segments, with diamond-set thumbpiece; gold, with French assay marks

Signed Cartier, Paris Londres New York, 4742
Measurements: 9.0 x 5.6 x 1.5 cm, 3 1/2 x 2 3/16 x 9/16 inches

The use of translucent agate in this cigarette case looks back to earlier examples of translucent stone boxes carved from a single block of stone [37, 72, 73]. However in this piece, Cartier modernizes the use of the agate by setting it into a gold and black enamel box like a precious stone, rather than using it as the box material. When the case is opened, the light pours through, illuminating the striations in the stone. The agate is sided by coral panels with Asian foliate motifs that have caught cabochon emerald bubbles in a seemingly random way.

18

Koi and Dragon Compact by Cartier, Paris, circa 1930

A compact featuring carved jadeite disks depicting an aquatic scene with a fish and dragon, studded with cabochon sapphires, framed by black enamel trim, the sides set with carved coral segments, with diamond accents and diamond-set thumbpiece; interior with fitted mirror and powder compartment, with removable gold powder screen with a pierced flower motif; gold, with French assay marks

Signed Cartier, Paris Londres, New York, Made in France, 0940
Measurements: 7.3 x 7.0 x 2.4 cm, 2 7/8 x 2 3/4 x 15/16 inches

This compact depicts the myth of the carp (koi) leaping over the Dragon's Gate (see also 35). According to Chinese mythology, the Dragon's Gate is located at the top of a waterfall cascading from a legendary mountain. Carp swim upstream against the river's strong current, but only a few are brave and capable enough for the final leap over the waterfall to transform into the dragon, a symbol of power and courage.

19

The Dragon and the Pearl Vanity Case by Cartier, Paris, circa 1927, with Mosaic by Vladimir Makovsky

A vanity case, the front and reverse each decorated with a mosaic depicting a red and black enamel dragon with gold detail summiting malachite peaks surrounded by mother-of-pearl clouds and mist, the front with a cabochon ruby, the scenes are edged in gold with cloud motifs on the sides and diamond details at the corners, the edges in black enamel, the terminals with carved coral and the sides with mother-of-pearl panels, with a coral and diamond thumbpiece; interior with two compartments and a fitted mirror; gold and platinum, with French assay marks

Signed Cartier, 8155, 0875, 21008
Measurements: 10.0 x 5.0 x 1.5 cm, 3 15/16 x 2 x 9/16 inches

This dynamic depiction of a dragon scene was created by Vladimir Makovsky, a master of hardstone miniatures. While this mosaic is unsigned, or possibly the signature is obscured by the diamonds at the corners, Makovsky created a handful of similar dragon mosaics for Cartier boxes and one for a clock by Verger Frères for Charlton & Co. This box contains the most elaborate and detailed of the dragon mosaics.

In Asian culture dragons are a divine mythical creature representing strength, good fortune, and transformation. This box depicts a traditional scene from Chinese mythology known as the "cloud dragon chasing the pearl." On the front of the box, the dragon is reaching for a ruby sun, a depiction of an eclipse, known in Chinese as *re she* or "sun-eat"; on the reverse the dragon is in a different position with a gold sun. The mystical flaming pearl, or sun, represents wisdom and enlightenment. The clouds are purposely treated to evoke water and the feeling that the creature is swimming in a turbulent sea to reach an elusive goal.

20

Dragon Compact by Cartier, Paris, 1924

A compact with mother-of-pearl panels on the front and back, the lid bordered by black enamel and small natural pearls, centering a rectangular plaque of gold, shell, and black enamel decorated with the figure of a dragon, held within four sets of rose-cut diamonds, flanked by two corals carved with a *ruyi* and set with round cabochon emeralds, the sides decorated with a gold and black enamel frieze of geometric dragon design, completed by a coral and diamond thumbpiece; interior with fitted mirror and powder compartment; gold, with French assay marks

Signed Cartier
Measurements: 5.9 x 4.3 x 1.5 cm, 2 5/16 x 1 11/16 x 9/16 inches

The long-whiskered dragon with sinuous body and claw hands in front of gold clouds depicted on this compact is similar in form to the Dragon and the Pearl Vanity Case [19]. The choice of a limited palette here sets it apart from that colorful work. The materials used, the deep blue shell against black enamel, reference the *lac burgauté* pieces produced for centuries in China, and used by Cartier and other jewelers in the Art Deco period [23]. Cartier set the mosaic panel into a box with other Chinese-inspired details, including carved coral *ruyi*, auspicious symbols, and, in a subtle clever detail, the meander pattern on the sides of the box has been turned into a geometric interpretation of the Chinese dragon.

This compact was purchased from Cartier by T'hami El Glaoui, Pasha of Marrakesh, in 1930 and he had it modified to his specifications. Once a mountain warlord controlling profitable desert trade routes, T'hami El Glaoui, a Berber and a notorious Lord of the Atlas, was installed by the French (along with his brother) to rule Marrakesh and central Morocco, which they did until Moroccan independence in 1956. During his reign, El Glaoui was thought to be the richest man in the world. A man who ruled with terror and cruelty, El Glaoui was also an aesthete who built extravagant palaces, had a 150-woman harem, and a love of Western cinema, American jazz, and lavish gifts. His style, charm, and prodigious wealth made him a popular entertainer when he visited European capitals, and at home. His palace at Telouet contained some of the finest tilework in the world. He was well known at Cartier, and even today there is a line of Pasha wristwatches, the first designed in 1943 when El Glaoui requested a watch he could wear while swimming.

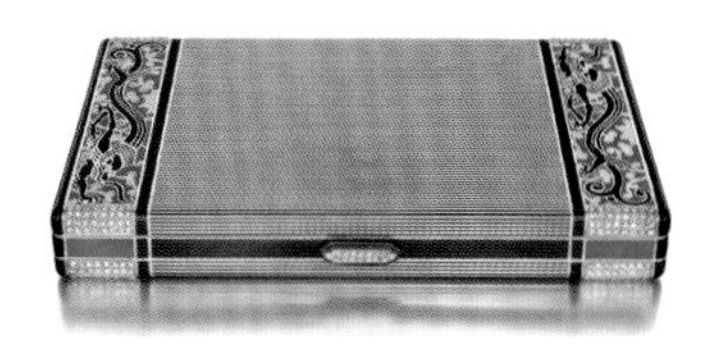

21

Dragon Vanity Case by Cartier, Paris, circa 1927, Manufactured by Renault

A vanity case, the front and back with small black enamel bands on gold, bordered by rectangular sections depicting dragons among floral vines applied with red, black, and cream enamel flanked by corners set with rose-cut diamonds, the sides applied with black and red enamel sections, with diamond-set thumbpiece; interior with fitted mirror, small powder compartment, and larger open compartment; gold, with French assay marks

Signed Cartier Paris Londres New York, 0743, with mark for Renault
Measurements: 11.0 x 6.5 x 1.4 cm, 4 3/8 x 2 9/16 x 9/16 inches

The dragon motif on the bands of this vanity case is a copy of the Chinese Kui dragons from the ancient bronzes in the Shang-Zhou periods (1600–770 BCE). The general characteristics are a large head, sinuous torso, and forked curling tail. Designs of Kui or *kuilong* dragons can be widely seen in Chinese jade, ceramics, and furniture, often entwined with a floral pattern. The dragon is an auspicious symbol of imperial power, as is the red enamel meant to evoke ancient Chinese red lacquer. The Cartier Collection contains a nearly identical case purchased by King Alexander of Yugoslavia in 1928.

22

Lac Burgauté Box by Cartier, Paris, circa 1927

A rectangular box decorated with *lac burgauté* panels, the lid accented with three round diamonds, the hinges and clasp of semicircular fluted coral outlined in black enamel, with cabochon emeralds, additional cabochon emeralds at the sides, the corners of fluted nephrite within coral borders; interior with fitted mirror; gold, with French assay marks

Signed Cartier Paris Londres New York, Made in France, OCC 434
Measurements: 8.7 x 5.9 x 2.5 cm, 3 7/16 x 2 5/16 x 1 inches

This chinoiserie scene is likely drawn directly from a Chinese literary source and was created in Japan for use in the West. Cartier accented the panels beautifully, drawing out the colors with use of coral, black enamel, and nephrite, as well as diamond and emerald accents. See the Lac Burgauté Garden Scene Vanity Case [89] and the Lac Burgauté Vanity Case [23] for discussion of *lac burgauté*.

23

Lac Burgauté Vanity Case by Cartier, Paris, circa 1928, Manufactured by Auguste Peyroula

A vanity case with *lac burgauté* panels framed by polished gold and geometric mother-of-pearl borders accented by blue enamel, the edges applied with blue enamel, the front accented by bands set with cabochon turquoise and lapis lazuli segments and diamonds, the sides composed of mother-of-pearl segments set in a checkerboard pattern accented by two shades of blue enamel, with diamond-set thumbpiece; interior with fitted mirror, powder compartment, and detachable lipstick holder; gold, with French assay marks

Signed Cartier, Made in France, 0626, with maker's mark for Auguste Peyroula
Measurements: 6.2 x 4.4 x 1.8 cm, 2 7/16 x 1 3/4 x 11/16 inches

In a number of Art Deco boxes, Cartier used small imported *lac burgauté* panels (see 89 and 22). According to Judy Rudoe, they "were made in the nineteenth century either on the Ryukyu islands between China and Japan, or in Nagasaki, the main center of production in Japan itself. The mother-of-pearl was partly tinted in purple and green. After the lacquer had been brought level with the mother-of-pearl inlay, a final layer of lacquer was applied to the whole object, thus concealing the mother-of-pearl. The surface was then rubbed with pumice stone until the inlay was once more exposed. In this way, a perfectly smooth surface was obtained."

This box features a love story of the type seen in woodblock illustrations. The woman in pink and the man in blue appear to be gazing out at each other when the box is flipped over. On the front, in a lush garden scene, the woman is with a friend who is gesturing toward the man who is accompanied by a monk and appears to be on a porch structure. There is evidence of Chinese motifs in the dress and architecture, and of Japanese style in the hair, which points to these plaques being created in nineteenth-century Japan for the Western market. The *lac burgauté* on this case is beautifully accented by an unusual geometric design of scored mother-of-pearl filled with blue enamel.

24

Landscape Vanity Case by Black, Starr & Frost, New York, circa 1929, with Mosaic by Vladimir Makovsky

A vanity case with stepped sides, the central mosaic composed of various shades of mother-of-pearl depicting a tree in front of a placid lake within a mountainous range with billowing clouds above, framed by an ornate geometric border set with rose-cut diamonds and square-cut rubies, further accented on the front and back with a geometric pattern of light and dark blue and black enamel, the sides accented by light blue enamel bands; interior with fitted mirror, powder compartment, and detachable lipstick holder; gold and platinum, with British importation marks

Although this case is unsigned, a similar example, the Persian Mosque Vanity Case [4], is both stamped Black, Starr & Frost and with the mosaic signed by Makovsky
Measurements: 7.4 x 4.8 x 1.3 cm, 2 15/16 x 1 7/8 x 1/2 inches

25

Landscape Vanity Case by Black, Starr & Frost, New York, circa 1929, with Mosaic probably by Vladimir Makovsky

A vanity case with a carved and tinted mother-of-pearl mosaic landscape, within borders of gold ribbing alternating with segments of black enamel and gold stylized clouds at the corners, further enhanced with bands of diamonds, the reverse decorated in polychrome enamel landscape, within a similar border to the obverse, completed by a diamond-set thumbpiece; interior with fitted mirror, powder compartment, and lipstick holder; gold and platinum (see also 24 and 4)

Signed Black, Starr & Frost
Measurements: 8.3 x 5.6 x 2.0 cm, 3 1/4 x 2 1/4 x 3/4 inches

This case is interesting for the juxtaposition of the mosaic landscape with the enamel interpretation on the back. The mosaic depicts a Chinese junk and a fishing boat in a watery landscape with mountains in the background and clouds overhead. On the reverse, in enamel, appears another watery landscape depicting two figures in a boat and a third figure waiting on the shore, against a background of mountains. The mosaic was probably completed by Vladimir Makovsky and resembles other pieces completed for Black, Starr & Frost (see 24). The enamelwork was likely completed by another hand, perhaps the box maker, thinking to complement the intricate mosaic. Both display a certain skill level, but the subtleties of color achieved in the mosaic far outshine the solid fields of enamel color.

26

Mountain Landscape Vanity Case by Boucheron, Paris, circa 1928

A vanity case in green enamel inlaid with a mother-of-pearl plaque depicting a landscape with mountains, river, and tree, embellished with black enamel and diamond details, the sides composed of onyx rectangles, with a diamond-set button clasp; interior with fitted mirror, two powder compartments, and a lipstick holder; gold, with French assay marks

Signed Boucheron Paris
Measurements: 9.0 x 5.0 x 1.4 cm, $3\frac{9}{16}$ x 2 x $\frac{1}{2}$ inches

The design of the mosaic on this case is based on a typical Chinese landscape of the type painted on a hanging scroll. The flattened perspective of the landscape and the curved contours of the rocks and mountains are deliberate choices that reflect the aesthetics of traditional Chinese paintings, realized here in mother-of-pearl. The mosaic was then set into a vanity case with the color of the green enamel matched to flashes of green in the mother-of-pearl. The geometric diamond, black enamel, and gold embellishments juxtapose the aesthetics of Art Deco against the form of a classical Chinese painting to great effect.

27

Fox Vanity Case, France, circa 1928

A vanity case composed of jadeite, the front adorned with a mosaic scene of carved coral, textured gold, and mother-of-pearl, with a diamond frame and diamond-set thumbpiece; interior with fitted mirror, powder compartment, and detachable lipstick holder; gold and platinum, with French assay marks

Measurements: 4.8 x 4.3 x 1.3 cm, $1\frac{7}{8}$ x $1\frac{11}{16}$ x $\frac{1}{2}$ inches

The mosaic scene likely depicts a Chinese fox spirit standing on a rocky ledge illuminated by moonlight and surrounded by trees. The mythological fox spirit, a trickster akin to a faerie, takes its energy from the moon. The fox is composed of carved coral and textured gold, and the tree, ground, and background are composed of shades of mother-of-pearl.

28

Imperial Door Vanity Case by Lacloche Frères, Paris, circa 1924, Manufactured by Strauss, Allard & Meyer

A vanity case in the form of two doors, with red and black lacquer, the front featuring two circular door-handle motifs of carved onyx and coral studded with diamonds, supporting diamond-set rings, the base accented by a band of diamonds, with diamond thumbpiece that releases both lids simultaneously; interior with two fitted mirrors and two compartments, gold and platinum, with French assay marks and British importation marks

Signed Lacloche Frères Paris, 3332, with maker's mark for Strauss, Allard & Meyer
Measurements: 8.3 x 4.8 x 1.7 cm, $3\frac{1}{4}$ x $1\frac{15}{16}$ x $\frac{11}{16}$ inches

The design of this vanity case is inspired by the traditional red doors of Chinese royalty. Only families with royal lineage or imperial titles could have the door at the main gate painted this deep red. Designed to stand when displayed on a table, the case is laid down to open and reveal two compartments.

29

Vanity Case, circa 1925

A vanity case of black and red lacquer, the front decorated with a stylized gong motif of black and green enamel accented by diamonds; interior fitted with large compartment, with sliding lipstick holder and perfume baton on either side; gold and platinum

Measurements: 6.0 x 4.6 x 1.4 cm, $2\frac{3}{8}$ x $1\frac{13}{16}$ x $\frac{9}{16}$ inches

30

Cloud Vanity Case, France, circa 1925

A vanity case of Asian inspiration decorated on the front and back with gold stylized clouds within a black lacquer ground, the ends applied with red lacquer, the clasp and hinges set with openwork platinum diamond-set plaques, with seed pearl thumbpiece; interior with fitted mirror, three compartments for powder and detachable lipstick holders, writing tablet and clip; gold, with French assay marks

Maker's mark EC (unknown)
Measurements: 7.9 x 5.2 x 1.4 cm, $3\frac{1}{8}$ x $2\frac{1}{16}$ x $\frac{9}{16}$ inches

Stylized clouds are one of the oldest forms in Chinese art and architecture. They are an auspicious symbol and the word for cloud sounds the same as the word for good fortune.

31

Jardinière Vanity Case by Cartier, Paris, circa 1928, Manufactured by Ploujavy

A vanity case composed of ribbed gold, the front accented by a central plaque depicting a carved turquoise pot, buff-top cabochon ruby flowers with buff-top cabochon emerald leaves, within a dark blue enamel background and framed by white enamel and diamonds, the front and back bordered by black-and-white enamel bands, with pagoda-shaped black-and-white enamel accents set with square-cut diamonds extending toward the center of the case, the sides decorated with a black enamel geometric pattern, with diamond-set thumbpiece; interior with fitted mirror, powder compartment, and detachable lipstick holder; gold, with French assay marks

Signed Cartier, Made in France, 70084, with maker's mark for Ploujavy
Measurements: 7.0 x 4.5 x 1.5 cm, $2\frac{3}{4}$ x $1\frac{3}{4}$ x $\frac{9}{16}$ inches

32

Cigarette Case by Cartier, Paris, circa 1929

A cigarette case composed of agate panels on the front and reverse within blue enamel trim, the front decorated with a square nephrite plaque accented by a tablescape set with a carved coral segment, two small carved rubies, and rose-cut diamonds, applied with blue, black, green, and red enamel, framed by rose-cut diamonds, the sides applied with a blue enamel geometric pattern flanked by cream-colored enamel bands, the thumbpiece composed of a carved cabochon ruby; gold, with French assay marks and British importation marks

Signed Cartier Paris Londres New York, Made in France, 21443, stamped JC for Jacques Cartier
Measurements: 8.0 x 5.7 x 1.6 cm, $3\frac{3}{16}$ x $2\frac{1}{4}$ x $\frac{5}{8}$ inches

The central panel on this cigarette case is based on the traditional image of the Chinese New Year offering. An auspicious setup in a prominent position in the household, the arrangement is meant to bring a year of luck and prosperity.

33

Vanity and Cigarette Case by Cartier, Paris, circa 1920

A vanity case of black enamel, the front set with an amber plaque centering a diamond-set Chinese symbol, enhanced by a meander pattern of diamonds at the top and bottom, one end featuring a diamond-set stylized pagoda roof completed by an oval cabochon chrysoprase, the other end composed of a fluted amber flower surmounted by an oval cabochon chrysoprase with diamond rim, the sides set with square amber segments; interior fitted on one side with a mirror and two compartments, the other side opening to reveal a cigarette case and match holder; gold and platinum, with French assay marks

Signed Cartier, 10838
Measurements: 10.4 x 4.4 x 2.2 cm, $4\frac{1}{8}$ x $1\frac{3}{4}$ x $\frac{7}{8}$ inches

This vanity case unifies a mix of Asian motifs. One end replicates the sloping roof and spirals of a pagoda. The flower pattern on the other end is a modified chrysanthemum, the symbol of imperial Japan. The character on the front is an artistic interpretation of the Chinese character "joy" or *xi*. The meander pattern of the diamonds is a common motif throughout Asian art.

34

Zen Garden Vanity Case by Linzeler & Marchak, Paris, circa 1925, with Mosaic by Vladimir Makovsky, Manufactured by Strauss, Allard & Meyer

A vanity case in red enamel, the central panel with a hardstone and tinted mother-of-pearl mosaic, the panel is outlined in calligraphy-like stylized black enamel lines that overlap at the corners, the edges of the case are decorated in purple, red, and black enamel accented with round diamonds, with a diamond-set button clasp; interior with fitted mirror, two compartments, and lipstick holder; gold and platinum, with French assay marks

Case signed R Linzeler Marchak, 1542, 3961, with maker's mark for Strauss, Allard & Meyer, mosaic signed with an M for Vladimir Makovsky
Measurements: 9.5 x 5.3 x 1.2 cm, 3¾ x 2⅛ x 9/16 inches

Joseph Marchak and Robert Linzeler collaborated for only three years, from 1922 to 1925, but in that time they produced spectacular Art Deco works of superior technical quality. This vanity case is technically superior, with an unusual curved design and inverted corners as well as a beautifully fitted interior conforming to the outline. The layered design on the cover centers on a panel by Vladimir Makovsky, depicting a monk meditating in front of a Zen rock garden in a Japanese mountain scene composed of hardstone and tinted mother-of-pearl in a riot of color. The scene is framed by black, purple, and red enamel, accented with diamonds in the form of traditional Japanese gates, or torii, found at the entrance to a shrine.

35

Koi Vanity Case by Cartier, Paris, circa 1930

A vanity case featuring black enamel koi with red enamel eyes in stylized cream enamel and gold water, outlined in black enamel, with further black enamel details accented at the corners with square cabochon rubies, the underside of the case featuring a gold plaque of Persian design engraved with lines on a white enamel ground outlined in black enamel, push-button clasp set with rose-cut diamonds; interior with two compartments for powder, a central detachable lipstick holder, and a fitted mirror; gold, with French assay marks

Signed Cartier, Paris
Measurements: 8.8 x 5.2 x 1.2 cm, 3½ x 2 x ⅝ inches

Inspired by Chinese and Japanese woodblock prints, this vanity case features both the flattened perspective and bold curvaceousness of this ancient art form. The koi (or carp), a common theme in Asian art, appear to be swimming upstream through raging waters of gold and white enamel. Chinese mythology contains a story of the golden carp that climbs the rapids of the Yellow River. If the carp succeeds, it transforms into a dragon. The same sentiment is echoed in the Japanese saying *"koi no taki-nobori"* ("koi climbing the rapids"), which indicates that a carp is spirited and strong, determined to overcome all obstacles (see also 18).

Feminine Elegance:
Jeweled Accessories for the Modern Woman

Stephen Harrison

The cigarette cases and vanity accessories from the 1920s and 1930s in the Prince Sadruddin and Princess Catherine Aga Khan Collection present powerful emblems of status, as well as markers of taste and fashion during a period of dramatic change in societal attitudes toward the public persona of women. Bejeweled luxuries of great expense, these cases and vanities owned by the wealthiest and most fashionable men and women of their day mark a world apart from the vastly cheaper versions kept by millions of other less affluent women, who by 1920 were fast becoming the mainstay of a burgeoning tobacco industry.[1] The world's most renowned purveyors of artistic luxury created such precious objects, ostensibly to be used, but also given, kept, and prized as works of art. These works reveal the widening gulf between rich and poor as well as emerging contrasts between the traditional and modern, or rather, conservative and avant-garde taste between the two world wars. These contrasts characterize the quest for a new vocabulary of design, a way to finally brush off the constraints of the last century and allow for modernity to be seen in the context of the changing role of society.

Defining the Modern Woman

Early in the twentieth century, long before medical research revealed a direct causal link between smoking and lung disease,[2] cigarettes were more closely associated with the modernity of a new century. Cigarettes were a relatively new phenomenon around 1900, and prior to James Bonsack's invention in 1881 of a machine to mechanically produce them, cigarettes were rolled by hand, limiting output and consequently consumption to a relatively small, rarified market. The introduction throughout the 1880s of Bonsack's technology into the East Coast manufactories of America's tobacco producers streamlined the process and resulted in high supply in both the United States and abroad.[3]

At the same time, tobacco companies focused on the creation of high demand, stimulating the desire to indulge in the smoking of cigarettes with colorful, artistic packaging and novelties such as cigarette cards, which served as enduring advertisements of the brand, long after the cigarettes were smoked. One of the most successful American tobacco producers, James Buchanan "Buck" Duke, issued these cards in series, creating instant consumer collectors and reinforcing brand loyalty.[4] By 1900, the branding of cigarettes had become one of the most important methods of creating demand and increasing sales.[5]

36
Cylindrical Vanity and Cigarette Case by Cartier, Paris, circa 1913

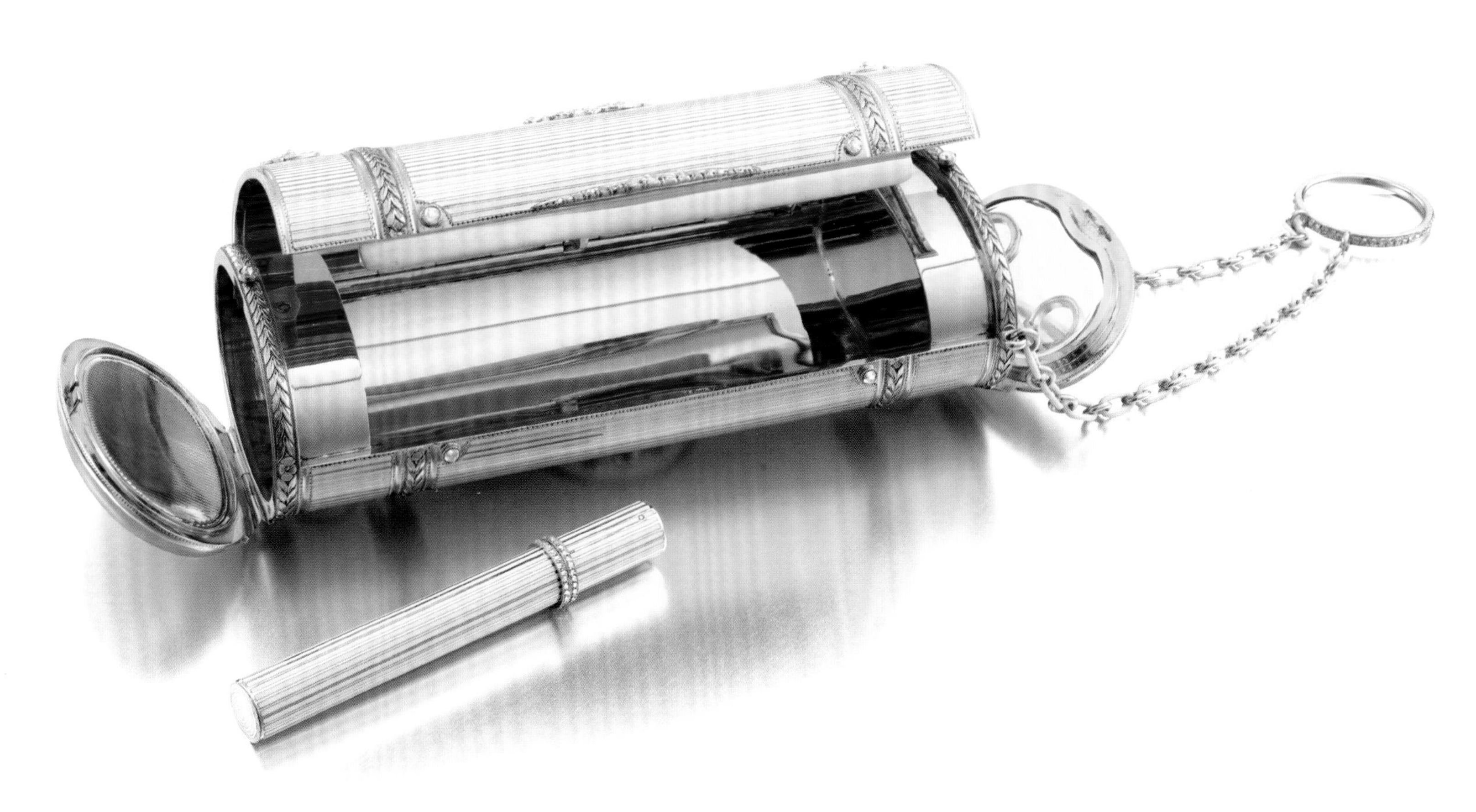

A collector's card from Wills's cigarettes depicting the Convent of the Annunciation, Nizhny-Novgorod, from the series "Gems of Russian Architecture" issued in 1917. Cigarette makers used these cards as a marketing tool to encourage smoking and brand loyalty.

Opposite:
Two advertising posters for cigarettes from the early twentieth century featuring exotic motifs and beautiful women smoking. Top: Advertisement incorporating oriental motifs, for Cigarettes Saphir by Stephano, 1908. Bottom: Advertising poster for Cigarettes Egyptiennes from Nerma brand by Gaspar Camps, 1924.

Not surprisingly, early visual marketing of tobacco began to follow artistic trends at the end of the nineteenth century, specifically a renewed emphasis on Asian aesthetics that would endure well into the twentieth century. The Aesthetic Movement dominated the discourse of household taste during the 1880s after the momentous introduction of Japanese art at the United States Centennial in 1876. All across America, and simultaneously in urban centers around Europe, architects, designers, and their clients showed a renewed enthusiasm for the aesthetics of faraway lands, considered mysterious and exotic by those who had never visited them. Close associations with foreign cultural motifs became coordinated with the function of certain rooms as consumers sought to portray their familiarity with, if not their direct knowledge of, these cultures and their decor. In "Japanese" parlors, collectors were encouraged to display Asian porcelains, painting, and sculpture. Asian elements of design were introduced within every genre of decorative art.

The aesthetic most synonymous with the practice of smoking during this period was a broadly Middle Eastern style. Smoking rooms were incorporated into new designs for large houses, while Turkish-inspired nooks at the top of the stairs were to be found in smaller domains. Tobacco companies capitalized on this trend and exploited the exotic nature of smoking. The finest tobacco was thought to come from Egypt or Turkey, although American tobacco was by far the most consumed and recognizable. To capitalize on this fervor for the Orient, some companies shifted their branding toward an orientalist perspective.[6] One of the most successful of these campaigns was the introduction of the Camel brand in 1913 by R. J. Reynolds. With its seductively attractive packaging featuring a quintessential image of the Orient, an Egyptian camel framed by the pyramids, R. J. Reynolds quickly captured an enormous market share before the First World War.[7] Authenticity was not of prime concern: the camel, which served as the inspiration for the image on the pack, wasn't even Egyptian. It was drawn apparently from a beast named "Old Joe," traveling through North Carolina in the Barnum & Bailey circus.[8] French manufacturers also adopted orientalist motifs, with an advertisement for Saphir cigarettes from around 1910 featuring a turbaned genie holding a cigarette in a haze of smoke. Likewise, a poster for Nerma from 1924, titled "Cigarettes Egyptiennes," features a smoking girl in exotic dress sitting atop a sphinx-like figure with Egyptian columns in the background.

Orientalism and its association with smoking in the late nineteenth century initially connoted a masculine sensibility. Smoking rooms in great houses were the exclusive domains of men and were almost always decorated in the orientalist taste. With a dark, sensual mix of overstuffed chairs, divans, ottoman stools, and Turkish carpets draped one over another, this decor created the perfect ambiance for a languid smoke with friends. Masculine associations with smoking extended to accessories as well, with cigar and cigarette cases becoming a staple of a gentleman's wardrobe. Makers of luxury goods, such as Tiffany & Co. in New York, London, and Paris, and the House of Fabergé in St. Petersburg and Moscow in Russia, supplied accessories for every smoking need, including humidors, cutters, lighters, and cases.[9]

Because of Fabergé's association with the Russian imperial family, many commissions for luxury objects were ordered from the firm by the government to be used as personal or diplomatic gifts on behalf of the tsar. Cigar and cigarette cases were ideal presentation objects as they could easily be personalized with engraved sentiments and commemorative messages or itineraries of travels and voyages undertaken.[10] Fabergé's cases were sumptuous creations, usually in gold but also wrought in silver, mixed metals, or Karelian birch, and almost always embellished with lavish enameled and jeweled decorations. In this way, Fabergé's cases provided a bridge to the glories of the Romanov past, particularly the eighteenth-century reign of Catherine the Great. Whether through the adaptation of historicist designs or just the spirit of presenting a snuffbox as a gift, these direct links to earlier royal patronage provided continuity with the past in the vain hope of maintaining a stable future.[11]

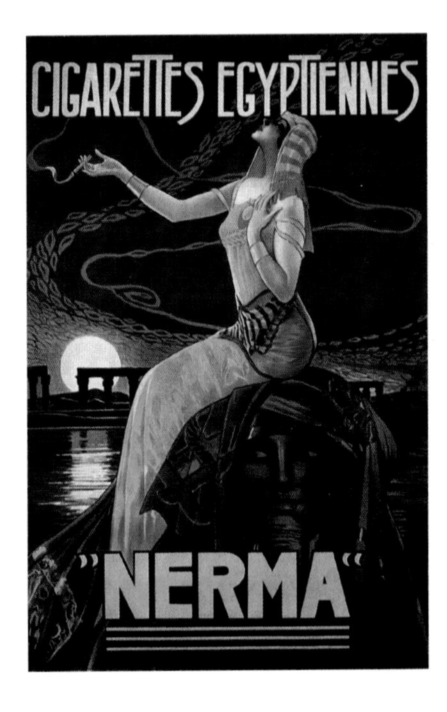

As Europe devolved into the First World War, the old nineteenth-century order, based on strict conventions of morality and hierarchy that had governed society into the first decade of the twentieth century, was literally swept away on a river of blood.[12] The so-called Great War was a long, costly battle, which thrust a generation of young men not used to mortal combat into lonely, infested trenches, where so many would meet their end. There was enormous support for the troops back home, where women took on greater roles in providing for their families and themselves while rolling bandages for the Red Cross and preparing packages for those at war. Packs of cigarettes, provided by both the government and those at home, became a mainstay of comfort for the soldier at the front.[13] It was largely this boost in consumption by the troops that caused cigarettes to outpace sales of all other forms of tobacco as the war came to an end in 1918.[14]

The most dramatic change in cigarette consumption from the period before World War I to 1920 was not so much the higher numbers of cigarettes consumed but who was consuming them—women. Historians note "women who bought cigarettes for their husbands overseas now bought packs for themselves."[15] Armed with the hard-won right to vote, women began to assert a sense of liberation just as a new era of prosperity began. While the timeline of voter's rights varied in the Western world, a new sense of freedom for women prevailed. Undergarments relaxed; hemlines were raised; and hair was chopped off and bobbed. A new more confident woman emerged, more defiant of previous social norms and willing to challenge a masculine-dominated world.[16] Whereas before the war everyone who smoked, especially women, smoked largely in private, the 1920s saw a dramatic increase in public smoking not only by men but also by women, in particular.[17] Even before the war, Edith Wharton and Ogden Codman Jr. observed in their landmark treatise on interior design, *The Decoration of Houses* (1902), that "the smoking-room proper, with its *mise-en-scène* of Turkish divans, nargilehs, brass coffee-trays, and other Oriental properties, is no longer considered a necessity in the modern house. . . ."[18] Their observation suggests that smoking was becoming so acceptable and commonplace that special rooms reserved for smoking in the domestic sphere were a thing of the past.

Just as clever, attractive marketing played a major role in introducing cigarettes to the consumer in the late nineteenth century, a renewed and more targeted pitch

Vogue magazine covers from 1926, depicting the new fashions for smoking and bold makeup, both requiring beautiful accessories.

encouraging the smoking of cigarettes by women dominated tobacco advertising in the 1920s. Companies sought to associate smoking with "beauty, glamour, and sexuality"[19] through campaigns such as the "Blow Some My Way" pitch of Chesterfield in the mid-1920s. This advertisement promoted smoking as sexually daring and to be shared with a man to entice him. Such ideas appealed to the modern woman, now liberated from the constraints of her grandmother's generation and free to take matters into her own hands. Smoking became a sociable pursuit, to be enjoyed in rail cars, offices, and libraries as well as fashionable restaurants, the theater, and nightclubs.[20] Accessories to enable social smoking quickly followed suit. Some furniture companies even provided special smoking tables with compartments for humidors and lighting equipment.[21]

This rise in smoking among men and women, however, did not come without opposition. Major scions of industry in America, Henry Ford and Thomas Edison, who ironically produced the most modern innovations—the motorcar and the light bulb—despised the use of tobacco. Ford went so far as to ban smoking by his employees at all seven thousand dealerships around the country.[22] Other opposition came from an older generation of women who were veterans of the successful, if not long-lived effort to force prohibition on the American people. However, unlike their fight to ban alcohol, which was based largely on moral grounds, tobacco prohibitionists appealed to aesthetics: smoking was ugly, dirty, and made one's breath smell bad.[23] Tobacco companies countered with a barrage of advertisements in fashion magazines, billboards, and other press showing not just the normalcy of women smoking in public, but the glamour and elegance of a woman surrounded by a wafting cloud of smoke.[24]

It was this new image of the modern woman that won out in the end. In both America and Europe, women were entering the professional workforce in record numbers by day and living an urban lifestyle by night. Dance halls and public ballrooms shared the stage with speakeasies and illicit gin-joints. The wealthiest young couples left their drawing rooms and traveled late at night to jazz clubs in Harlem in New York or Montmartre and the Latin Quarter in Paris. As essential as a glittering wisp of a dress was to the flapper—the ultimate modern icon of the Roaring Twenties—the bejeweled cigarette and vanity accessories became the necessities of the night for the most fashionable society elite. They held the essentials, rouge powder, perfume, lipstick, or cigarettes, at the ready for a quick dab or a short puff. The modern woman was now in charge of her own image: her clothes were the length she wanted; her hair was short and easy to style; and she could indulge any luxury she desired.[25]

Jewelers responded with exquisitely crafted vanity cases, called *nécessaires*, containing divided interior compartments to conceal face powder, lipsticks, and eye mascaras developed some years earlier by a burgeoning cosmetics industry before the First World War. One such vanity case made in 1926 by the Brooklyn, New York, firm Gold, Most & Fogel [67], is cleverly shaped like a small handbag decorated in brilliant red and blue enamel, offset by garlands of tiny diamonds, sapphires, rubies, and emeralds on the face. Opening to reveal a mirror and two compartments for cosmetics, this case typifies the combination of whimsy and practicality these *nécessaires* provided the sophisticated modern woman. As the motion picture industry began to capture the world's imagination, their goddesses—the Hollywood stars—became iconic models for a glamorous world of luxurious living. These lucky few were depicted in magazines or on the cover of sheet music and movie posters smoking and wearing distinctive makeup as emblems of a changing society, even if only imagined by most. Actress Clara Bow favored the Japanese Kabuki red lipstick supplied by

Helena Rubinstein which, when combined with a highly powdered face, produced a doll-like appearance on the black-and-white screens of the silent movie theaters.

Maintaining her beauty throughout a long night required the fashionable woman to carry necessities to be used side by side with other women in the ladies' lounge, instantly transforming these little utilitarian boxes into artistic symbols of status, wealth, and privilege. Cigarette cases served the same purpose because of what they symbolized: emblems of taste, independence, and the means to achieve both. Just as, a decade earlier, Fabergé and his Russian counterparts had created boxes and bibelots in the spirit of the eighteenth-century court for royalty, Cartier, Tiffany, Van Cleef & Arpels, Boucheron, Black, Starr & Frost, and many others did the same for the modern woman.[26]

While major firms maintained retail establishments in the urban style centers of the world where their clients could visit each separately, one event brought the European firms together in Paris: the 1925 Exposition internationale des Arts décoratifs et industriels modernes.[27] Enormously influential in the progress of modern style and taste in the 1920s, the official exhibition committee expressed their desire to show only works of modern artistic achievement. This fair was to be the ultimate synthesis of all that was thought to be modern in the moment. For reasons still not fully discernible, but mostly political, the United States commissioners declined the invitation from the French government to participate. Thus, American designers were not represented, although most of the rest of the Western nations did participate. There was an enormous amalgamation of ideas and currents of taste represented, notably those pavilions hosted by Austria, Germany, and Scandinavia. Against this backdrop, the French firms dominated with individual pavilions for large firms and ideal living experiences, such as the pavilion of "a collector" that showcased fashionable interiors by Parisian cabinetmaker Émile-Jacques Ruhlmann.[28] Smaller firms were arrayed in stands along the sides of the bridges crossing the Seine, and at the nexus of lanes in the middle stood a giant fountain of glass, lit brilliantly by night, created by René Lalique, who had been the undisputed king of Art Nouveau jewelry at the world's fair of the 1900 Exposition universelle in Paris and was now designing only in glass. There was no mistaking the metaphor—modernity and the fountain of youth. This motif of cascading water effectively served as an emblem of the fair and was repeated over and over in designs throughout the grounds and exhibits.

Modernity in 1925 was anything but defined. As British author Aldous Huxley asked in a May 1925 issue of *Vanity Fair*: "What, exactly, is modern?"[29] In his estimation, "only that which is really new, which has no counterpart in antiquity, is modern."[30] At the 1925 Exposition, several approaches to contemporary design combined to create a stylized modern aesthetic on the one hand, highly fluid with references to nature, figuration, and antique cultures, and a more abstract, streamlined modernity on the other, influenced not by nature but by the rational use of geometry and technological inspiration. Virtually shunned as too modern was the avant-garde—the artistic fringe, which took its inspiration from art movements such as Cubism, Futurism, German Expressionism, and the Dutch De Stijl. These differing aspects of modern design all live somewhat uncomfortably now under the large umbrella of "Art Deco," a later term derived from the title of the 1925 Exposition. However, contemporary observers and critics could see their distinctions. Writing some forty years later about her observations of the fair in 1925, Katharine McClinton described three types of Art Deco from that period: "the graceful, curvilinear type . . . ; the functional machine-inspired type . . . ; and [a type] tied to the rhythm of the times . . . [which] produced a

A fashion image by Thayaht titled "De la fumée," from *Gazette du bon ton*, 1922, depicting a dress by Madeleine Vionnet that appears to be made from the smoke of the woman's cigarette.

Plates by Paul Iribe from *Les robes de Paul Poiret*, 1908, showing the influential modern silhouette for women in a colorful palette.

gay, fanciful style but one that was still based on genuine values."[31] These categories of modern design that McClinton observed in the 1920s are to be found in the myriad designs for cigarette cases and vanity *nécessaires* of the Prince Sadruddin and Princess Catherine Aga Khan Collection. These works tell a story not only of the advancing independence and changing role of women in Western society between the two world wars but also of the corresponding development of artistic design during this period as well. Accessories of well-dressed occasions, these calling cards of wealth closely followed the aesthetics of the era.

Historicism

Paris after 1900 was just beginning to settle into the vast architectural changes undertaken fifty years earlier (1853–1875) by Napoleon III and his Prefect of the Seine, Eugène Haussmann. This unprecedented remaking of the central core of Paris transformed the previously crumbling medieval town into a glorious (some said vainglorious), shiny, new capital city. Haussmann was charged with creating grand boulevards leading to open plazas, bringing light and broad patterns of circulation into the once dark, narrow alleyways. Lined with commodious new apartment blocks, designed in a harmonious baroque style, Haussmann's boulevards and buildings, such as the Champs-Élysées and the Palais Garnier (Opéra), uplifted the character of the Parisian landscape. This era before the First World War came to be known as the Belle Époque, and Haussmann's Paris served as the backdrop for a grand aristocratic society, which it attracted. The city's new buildings were laden with mansard roofs and carved limestone in the form of Neoclassical decoration. Garlands, swags, cornucopias, classical figures, and Palladian arches were in abundance, dictating the visual aesthetic of everyday life. Opening nights at the Opéra were dubbed "tiara nights" by critics who noted that more interesting dramas played out in the lobbies and on the grand staircase than on the stage itself, animated by a glittering array of white diamonds and pearls.[32]

Parisian jewelers responded with jewels that reflected this taste for an earlier eighteenth-century grandeur: necklaces and brooches with garlands of white diamonds, long ropes of pearls, and elaborate Louis XVI–style hair ornaments. The opening of diamond mines in South Africa in the 1870s had made the procurement of spectacular stones more desirable. Louis Cartier's development of a platinum setting enhanced the lightness of the firm's creations, allowing for greater scale without becoming ponderous.[33] Important royal events around 1900, including the coronations of Nicholas II of Russia (1896) and Edward VII of Great Britain (1902), reinforced the Neoclassical style among society at all levels, whether participants or observers. Cartier's use of Neoclassicism continued to flourish throughout the teens and into the twenties as the most conservative and traditional form of good taste.[34]

While Neoclassicism reflected the Belle Époque sensibilities of established society, it also became a bridge over the naturalistic fervor of the Art Nouveau toward a more refined interpretation of modernity. Arguably the most influential fashion designer in Paris in the early teens was Paul Poiret, who, along with Paul Iribe, published an album of fashion plates in 1908 that featured natural waistlines free of corsets and silhouettes inspired by Directoire and Empire designs.[35] In this way, Iribe and Poiret contributed to a shift toward modernity that would have a lasting effect.[36] An enameled cylindrical vanity case by Cartier from around 1913 [36] reflects the symmetry, the use of *trophée* reserves (the round plaques set here with flowers), and white enameled stripes associated with late eighteenth-century Neoclassical decoration. In its economy of form and its use as a modern convenience to hold cosmetics, the design transcends mere imitation. This type of decoration was favored across Europe and could be found in the work of Henrik Wigström for the House of Fabergé as well.[37]

Cartier competed vigorously with Fabergé for the Russian market, establishing an outpost in St. Petersburg in 1907, and counting many Russian aristocrats, members of the imperial court, and the imperial family as clients. A box in hardstone affixed with diamond ribbons reflects designs for boxes by Russian makers [37]. Two vanity cases in the collection, one likely Russian by an unknown maker [38] and the other attributed to Cartier [39], share a similar use of a featured engraved panel depicting frolicking cherubs. This use of carved plaques was also a trait of the renowned Parisian jeweler René Lalique, who first used carved rock crystal around 1900, continuing into the 1920s. The Cartier case also features a contrasting black-and-white aesthetic that was a distinctly Viennese trait, having been used by Koloman Moser and Josef Hoffmann in the early years of the Viennese Secessionist movement after 1900 to imbue small objects with a sense of monumentality.[38] This fascination with the contrast between white and black, light and dark, continues throughout the twenties especially as a metaphor for day and night. A Cartier mechanical pencil and a Bulgari vanity case, both from around 1930 [40, 41], display this effect in their stark use of white diamonds and pearls, at the edge of the pencil, against black enameled surfaces, one matte, the other highly polished. The Bulgari case employs the use of a *giardinetto* device, or "little garden," which is in the form of a basket of stylized flowers. The plants themselves are indiscernible, but the effect is the same—an evocation of nature transformed, abstracted, and harnessed—all characteristics of Viennese decoration that were espoused earlier in the century and applied throughout the 1920s to create an accessible style of modernism that adapted established forms in new ways.

François Boucher, *The Toilette of Venus*, 1751.
The influence of eighteenth-century Romantic grandeur can be seen in the ribbon and cupid motifs of early Art Deco designs.

37
Ribbon Box, France, circa 1915

38

Putto and Lady Vanity Case, probably Russia, circa 1920

39
Putti Vanity Case Attributable to Cartier, circa 1920

40
Mechanical Pencil by Cartier, circa 1929

41
Giardinetto Vanity Case by Bulgari, Rome, circa 1930

Stylistic Modern

One of the most influential, over-arching tenets of design during the first half of the twentieth century was the concept of *Gesamtkunstwerk*, meaning a total or harmonious work of art.[39] Especially strong in Austria and Germany, this ideal of a completely unified aesthetic scheme—from architecture to interior arrangement, furniture to furnishing fabrics, dishes to cutlery—extended to fashion and accessories as well. The same patterns and motifs used to adorn buildings and decorative furnishings found their way into the visual language of everyday life through graphic design, set design, and fashion. Viennese design from the first decades of the twentieth century represented a counterpoint to the dominant forces of the Art Nouveau practiced elsewhere around Europe, especially France and Belgium. Indeed, those artists and artisans who raised a voice of dissent against the proponents of whiplash lines and saccharine symbolism resigned from the Association of Austrian Artists and came together in 1897 as the Secessionists. Eventually attracting patrons and staging their own exhibitions of architecture and applied arts, these designers became enormously influential on the world stage with others either embracing or rejecting their tenets. While Art Nouveau waned before 1910, the work of the collective known as the Wiener Werkstätte, founded in 1903, would continue to dominate the discourse of design well into the 1920s.

Like all students of art around 1900, Secessionist designers led by Moser and Hoffmann looked to Japanese art for a path out of what they felt was the oppressiveness of historicism that had long dominated art and design during the nineteenth century. Through reimagining Japanese design and adapting certain qualities like a reduction of form, the Secessionists were able to avoid the excesses of the literal translation of Japanese decoration found in the *japonisme* of the 1880s and 1890s, to create a more sophisticated approach, based on pattern and repetition.[40] The result was a heavy emphasis on stripes, dots, and cubes—all manner of shapes and patterns repeated in lines of contrasting colors and values. Art historian Kirk Varnedoe describes this trait as "order directing natural energies,"[41] an apt observation given the rigid linear quality of much early Secessionist decoration.

The influence of this aesthetic can be seen in two cigarette cases in the collection that feature such a pulsing energy, in these cases both achieved through parallel lines of channel-set sapphires [43, 42]. The translucency of the stones gives an added three-dimensional quality to an otherwise flat pattern, contrasted in one of the two cases with the use of mother-of-pearl panels, further enhancing this depth and texture. With two other cases made in France [44, 45], the diagonal stripes form a trellis pattern, offset at the juncture of lines with repeated dots of rubies and lozenges of sapphires. Both rely on additional contrasting backgrounds, one of smooth polished rock crystal, the other of pebbly seed pearls, to relieve the visual tension of repetition. A Cartier perfume bottle similarly exploits the contrast between polished and frosted rock crystal on the fluted container against a black enamel setting studded with stones [46]. These containers reveal a mannered approach to Viennese aesthetics through this use of materials to achieve an added dimensional effect.

42
Cigarette Case, probably Russia, circa 1910

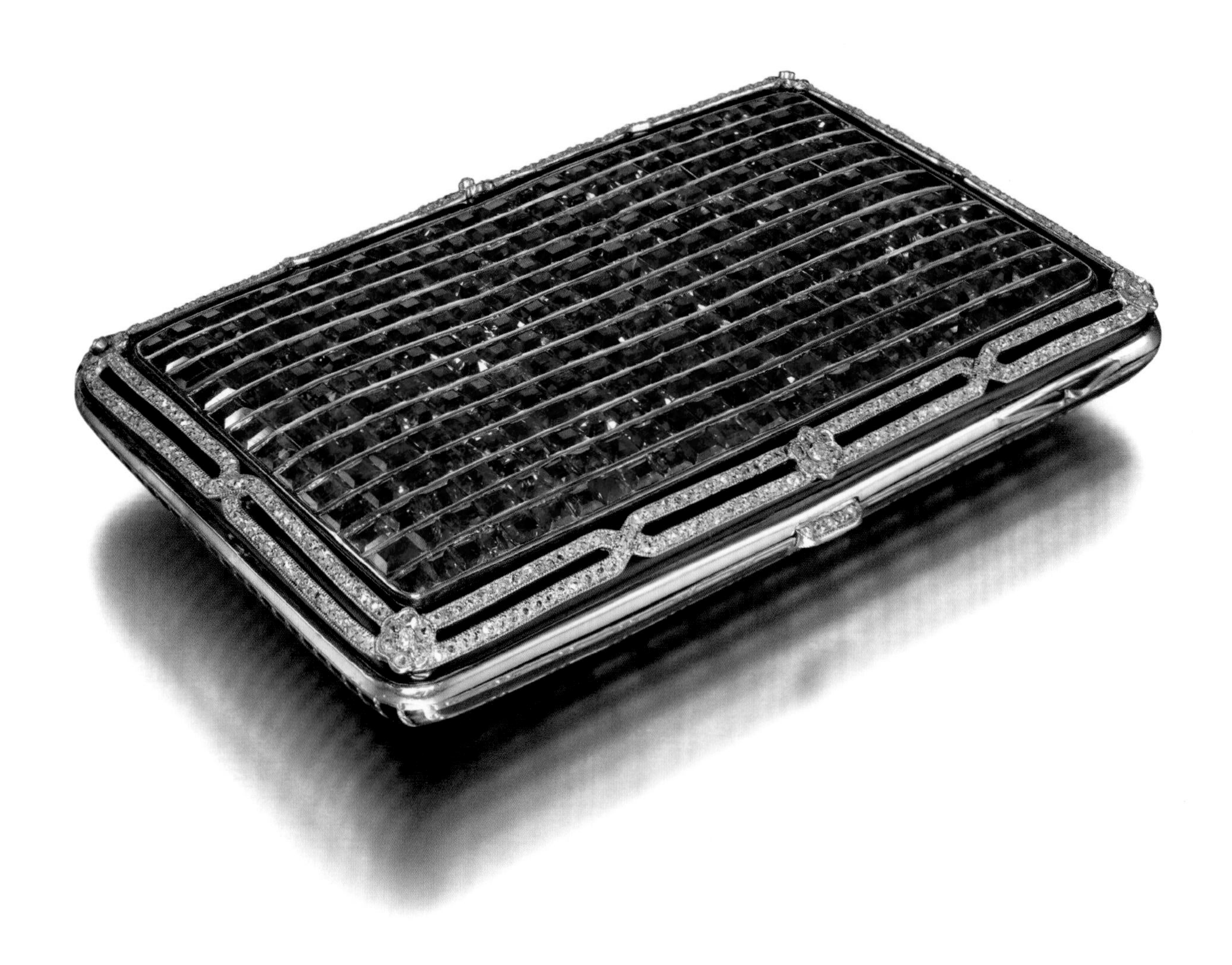

43
Cigarette Case, circa 1920

Opposite:
44
Rabbit Vanity Case by Cartier, Paris, circa 1924

45
Cigarette Case and Match Box, France, circa 1920

Another group of cases adheres more closely to a later 1920s Secessionist approach of using smaller repetitive patterns to achieve subtle rhythms of decoration. Two cases by Cartier from around 1927–30 produce a carpeted effect through a wrap-around pattern of black-and-white stylized chevrons enameled within a plain gold ground [47, 48]. The addition of color to the patterns in two similar works by Cartier and Van Cleef & Arpels [49, 50] creates a rich, two-dimensional effect by layering the patterns. Employing an even bolder use of red, black, and yellow in a cigarette case [51] from 1927, Van Cleef & Arpels achieves a strong visual rhythm, enhanced by the diagonal stripes, in an abstracted "leaf" pattern, though no discernible plant is apparent. All of these cases display an intimate knowledge of Viennese design principles by their makers and an understanding of the popularity of these motifs among their clients.

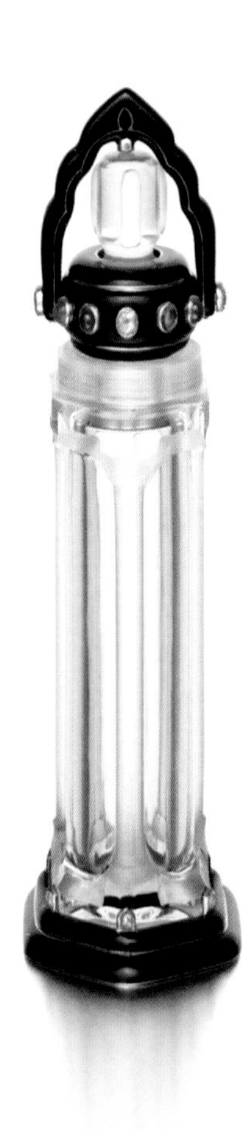

46
Perfume-Extract Bottle by Cartier, Paris, circa 1924

47
Geometric Pattern Cigarette Case by Cartier, Paris, circa 1930, Manufactured by Renault

48
Geometric Pattern Vanity Case by Cartier, Paris, circa 1927, Manufactured by Renault

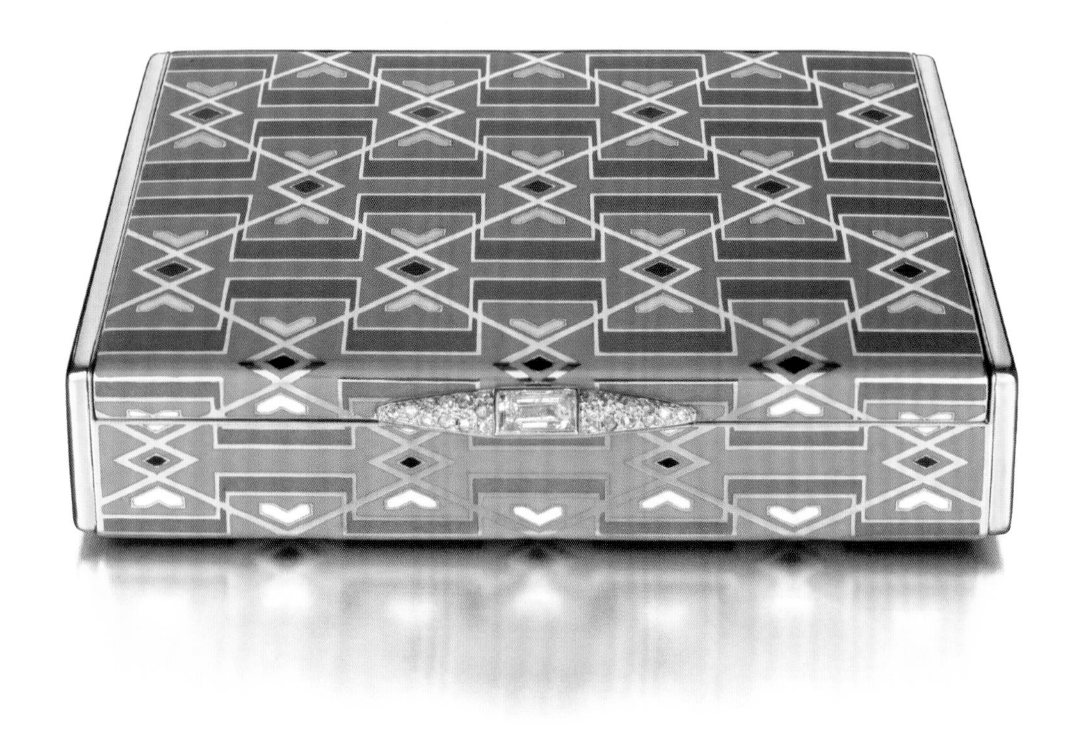

49
Geometric Vanity Case by Cartier, Paris, circa 1930

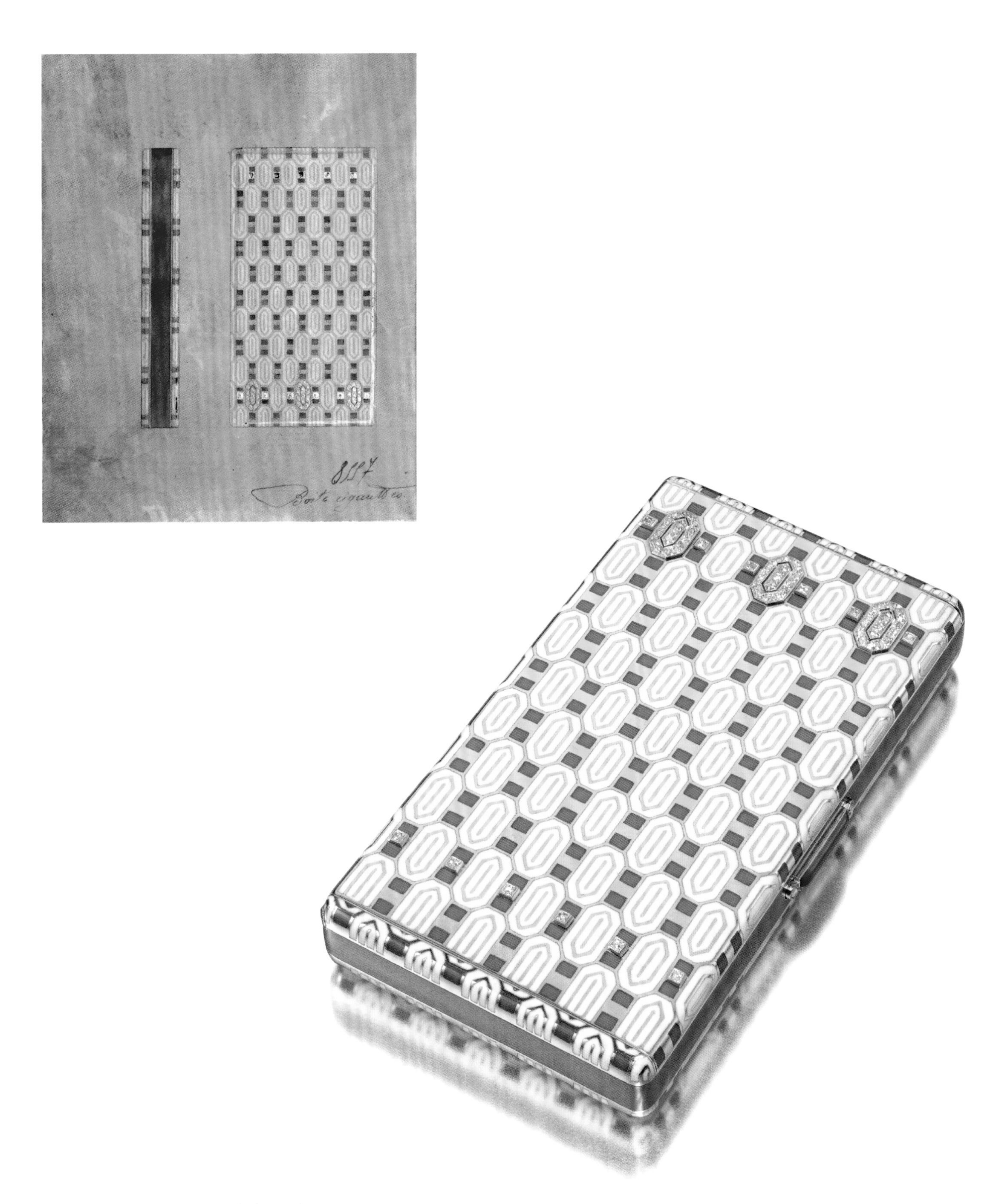

Original retail book drawing, Van Cleef & Arpels, Paris, 1927.

50
"Aubergine Motif" Cigarette Case by Van Cleef & Arpels, Paris, 1927, Manufactured by Alfred Langlois

Original retail book drawing, Van Cleef & Arpels, Paris, 1925.

51
"Feuilles" Cigarette Case by Van Cleef & Arpels, Paris, 1927, Manufactured by Alfred Langlois

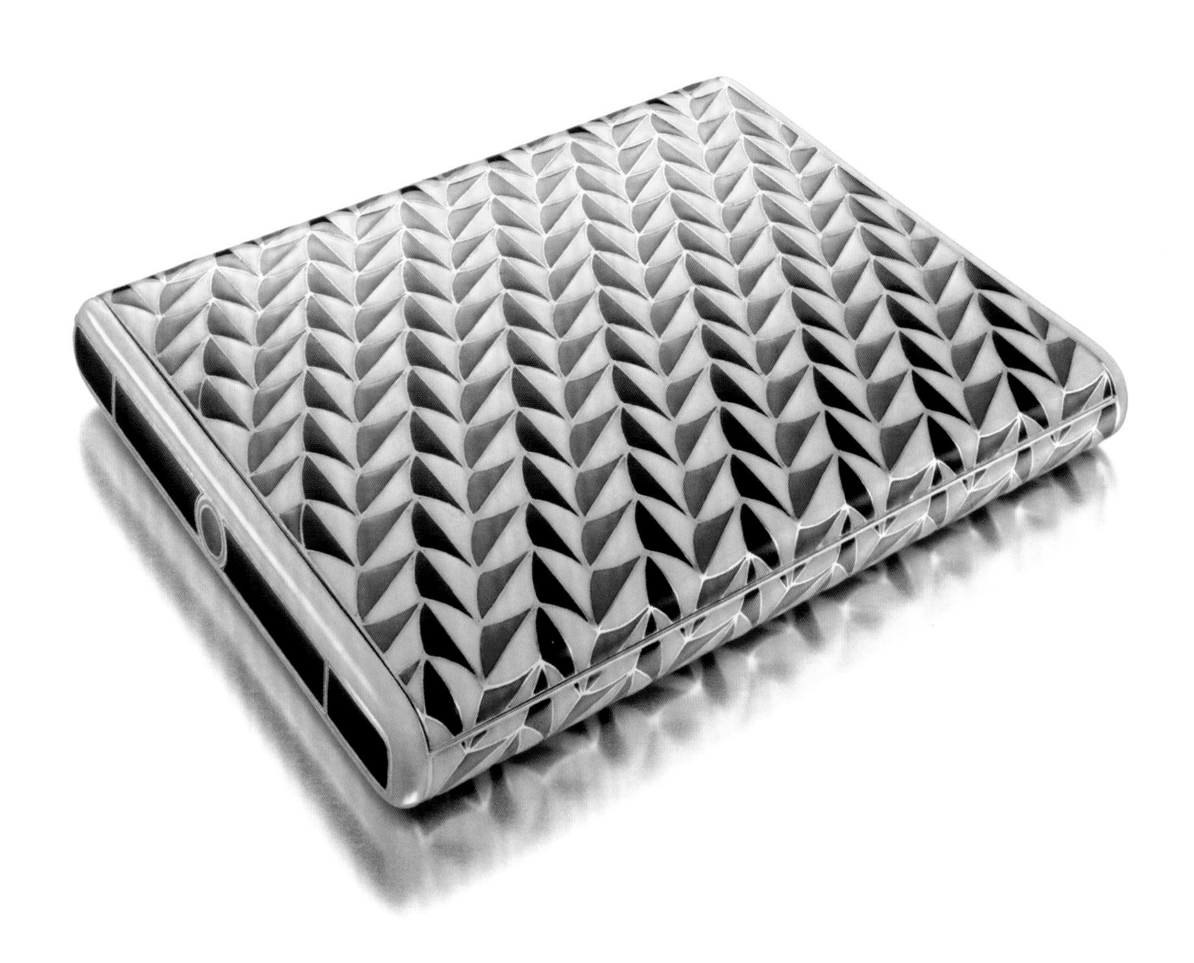

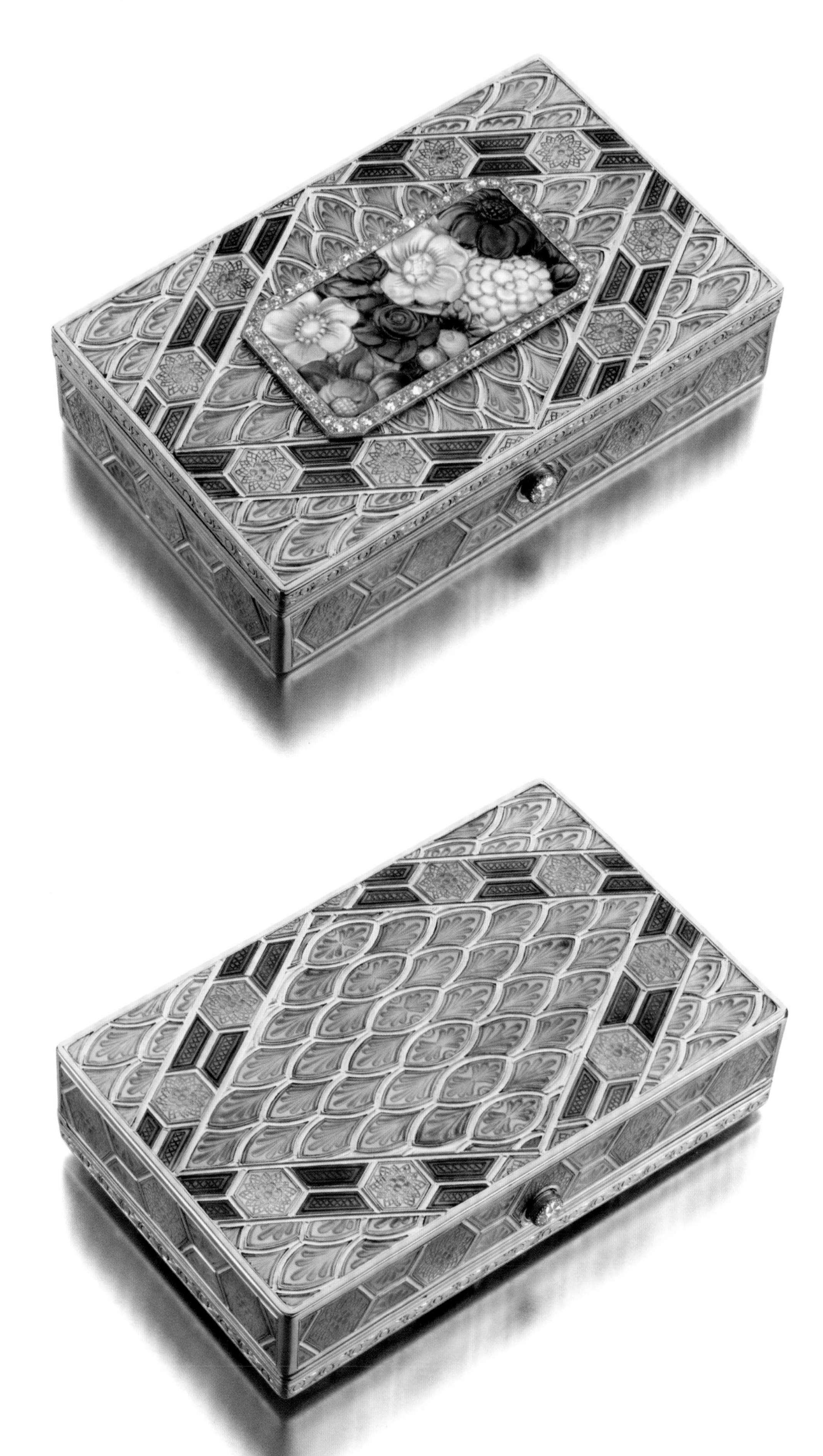

52
Vanity Case by Bensimon, Paris, circa 1920

After the founding of the Wiener Werkstätte in 1903, the use of pure geometric forms in Viennese design, such as the repetition of circles and squares, moved toward a more stylized, abstracted treatment of naturalistic ornament than had been seen before.[42] Varnedoe observes that much of this shift resulted from an increased fascination with folk traditions in Eastern Europe in much the same way that the Arts and Crafts Movement impacted British design.[43] The same held true in France. After a trip to Austria, Germany, and Belgium in 1910, Paul Poiret returned home to open the Atelier Martine, a collaborative art school in which young women with no training at all were encouraged to draw patterns derived from nature.[44] The aim was to arrive at fresh, bold, naïve patterns for textiles, which resulted in a mélange of new color combinations and boldly shaped patterns. The stylized floral patterning superimposed over a geometric ground in a vanity case by Bensimon [52] reflects this approach, first expressed in Vienna then translated to Paris by Poiret. Likewise, a *nécessaire* by Strauss, Allard & Meyer for Lacloche Frères of 1927 [53] includes the same concept but realized in a much bolder way with contrasting coral, lapis lazuli, and semi-precious stones. The naturalistic color combination of jadeite, coral, amethyst, and sapphires, against a background of sea-green aventurine, dominates the top of a vanity case [81] retailed by Janesich in Paris around 1928, also manufactured by the firm Strauss, Allard & Meyer. These abstracted depictions of nature were seen as modern in the eyes of the luxury consumer and were instantly recognized as motifs found in every genre of decorative arts.

53
Flower Vanity Case by Lacloche Frères, Paris, circa 1927, Manufactured by Strauss, Allard & Meyer

Wall decoration at the tomb of I'timad ud-Daulah in Agra, Uttar Pradesh, India, 1622–28. A Mughal mausoleum often described as the "Baby Taj," it displays a variety of wall patterns, including honeycomb motif.

Cultural Styles

A counterpoint to classically derived designs from the teens and twenties as well as the more stylized modern adaptations of nature and geometry found in Viennese-inspired designs were those that explored cultures relatively unknown to the average consumer. African, Egyptian, Mayan, Native North American (American Indian), Chinese, Japanese, Indian, and Near Eastern—these modes were all ones that held the popular fascination of Western culture during the Roaring Twenties. Some styles were prompted by popular events such as the discovery and opening of Pharaoh Tutankhamun's tomb in Egypt between 1922 and 1925, after which no genre of design was immune to the layering on of Egyptian decoration. Others were less inspired by events than by association, such as that of Turkish tobacco with smoking and its accessories. Still other modes, mainly those derived from Asian and Near Eastern cultures, were continuations of long-revered decorative schemes, which had enjoyed moments of popularity in nearly every century past.

Europeans had been trading with the East since the seventeenth century and shortly after that with China. Though Japan had been opened to the West only from the mid-nineteenth century, the impact of Japanese art and culture on Western thought and creativity cannot be overstated. In the 1920s these influences profoundly affected the progress of artistic production, particularly in the area of applied arts. More and more, Western tourists were making journeys to Asia and the East, but by far the biggest exposure was to be found in the collections amassed at large metropolitan art museums around the world, particularly in New York, London, and Paris. Jewelers such as Louis Comfort Tiffany and Louis Cartier encouraged their designers to draw from these collections and to learn about new materials and decorative schemes.[45] Orchestral, ballet, and theater productions brought the sounds and settings of these faraway lands to life as well.[46] The most influential of all these sources was the Ballets Russes in Paris in the years before the First World War. Its founder, Sergei Diaghilev, staged many productions of diverse foreign cultural themes from 1909 until 1929, with elaborate sets, exotic costumes, and evocative scores. For many, particularly artistic Parisians, the Ballets Russes brought the Eastern world to life, even if accuracy took a back seat to creative imagination.

By this period, India had become a rich source of precious stones and an inspiration for setting designs. While elaborate and often enormously scaled jewels in the Indian taste were created for specific clients in Europe and America, as well as in India itself, a more subtle use of patterning, reflecting a fresh approach to the design, can be found in the luxury accessories designed in this mode within the collection. The Cartier honeycomb patterned cigarette case of 1929 [54] depicts the ennobled structure produced by the honeybee used to adorn buildings throughout the ancient world, including the Taj Mahal. Its original owner may not have readily recognized such a reference, but certainly the geometry of the patterning conveyed a modern spirit easily understood. Two other cigarette cases [56, 55] produced by Cartier around 1930 use contrasting black, white, and gold elements to emphasize the perfectly proportioned Islamic motifs at each side. Likely taken from textile patterns, these elements would have been instantly identified with Near Eastern cultures. A more elaborate example using similar motifs is the Cartier box [57] with stylized orientalist motifs of white diamonds in each corner surrounding a central lozenge of similar pattern against a finely enameled ground of white stripes. Here the decorative elements are more abstract and share an affinity with both Islamic and Asian aesthetics.

54
Honeycomb Pattern Cigarette Case by Cartier, Paris, circa 1929

55
Cigarette Case and Lighter, Cartier, circa 1932

56
Cigarette Case by Cartier, Paris, circa 1929

57
Box by Cartier, circa 1928

58
Cigarette and Vanity Case by Cartier, Paris, circa 1925

59
Box by Cartier, Paris, circa 1927

In a similar, but perhaps more overt way, the Cartier combination cigarette and vanity case [58] in black enamel of around 1925 blends several cultures. The form derives from Japanese inro boxes, which were small, compartmented cases designed to carry several necessities at once. The central section is flanked at either end by patterns inspired by Islamic lambrequins outlined in diamonds and featuring small cabochon emeralds. Parallel Grecian meandering borders complete the composition. Likewise, the white marble Cartier box [59], which belonged to the designer Jean-Charles Worth, displays a similar combination of elements as the little vanity case, with its Islamic-patterned hinges on a Chinese form resembling carved jade. This melding of cultures could be seen as a metaphor of the times, particularly in light of the cacophony of influences to be absorbed in Paris of the 1920s.

Chinese decorative motifs on luxury cases were the most recognizable in this period as they were largely inspired by patterns found on objects from the trade that any client might have owned, such as bronzes, textiles, lacquer boxes, and export ceramics. The Cartier vanity case of 1925 [60] in multicolored Chinese patterning uses enameled decoration in exactly the same way as could be found on a *famille verte* Chinese export vase, with its central trellis pattern flanked by two boldly worked vines. Evocative of a Chinese silk textile, the fern compact [61] was made in France by an unknown maker about 1929. Cartier produced a cigarette case [62] with a small-scaled honeycomb pattern, so small in fact that it resembles a screen rather than a beehive, taken almost directly from the ground pattern found on a seventeenth-century Chinese box. Two works manufactured by Strauss, Allard & Meyer [64, 63] depict the delicate asymmetry of plum blossoms often seen in Japanese woodblock prints, painted screens, or ceramics. Even if they were not adorned with such a recognizable motif, their coloration, one jet-black with diamonds, the other brilliant red with black accents, has long been emblematic of the Chinese aesthetic as popularized in the West. The use of red and black in Chinese lacquerware dates back to ancient practice, with the color red corresponding to fire and symbolizing joy and good luck, while black corresponds to water and connotes the mystery of life. These same colors of red and black, in imitation of Chinese lacquers, can be seen in two boxes resembling valises with diamond straps [65, 66], in which the primary focus is the purity of color and simplicity of form.

Design by Owen Jones showing the floral vine pattern from *Examples of Chinese Ornament*, 1867.

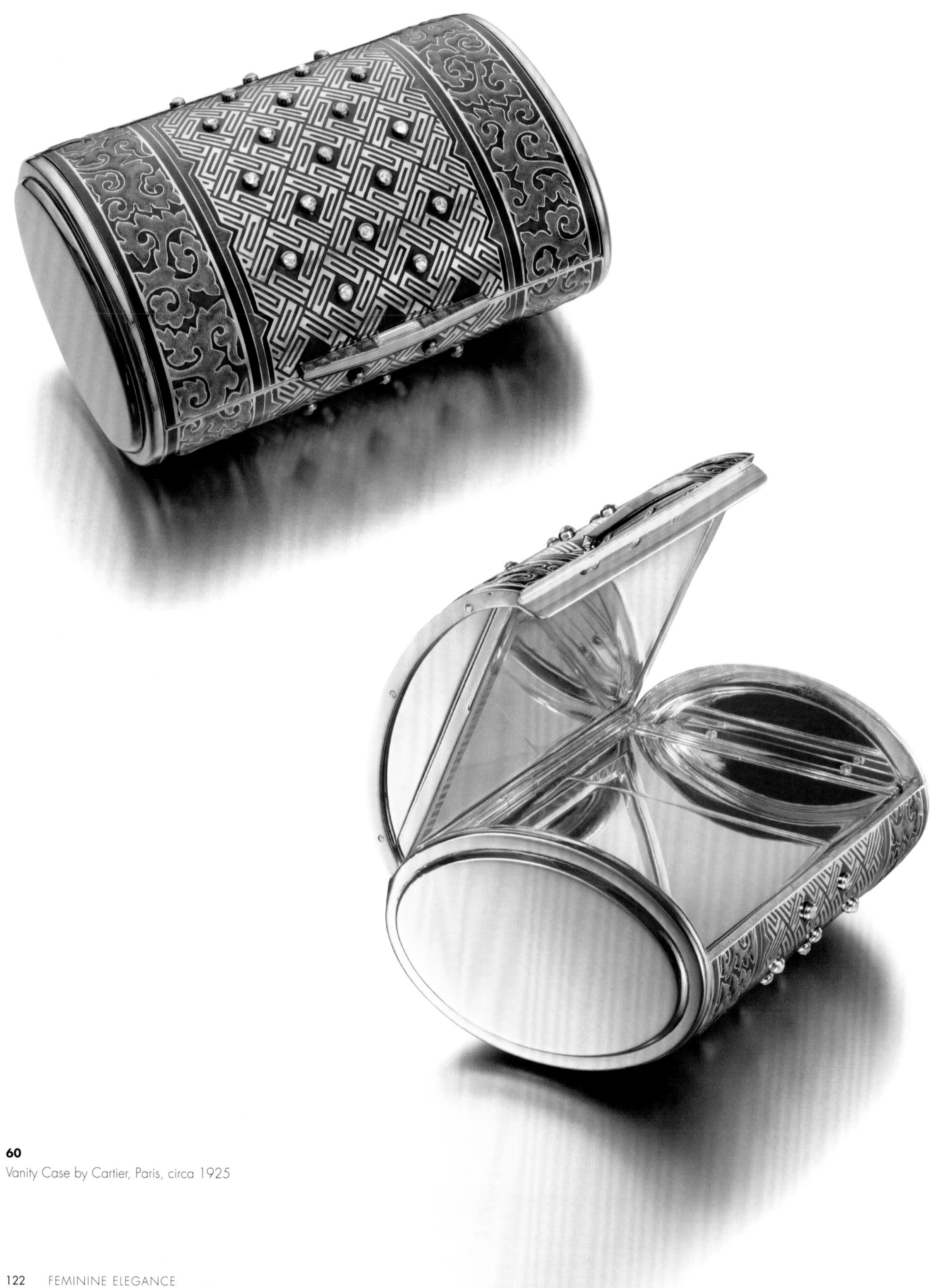

60
Vanity Case by Cartier, Paris, circa 1925

61
Fern Compact, France, circa 1929

62
Dot Pattern Cigarette Case by Cartier, Paris, circa 1930

63
Plum Blossom Vanity Case and Lipstick Holder by Strauss, Allard & Meyer, Paris, circa 1925

64
Plum Blossom Vanity Case by Lacloche Frères, Paris, circa 1925, Manufactured by Strauss, Allard & Meyer

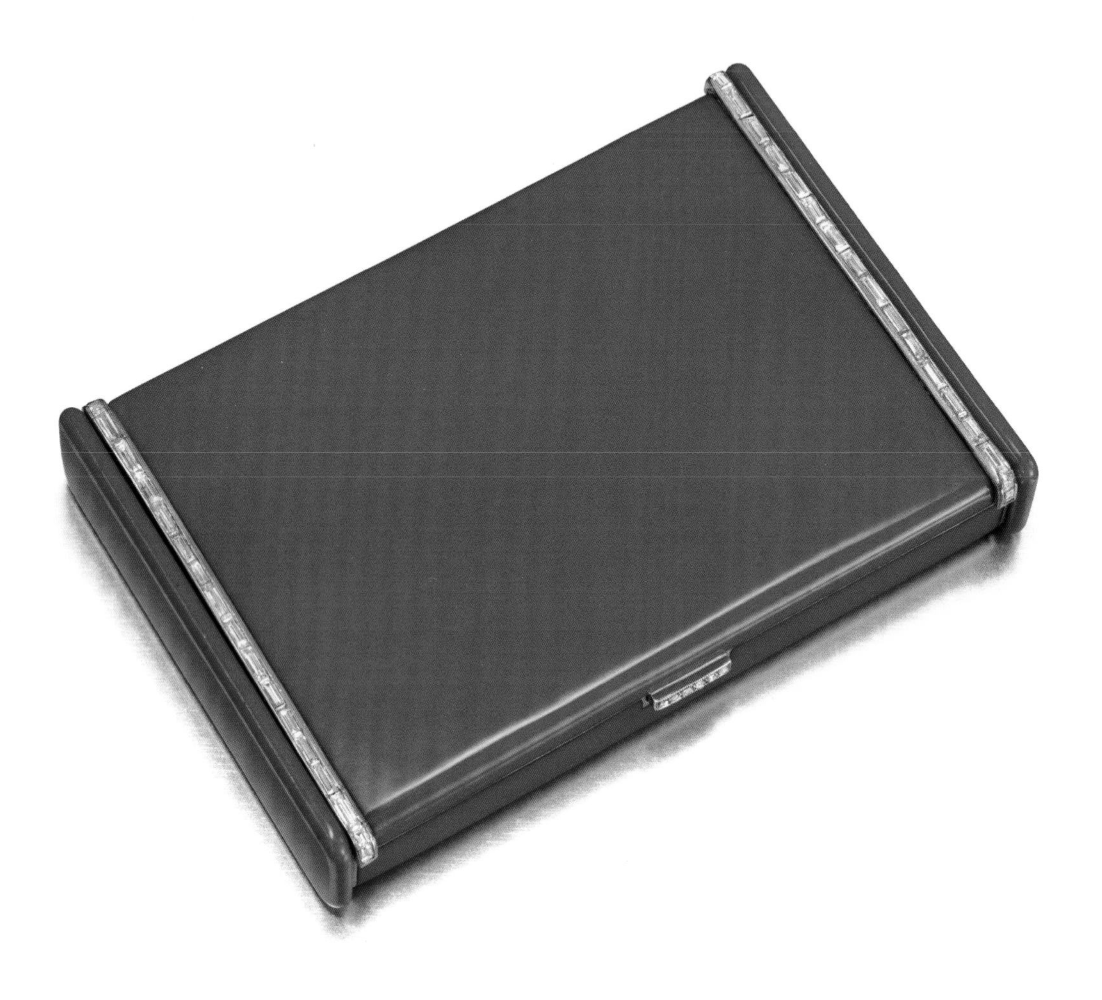

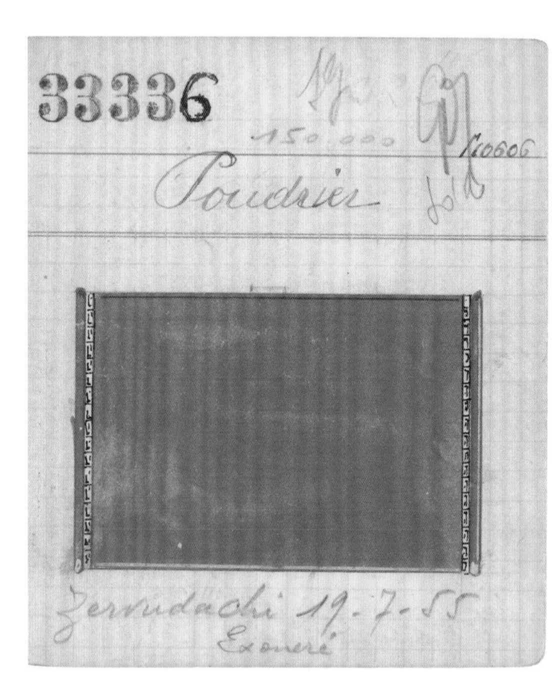

65
Vanity Case by Van Cleef & Arpels, Paris, 1930,
Manufactured by Strauss, Allard & Meyer

Original stock card, Van Cleef & Arpels, Paris, 1930.

66
Vanity Case by Janesich, Paris, circa 1928, Manufactured by Strauss, Allard & Meyer

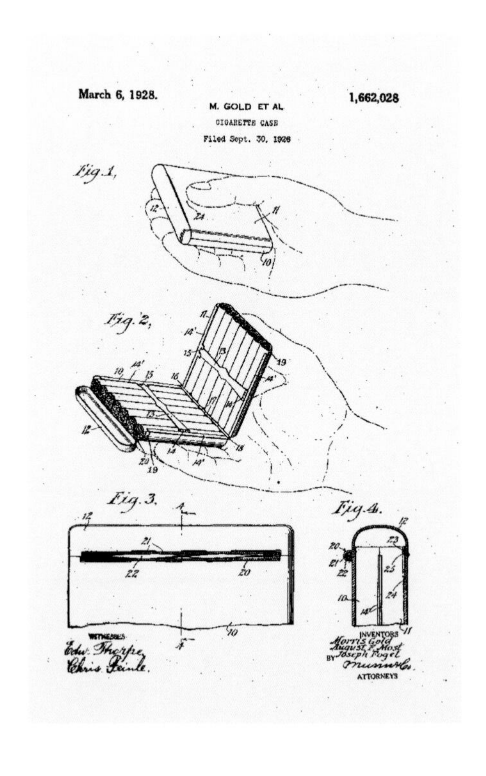

67

Vanity Case by Gold, Most & Fogel, New York, circa 1926

A patent filed by Gold, Most & Fogel for the one-handed closing mechanism employed on this box, 1926.

Abstracted Modern

Commissioning work from avant-garde painters and sculptors is one reason the Ballets Russes is so often cited as a moving force in the progress of modern design in Paris during the twenties.[47] Among those whose work was seen by a wider audience as a result of their association with Diaghilev's company were Léon Bakst, Georges Braque, André Derain, Juan Gris, Natalia Goncharova, Henri Matisse, and Pablo Picasso. Through the publicity and popularity that surrounded each production, Parisians became aware of artistic movements outside the rarified world of the salon, such as Futurism, Cubism, and Expressionism.[48] These ideas were further advanced through the forming of ateliers of design at major department stores in both New York and Paris promoting modern design. Likewise, jewelers infused their creations with an eclectic blend of cultural and artistic motifs "moderated by a geometrical treatment of shapes."[49] Two vanity cases, one by Tiffany & Co. and the other by Gold, Most & Fogel [68, 67], produced around 1925, exemplify the push toward more overtly abstracted design against the pull of accessible, recognizable decoration. On the Tiffany box, the rectangular form itself is a conventional geometric shape, enhanced with faceted sides, repeated in a stepped-form lapis inlay on the top. However, just as the central decorative element, while composed of geometric shapes in precious stones, is nonetheless an easily recognizable basket of flowers, on the other box, the central element seems to be floral, composed of a complicated hanging mechanism made up of geometric parts. The combinations may seem confused, but they typify the restrained modernism of the early and mid-1920s in which commercial designers sought to temper their artistic impulses with an eye toward the taste of their consumer.

68
Vanity Case by Tiffany & Co., Paris, circa 1925

Similarly, a combination vanity and cigarette case, commissioned for Princess Andrée Aga Khan from Cartier [69], uses geometricized elements of decoration, but the form is that of a traditional eighteenth-century etui, and the ground is a complete wash of black enamel evoking an association with traditional Chinese lacquer. By contrast, a compact by Cartier from later in the decade [70] displays no such restraint in its use of modernism. Stepped elements, now fully assimilated into the vocabulary of design as the result of the surge in skyscraper architecture, such as the Chrysler Building in New York of 1928–30, form the central unifying element of the composition without the use of other traditional design motifs.

69
Princess Andrée Aga Khan's Vanity Case and Cigarette Box by Cartier, Paris, circa 1925

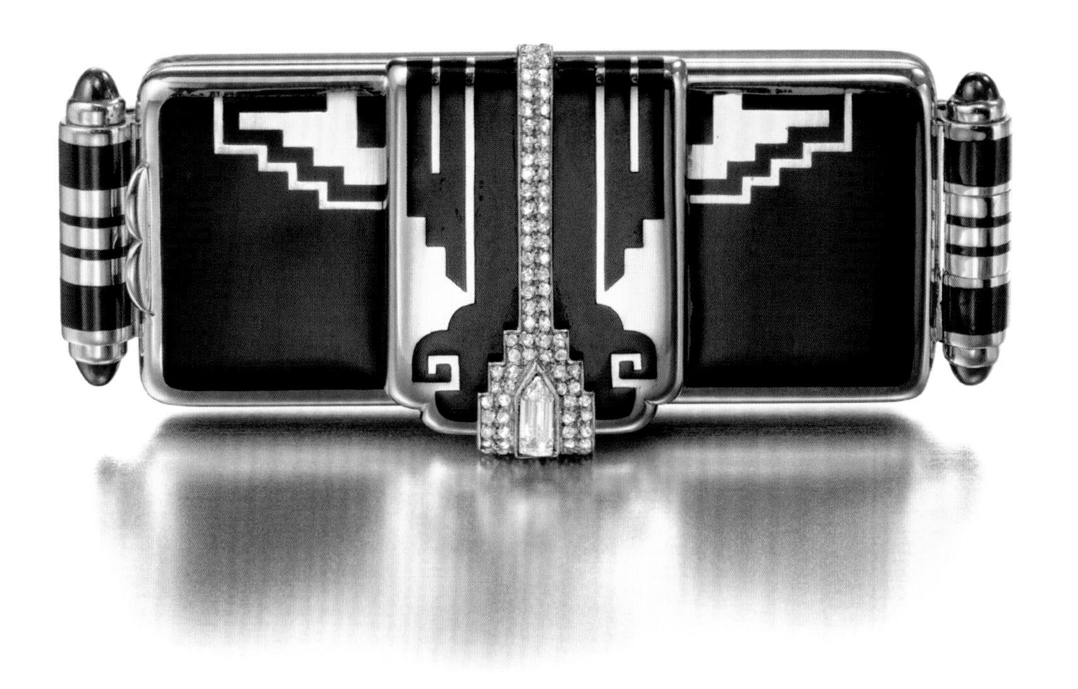

70
Compact Brooch by Cartier, Paris, 1929,
Manufactured by Ploujavy

Pure geometric form was a fully integrated concept in modern design by the 1920s, having triumphed over other modes of artistic reform, notably the organic abstraction of the Art Nouveau. A jabot brooch by Marzo displays the ideal of simplified geometric design in the two frosted rock crystal disks tied together with simple diamond, onyx, and enamel straps [71]. Russian jewelers, in particular, favored simple shapes that featured relatively unadorned materials, exquisitely worked. Two boxes in the collection, both probably French, but based on Russian hardstone box designs [72, 73], display this love of material in a thoroughly modern way: sleek forms, with rounded corners, featuring the beauty and purity of their carved agates. Their only embellishments are a clasp and two hinges of abstracted modern shapes realized in tiny precious stones.

A carved nephrite cigarette case by Cartier [74] uses only the tiniest border of enameled triangles to highlight the innate beauty of its panels of deep green hardstone. The asymmetrical arrangement of these lines and panels may show the influence of the Dutch De Stijl movement and its proponents Gerrit Rietveld and Piet Mondrian, who championed a mode of composition based on two-dimensional planes and lines in space meeting at points on a grid. Similarly, the pendant by Dusausoy [75], shown in a 1927 article in the French art journal *L'Illustration*,[50] captures the spirit of Cubism in its abstracted composition of angular lines and contrasting colors, while the inlaid malachite panels themselves reveal fractured patterns, mimicking the look of Cubist forms.

71
Jabot Brooch by Marzo, Paris, circa 1925

72
Striped Agate Box, circa 1919

73
Agate Box, circa 1919

74
Cigarette Case and Mechanical Pencil by Cartier, Paris, circa 1928, Manufactured by Renault

A page from Henri Clouzot's seminal article "Le Bijou moderne," from *L'Illustration*, December 3, 1927, featuring the Dusausoy pendant.

75
Tree Pendant by Dusausoy, Paris, circa 1925

As the Roaring Twenties moved into the more sober years of the 1930s, the world was plunged into a cauldron of economic depression, political instability, and a reordering of society at all levels. Those that had not lost their fortunes in the stock market crash, and there were plenty, continued to seek comfort in the glamour and elegance of a bejeweled existence. However, the colorful motifs of floral garlands and bubbling fountains, the wild eclectic pairings of cultural influences, and the frivolity imbedded in society took on a harder edge. Those at the top continued to enjoy luxurious evenings at the opera, theater, and nightclubs, but the contrasts between rich and poor became more pronounced. The economies, both literal and figurative, that were accepted in daily life began to be reflected in the aesthetic of luxury goods. Women's wear took on a simpler silhouette, with long straight lines offset by angular shoulder pads or curvilinear draping. Shapes in all aspects of design from architecture to decorative arts, including fashion and accessories, took on the streamlined look derived more from the rational, purpose-driven shapes demanded by industry than the organic lines found in nature. Some historians have termed this era in design the Machine Age, because of the appeal of progress as expressed in the ergonomic and aerodynamic innovations used by man to harness and exploit the power of earth's resources.[51] In 1929, the French critic Jean Gallotti described the work of such master jewelers as Raymond Templier, Jean Fouquet, and Jean Després as a "school of straight lines,"[52] to reflect their Futurist aesthetic, which relied on pure geometry, spatial relationships, contrasting textures, and an emphasis on white and black materials. These characteristics were instantly associated with the lines and aesthetics of machinery and were found in more luxurious combinations in the work of established luxury firms.

In two designs for a compact and a vanity case made around 1930 [76, 77], Cartier uses the strong contrast of white diamond pavé against a polished black enamel ground to transform otherwise mechanical-looking decorative elements into luxurious accompaniments. The same is true for a Cartier case from 1936 incorporating a coral baton into the strap clasp [78]. Here the shiny black surfaces are not meant to evoke Chinese lacquer. Rather, they provide the necessary foil to the blinding, fiery effect of the diamonds. An ironic twist is seen in these works as well as in a small lipstick case by Cartier from 1940 [79], in which the maker obliterates the precious nature of the gold base by completely covering the surface with black enamel. The effect is at once modern and abstract; the nature of the material is obscured, and the simplicity and purity of the form are supreme.

76
Compact by Cartier, Paris, circa 1929

77
Vanity Case by Cartier, London, circa 1930

Cartier London

The Art of Smoking

The dawning of a new century in 1900 brought the promise of new horizons for women in Europe and America. The fight for suffrage and the responsibilities that went along with taking a full stake in society meant that women were able to unlace their corsets, both literally and figuratively, and gain the freedom to think and be independent that their ancestors had been unable to claim. The ability to smoke was just one outward sign of this newfound freedom that, ironically, would ultimately become yet another shackle, binding their lives to an unhealthy future. Still, the act and art of smoking to achieve personal pleasure, social parity with men, and a modern sensibility created a lasting legacy in the accessories used to conduct such a titillating habit. Smoking accessories went hand in hand with vanity paraphernalia and together they became tokens of the heady nightlife that characterized the Jazz Age. As markers of high fashion these hand-held treasures were vehicles for personal expression and emblems of status and taste. Great firms of luxury goods produced cigarette and vanity *nécessaires* in all manner of precious materials, usually showcasing their finest techniques in jewelry setting, composition, artistic design, and mechanical innovation. Designs for cigarette and vanity cases closely paralleled trends in art and decoration between the two world wars. Examples of the finest artistry and workmanship from this era can be found in the Prince Sadruddin and Princess Catherine Aga Khan Collection and represent seminal aspects of the progress of modernity, from the historicism of the Belle Époque to the stylized modernism of the twenties. Cultural traditions, including works in the Persian, Japanese, and Chinese tastes, are numbered alongside those of an abstracted modernist aesthetic, emblematic of the Machine Age. Though the "art" of smoking has eventually faded as the harm of its destructive effects on the human body has become apparent, these remarkable objects of an era past are now what remain as art, a legacy of the progress of design in the twentieth century.

79
"Forget-Me-Not" Lipstick Case by Cartier, Paris, 1940

Opposite:
78
Vanity Case by Cartier, London, circa 1936

Catalogue Texts

Sarah Davis

HISTORICISM

36

Cylindrical Vanity and Cigarette Case by Cartier, Paris, circa 1913

A cylindrical vanity case decorated throughout with white enamel stripes (*émail pekin mille raies*), separated by four green and rose gold wreath bands, the front and back accented by white enamel plaques with diamond-set floral motifs, the ends set with pink agate, suspended from an alternating white enamel and gold link chain with a suspension ring set with rose-cut diamonds, with a diamond-set thumbpiece and two diamond-set push-pieces; interior fitted with a large compartment with matching removable lipstick case, one end opens to reveal a fitted mirror and powder compartment, the other end opens to reveal a strike-a-light; gold, with French assay marks

Signed Cartier Paris Londres New York, 607
Measurements: 11.6 x 5.2 x 3.1 cm, 4 9/16 x 2½ x 1¼ inches

One of the earliest boxes in the collection, this vanity case shows the transition away from the ornate "Garland Style" popular in the Belle Époque to a stripped-down geometry. At the turn of the century, jewelers created objects and jewelry with all-white color forming ornate floral garlands and ribbons. This box was designed at the end of that period and, while it incorporates some of those elements, according to *Retrospective Louis Cartier*, it was designed in the style of Louis XVI, or early Neoclassicism, which took its inspiration from the grandeur of Greece and Rome and the designs of Palladio and Vitruvius.

Neoclassical design was influenced by the grid system, as can be seen in the enamel lines and gold bands. The play of light and shadow is also explored in the use of enamel and gold lines. Neoclassical architectural references can be seen in the subtle treatment of the rosette plaques on either side of the lid. The rose gold border beautifully encircles one side of the plaque before overlapping with the other side of the border and returning to the green gold garland. These Neoclassical elements are precursors to the stripped-down geometry of the early Art Deco.

37

Ribbon Box, France, circa 1915

A box carved from a single block of translucent light brown agate, each of the corners decorated with a ribbon-tied floral spray set with small diamonds, further enhanced with diamond-set ribbons on the hinges and thumbpiece; gold and platinum, with French assay marks

Measurements: 8.9 x 6.9 x 2.4 cm, 3½ x 2¾ x 15/16 inches

Made in France, this box is inspired by the carved hardstone boxes of Russian makers including Fabergé. The delicate ribbon motif is a holdover from the Belle Époque and is juxtaposed against the beautiful simplicity of a box carved from a single block of agate.

38

Putto and Lady Vanity Case, probably Russia, circa 1920

A frosted rock crystal vanity case with a scene engraved on the underside of the cover, the geometric hinges and clasp set with rose-cut diamonds; interior fitted with two compartments; gold and platinum, with French owl importation marks

Measurements: 6.8 x 5.9 x 2 cm, 2 11/16 x 2 5/16 x ¾ inches

This box depicts a scene of romantic yearning as a young woman seated next to a fountain plucks a flower while a whispering putto approaches. A transitional piece, the scene on the box looks back to the romanticism of the Art Nouveau and the Rococo periods, which often featured mythological scenes of love and yearning with nudes and putti, while the hinge and clasp elements look forward to the geometry of the Art Deco.

39

Putti Vanity Case Attributable to Cartier, circa 1920

A vanity case, rounded at one end, centering a hexagonal engraved mother-of-pearl panel depicting putti surrounded by round diamonds and embellished with palmettes on a black enamel ground further outlined with round diamonds, loops set with round diamonds connected to a chain with four fluted rock crystal beads; interior with two compartments for powder, a central detachable lipstick holder, and a fitted mirror; gold and platinum, with British hallmarks

Vanity Case: 10.0 x 4.8 x 1.3 cm, $3\frac{15}{16}$ x $1\frac{7}{8}$ x $\frac{1}{2}$ inches; chain: 11.5 cm, $8\frac{1}{2}$ inches

A classic black-and-white box embellished with diamond details and a mother-of-pearl plaque depicting three playful putti. A smaller version of this box, signed by Cartier, was sold at Sotheby's in November 2013.

40

Mechanical Pencil by Cartier, circa 1929

A mechanical pencil in black enamel decorated at either end with a cap of rose-cut diamonds and a pearl, the center with rose-cut diamond-set band supporting a black silk tassel with enamel and diamond slide link, with a telescoping gold mechanical pencil that slides out from one end attached to the pearl and diamond cap; platinum and gold, with British hallmarks

Not signed but purchased directly from Cartier
Pencil: 5.6 x 1.4 x 1.4 cm, $2\frac{1}{4}$ x $\frac{9}{16}$ x $\frac{9}{16}$ inches; tassel: 14.8 cm, $5\frac{7}{8}$ inches

41

Giardinetto Vanity Case by Bulgari, Rome, circa 1930

A vanity case in black enamel, the front accented by a plaque designed as a potted flowering plant set with round and baguette diamonds; interior with fitted mirror and four compartments; silver with assay marks

Signed Bulgari, 05057
Measurements: 10.5 x 8.4 x 1.9 cm, $4\frac{1}{8}$ x $3\frac{5}{16}$ x $\frac{3}{4}$ inches

Giardinetto rings became popular in eighteenth-century Italy before spreading to the rest of Europe. Meaning "little garden," the rings feature a pot full of blooming flowers. *Giardinetto* jewelry was revived in the Art Deco period, often in the form of marvelous brooches, which Bulgari was known for. This demure box features a *giardinetto* composed of various shaped stones on an expanse of black enamel.

STYLISTIC MODERN

42

Cigarette Case, probably Russia, circa 1910

A cigarette case composed of alternating diagonal bands of channel-set calibré-cut sapphires and mother-of-pearl segments, the reverse composed of diagonal mother-of-pearl segments, the thumbpiece set with a cabochon sapphire; interior fitted with an elastic cigarette band; gold, with French owl importation marks

Measurements: 8.5 x 7.3 x 1.3 cm, $3\frac{3}{8}$ x $2\frac{7}{8}$ x $\frac{1}{2}$ inches

43

Cigarette Case, circa 1920

A cigarette case, the front channel-set with calibré-cut sapphires within a black enamel border, overlapped by an interlocking double frame accented with flowers all set with rose-cut diamonds, the reverse composed of alternating textured gold and black enamel bands, the thumbpiece set with rose-cut diamonds; interior fitted with a cigarette clip; white gold, with assay marks

Measurements: 7.9 x 5.2 x 1.2 cm, $3\frac{1}{8}$ x $2\frac{1}{16}$ x $\frac{1}{2}$ inches

Because the sapphires are channel-set with an open back, when the case is open the light shines through the stone with an effect like stained glass.

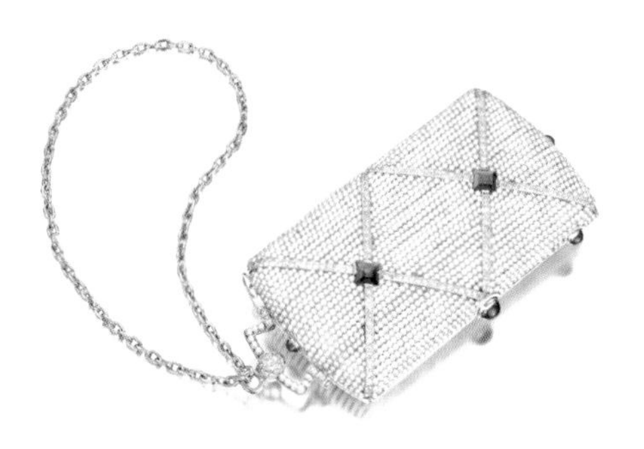

44

Rabbit Vanity Case by Cartier, Paris, circa 1924

A vanity case with curved ends suspended from an oval-link gold chain, the front with lines of seed pearls accented with a lattice motif set with brilliant diamonds, accented by two square-cut sapphires, the reverse applied with white enamel lines accented by a small rabbit set with rose-cut diamonds and a ruby eye, the sides set with four cabochon sapphires, one used as a thumbpiece and the remainder for operating the lids on the interior; interior with fitted mirror, which opens to reveal a writing pad beneath, a powder compartment and a compartment fitted with two lipstick holders, with a removable pencil; gold

Signed Cartier Paris
Measurements: 10.4 x 5 x 1.7 cm, $4\frac{1}{8}$ x 2 x $\frac{11}{16}$ inches

This vanity case by Cartier was the perfect lavish accessory to lay on a table at dinner or a nightclub. Wonderfully tactile, the warmth of the pearls on one side balances the cool enamel and metal on the reverse. A small diamond rabbit with a ruby eye, perhaps requested by a client for luck, is an unusually whimsical move by Cartier in this era.

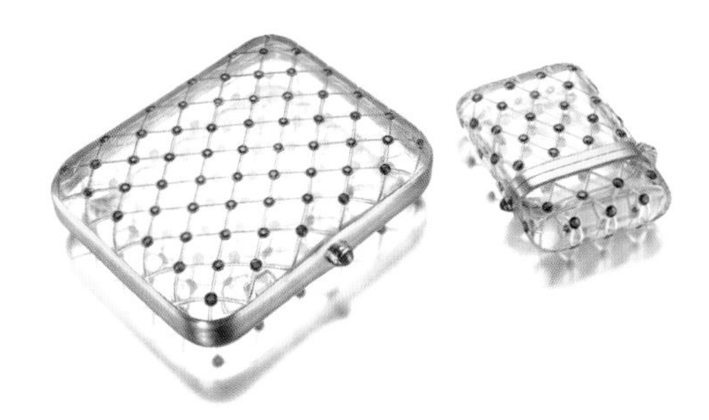

45

Cigarette Case and Match Box, France, circa 1920

A rectangular cigarette case with rounded corners and matching match box composed of carved rock crystal of lattice design studded with round rubies, both with cabochon ruby thumbpiece; gold, with French assay marks

Cigarette Case: 8.0 x 7.2 x 2 cm, $3\frac{3}{16}$ x $2\frac{7}{8}$ x $\frac{13}{16}$ inches
Match Box: 5.3 x 4.3 x 1.5 cm, $2\frac{1}{8}$ x $1\frac{11}{16}$ x $\frac{9}{16}$ inches

At the turn of the century, the Russian jeweler Fabergé was at the peak of its technical skill and created beautiful objects that made their way around the world. French jewelers were particularly inspired by the firm's creations, as were the wealthy Parisian clients who demanded similar work. Cartier had a famous rivalry with Fabergé, producing pieces in the Russian style that rivaled or exceeded the original. This box and match safe are unsigned, but the assay mark indicates they were made in France. The design is modeled after similar rock crystal boxes mounted in gold created by workmaster Michael Perchin for Fabergé around 1890.

46

Perfume-Extract Bottle by Cartier, Paris, circa 1924

A carved rock crystal bottle designed as a column of alternating clear and frosted crystal segments, the base, cover, and closing mechanism of platinum and black enamel, the cover further decorated with alternating diamonds, cabochon rubies, and emeralds, the base with rose-cut diamonds; with French assay marks

Signed Cartier Paris
Measurements: 7.0 x 2.4 x 2.4 cm, $2\frac{3}{4}$ x 1 x 1 inches

For thousands of years rock crystal has been a material used for luxury containers. There are examples dating from the tomb of Empress Maria of the Western Roman Empire, who died in 423 CE and was buried with thirty-nine rock crystal vessels. These early objects were monolithic, carved from a single block of rock crystal with no mountings. By 1000 CE, artisans were creating elaborate rock crystal carvings under the Fatimid caliphs of Egypt, who founded the city of Cairo (and were direct ancestors of Prince Sadruddin Aga Khan). During the Renaissance, and later, many of the rock crystal carvings of these earlier eras were set in elaborate mountings with precious stones and were prized by the church as reliquaries or by the royals of Europe as beautiful objects.

This Cartier scent bottle is based on the form of an Egyptian rock crystal flask set in a metal mounting accented with stones. The use of black enamel on the metal positions this piece as a sleek modern design referencing the past.

47

Geometric Pattern Cigarette Case by Cartier, Paris, circa 1930, Manufactured by Renault

A cigarette case decorated in black enamel with an abstract geometric pattern of squares and chevrons with black enamel borders (see 62), the corners decorated with rose-cut and baguette diamonds, two acting as push-pieces revealing a match safe and strike-a-light; gold and platinum, with French assay marks

Signed Cartier Paris Londres New York, Made in France, with maker's mark for Renault
Measurements: 10.0 x 5.8 x 1.4 cm, 3 15/16 x 2 5/16 x 9/16 inches

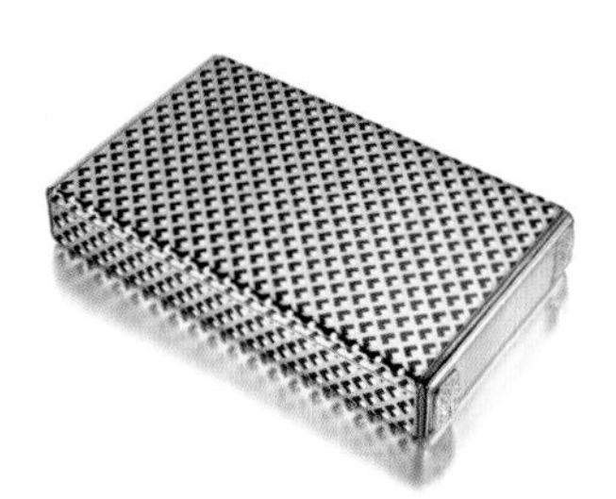

48

Geometric Pattern Vanity Case by Cartier, Paris, circa 1927, Manufactured by Renault

A vanity case with hinged lid decorated in black-and-white enamel with an allover chevron and dot stylized lattice motif (see 62 and 47), the sides accented with four diamond-set squares concealing the push-button opening mechanism; with a fitted mirror and compartments for powder, rouge, and lipstick; gold, with French assay marks

Signed Cartier Paris Londres New York, Made in France, 860868B, with maker's mark for Renault
Measurements: 9.9 x 5.7 x 1.6 cm, 3 7/8 x 2 1/4 x 5/8 inches

The push-button spring opening on this case is known as "Kodak" for its similarity to the famous shutter on a Kodak camera. "You press the button, we do the rest" was the advertising slogan coined by George Eastman, founder of Kodak, in 1888.

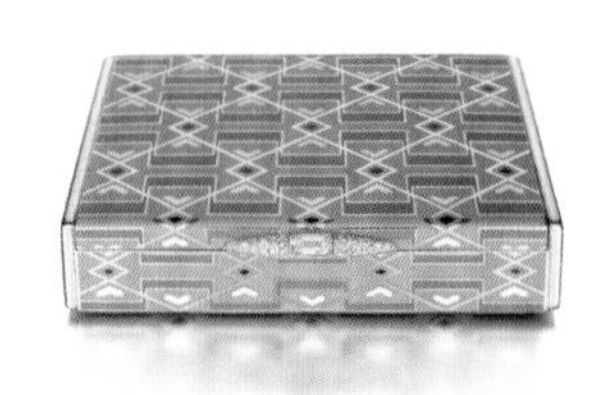

49

Geometric Vanity Case by Cartier, Paris, circa 1930

A vanity case with hinged lid decorated in blue-gray, black, and white enamel in a geometric pattern of interlocking gold diamonds, white chevrons, blue stepped lines, and black enamel diamond accents, with a diamond-set thumbpiece; interior with fitted mirror, powder compartment, and lipstick holder; gold and platinum, with French assay mark

Signed Cartier Paris Londres New York, Made in France, 01216, stamped JC for Jacques Cartier
Measurements: 7.6 x 5.7 x 1.7 cm, 3 x 2 1/4 x 11/16 inches

50

"Aubergine Motif" Cigarette Case by Van Cleef & Arpels, Paris, 1927, Manufactured by Alfred Langlois

A cigarette case decorated in an allover geometric design in lilac, white, and green enamel described in the Van Cleef & Arpel's archive as an "aubergine [eggplant] motif," one side of the lid enhanced with a band of rose-cut diamonds in conforming geometric shapes, the push-piece applied in green enamel; gold and platinum, with French assay marks

Signed Van Cleef & Arpels, Brevete S.G.D.G. 29726
Measurements: 7.8 x 4.5 x 1.2 cm, 3 1/16 x 1 3/4 x 1/2 inches

An anniversary gift engraved with an inscription from Prince Sadruddin to Princess Catherine: "Kate happy 25th, dearest love – S. 25.11.97." The prince chose another case with an abstracted natural motif manufactured by Alfred Langlois for Van Cleef & Arpels for their thirtieth anniversary [51].

51

"Feuilles" Cigarette Case by Van Cleef & Arpels, Paris, 1927, Manufactured by Alfred Langlois

A cigarette case decorated in red, black, and yellow enamel with a bold geometric pattern of rounded arrows arranged in diagonal stripes, the total effect resembling abstracted *feuilles*, or leaves, as described in the Van Cleef & Arpels archive; gold

Signed Van Cleef & Arpels, 29265
Measurements: 10.5 x 8.1 x 1.4 cm, 4 1/8 x 3 1/4 x 1/2 inches

An anniversary gift engraved "Kate from Sadri, Thirty years (and more) of happiness, 25 November 2002" (see also 50). This was the last anniversary gift Prince Sadruddin purchased for Princess Catherine, as he passed away the following May.

52
Vanity Case by Bensimon, Paris, circa 1920
A rectangular box decorated with segments of tinted mother-of-pearl in a geometric design, the lid applied with a medallion of stylized flowers in carved mother-of-pearl within a diamond-set border, completed by a diamond thumbpiece; interior with fitted mirror and two covered compartments for powder and an open compartment for a comb; gold and platinum, with French assay marks

Stamped Bensimon Paris
Measurements: 8.3 x 5.4 x 2 cm, 3¼ x 2⅛ x 13/16 inches

This box is a modern adaptation of Shibayama, a style of Japanese inlay used on small objects. This method was often used to create small boxes covered with pearl and shell flowers.

53
Flower Vanity Case by Lacloche Frères, Paris, circa 1927, Manufactured by Strauss, Allard & Meyer
A vanity case in dark blue enamel, the front accented by a circular medallion set in the center with a carved coral flowerhead with cabochon emerald pistils, accented by carved lapis lazuli leaves on a black enamel field, all framed by rose-cut diamonds, the top and bottom accented by bands of diamonds and reeded onyx segments, with diamond-set thumbpiece; interior with fitted mirror, compartments for powder and rouge, and detachable lipstick holder; gold and platinum, with French assay marks and British importation marks

Signed Lacloche Frères, 8501, with maker's mark for Strauss, Allard & Meyer
Measurements: 8.0 x 4.5 x 1.8 cm, 3 3/16 x 1¾ x ¾ inches

A brooch by Lacloche Frères with the same carved coral flower on a blue background was featured in Henri Clouzot's article "Le Bijou moderne" from *L'Illustration*, December 3, 1927. It is unusual to see a brooch and a cigarette case so closely related.

CULTURAL STYLES

54
Honeycomb Pattern Cigarette Case by Cartier, Paris, circa 1929
A rectangular case carved from a single piece of Siberian nephrite, the borders decorated with segments of carved lapis lazuli and turquoise in a honeycomb pattern, one lapis lazuli end hinged to open, the base and lid with lapis lazuli mosaic, the thumbpiece set with rose-cut diamonds; gold and platinum, with French assay marks and British importation marks

Signed Cartier New-York Paris Londres, Made in France, stamped JC for Jacques Cartier, 299
Measurements: 9.5 x 5.9 x 1.8 cm, 3⅝ x 2¼ x 11/16 inches

The hexagonal pattern of goldwork employed on this box replicates the honeycomb structure created by honeybees. It is an ancient form: the Greek historian Diodorus Siculus wrote in the first century BCE of the mythological Athenian sculptor and inventor Daedalus creating a lost wax casting of a honeycomb in gold so perfect as to be indistinguishable from the real thing. Long known to be an efficient means of engineering and building, the honeycomb also creates a beautiful lattice pattern as seen in the intricate *jali* (pierced stone screens) of Indian architecture, including the Taj Mahal (1632–53). Cartier employed the pattern here to great effect, filling the comb with lapis lazuli hexagons, with turquoise at the edge, against a nephrite field.

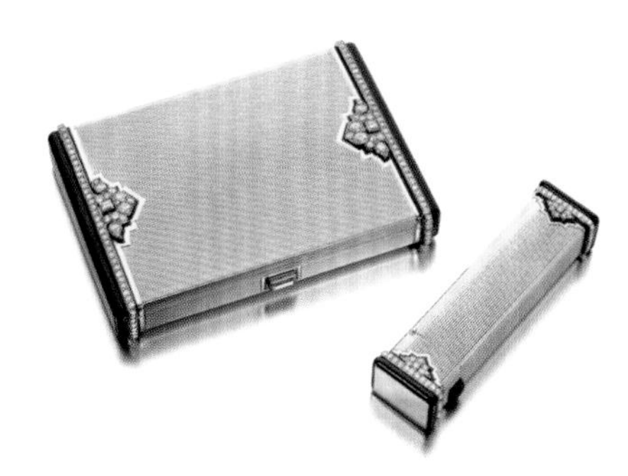

55
Cigarette Case and Lighter, Cartier, circa 1932
A cigarette case composed of ribbed yellow gold, accented at either end with raised edges applied with black enamel enhanced by stylized palmette motifs completed by diamond bands, with diamond push-piece; with matching lighter; both gold and platinum, with British hallmarks, the lighter with French assay marks

Cigarette Case signed Cartier London, stamped JC for Jacques Cartier, 22088, 686
Lighter signed Cartier, Made in France, BTE5606, stamped JC for Jacques Cartier, 22033, 6568
Cigarette Case: 8.1 x 5.7 x 1.3 cm, 3 3/16 x 2¼ x ½ inches
Lighter: 6.5 x 1.7 x 1.2 cm, 2 9/16 x 11/16 x 7/16 inches

56

Cigarette Case by Cartier, Paris, circa 1929

A cigarette case in black enamel with bands and stylized palmette motifs set with rose-cut diamonds and two hexagonal-cut diamonds, with a diamond-set thumbpiece, inscribed "Carla, 10th May 1937"; gold and platinum, with French assay marks and British hallmarks

Signed Cartier Paris Londres New York, Made in France, 4674, 4842, 2428, stamped JC for Jacques Cartier
Measurements: 7.7 x 5.8 x 1.4 cm, 3 x 2 1/4 x 9/16 inches

57

Box by Cartier, circa 1928

A cigar or cigarette box decorated on the front with white enamel stripes, the four corners and center accented by openwork diamond geometric plaques of oriental influence, the sides applied with rectangular sections of white enamel stripes, with diamond-set thumbpiece; gold and platinum

Signed Cartier
Measurements: 12.4 x 8.4 x 2.2 cm, 4 7/8 x 3 5/16 x 7/8 inches

58

Cigarette and Vanity Case by Cartier, Paris, circa 1925

A cylindrical vanity case applied throughout with black enamel, set at the top and bottom with rose-cut diamonds and jade cabochons in repeating architectural motif and black enamel meander trim, the black enamel cap with diamond-set accents and a cabochon jade bead, suspended from an onyx ring, with diamond-set thumbpiece at the side and two onyx thumbpieces at the top and bottom; interior center compartment, the top and bottom interior fitted with a mirror and compartments; gold and platinum

Signed Cartier Paris Londres New York, Made in France
Measurements: 14.3 x 4.6 x 3.6 cm, 5 5/8 x 1 13/16 x 1 7/16 inches

The form of this box, a container opening at each end and in the center, is taken from the Japanese inro (seal-basket), a traditional case for holding small objects that was suspended from the obi, or sash, not unlike the idea of a chatelaine in Europe. The inro was an enclosed series of nested boxes that could be made from a variety of materials including wood, ivory, bone, leather, or paper, covered in lacquer and inlaid with mother-of-pearl, gold, or silver. Originating at the end of the sixteenth century, these boxes evolved over time becoming elaborate works of art representing the status of the bearer.

Cartier modernized the form in this box with smooth black enamel accented by their interpretation of architectural elements including a Greek meander at the edges and a repeating motif in diamonds and jade evocative of an Islamic doorway.

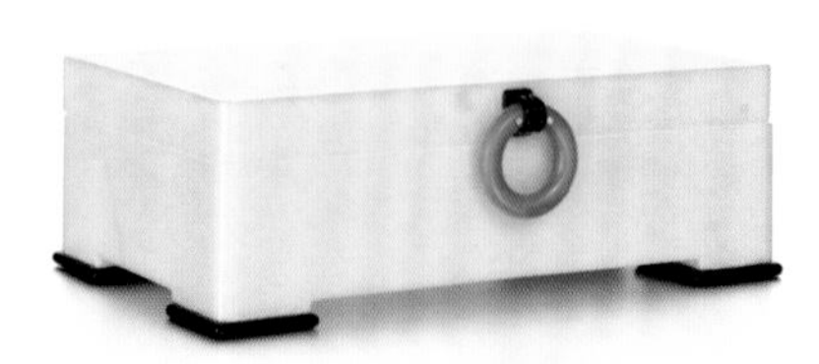

59

Box by Cartier, Paris, circa 1927

A box of white marble decorated with a coral ring handle enhanced with rose-cut diamonds and held within a black enamel mount, completed by three red and black enamel and diamond hinges, standing on four onyx feet

Not signed, but with a certificate from Cartier
Measurements: 16.9 x 10.8 x 5.4 cm, 7 11/16 x 4 1/4 x 2 1/8 inches

The first owner of this box was Jean-Charles Worth, head designer of the House of Worth from 1910–1935, succeeding his uncle Jean-Philippe Worth. The house was started by Charles Frederick Worth in 1858 and is considered to be the genesis of haute couture. When the Cartier family moved their store to the rue de la Paix in 1899, just steps from Worth, they came in contact with a global luxury empire that would have great impact on their company, and Alfred Cartier and Charles Frederick Worth became fast friends. According to Hans Nadelhoffer, it was Worth who "drew Cartier's attention to American hostesses" who had frequented Worth's establishment since the 1876 Philadelphia Exhibition. The families became deeply entwined when Louis Cartier married Jean-Philippe Worth's daughter, Andrée, in 1898, and Louis's sister, Suzanne, later married Jean-Charles's brother, Jacques.

60

Vanity Case by Cartier, Paris, circa 1925

A rounded vanity case decorated in blue enamel with a geometric motif in gold accented with collet-set diamonds, the borders decorated in green and blue enamel with a scrolling foliate motif, completed by a diamond and ruby thumbpiece; interior with fitted mirror, powder, and rouge compartments, with an additional hidden compartment behind the mirror; gold and platinum

Signed Cartier Paris Londres New York, Made in France, 01308
Measurements: 7.8 x 5.0 x 3.4 cm, 3 1/16 x 2 x 1 5/16 inches

This case incorporates three Chinese decorative motifs: a continuous-stem pattern seen in Chinese decorative arts such as enamel and porcelain, an abstracted geometric cloud pattern in the central gold and blue enamel, and the diamond studs derived from *ru ding*, the studs seen in regular geometric pattern on Chinese bronze vessels.

61

Fern Compact, France, circa 1929

A compact applied with blue and gold enamel replicating lapis lazuli, centering upon a continuous band depicting a meandering motif of stylized fern fronds applied with black, green, and white enamel, the front accented by circular plaques set with rose-cut diamonds, edged with black enamel; interior with fitted mirror and compartment; gold and platinum, with French assay marks

Measurements: 8.2 x 5.4 x 1.3 cm, 3 1/4 x 2 1/8 x 1/2 inches

62

Dot Pattern Cigarette Case by Cartier, Paris, circa 1930

A cigarette case decorated in a black enamel dot pattern, the ends applied with black enamel rectangles, interior with fitted mirror and match safe, inscribed "January 1936"; gold

Signed Cartier Paris Londres New York, Made in France, 02688
Measurements: 9.7 x 5.4 x 1.4 cm, 3 7/8 x 2 1/8 x 9/16 inches

At first glance, this box does not look to be inspired by Chinese art, however the source for the allover geometric gold and black enamel pattern cases of the 1930s was the ornate Chinese lacquer panels Cartier incorporated into their designs in the 1920s. The panels often had patterns built up from standard tesserae. According to Hans Nadelhoffer, "Cartier's designers covered the surface of their boxes with Chinese geometrical patterns," adapting the geometric mother-of-pearl patterns into gold and enamel works. (See also 47 and 48.)

63

Plum Blossom Vanity Case and Lipstick Holder by Strauss, Allard & Meyer, Paris, circa 1925

A vanity case in red enamel, the front accented by three half-moon-shaped black enamel sections with plum blossom floral motifs (see 64) set with rose-cut diamonds, with diamond-set thumbpiece, suspended from a red enamel chain connected to a lipstick holder applied also in red and black enamel, with removable lipstick tube; interior with fitted mirror, powder compartment, and rouge holder; gold and platinum, with French assay marks

Maker's mark for Strauss, Allard & Meyer
Vanity Case: 6.2 x 4.5 x 0.9 cm, 2 1/2 x 1 3/4 x 3/8 inches
Lipstick Holder: 5.3 x 1.6 x 1.5 cm, 2 1/8 x 5/8 x 5/8 inches

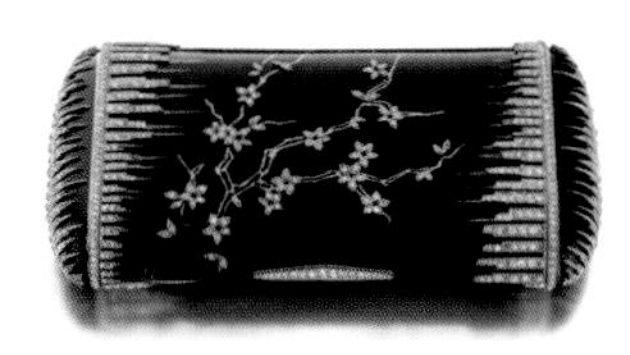

64

Plum Blossom Vanity Case by Lacloche Frères, Paris, circa 1925, Manufactured by Strauss, Allard & Meyer

A black enamel vanity case of Japanese inspiration decorated on the front with meandering silver branches set with rose-cut diamond blossoms, the borders and terminals highlighted with icicles set with rose-cut diamonds, with diamond-set button clasp; interior with fitted powder compartment and lipstick holder; gold and platinum, with French assay marks

Signed Lacloche Frères, Paris, 66126, 2171, with maker's mark for Strauss, Allard & Meyer
Measurements: 9.4 x 4.8 x 1.5 cm, 3 3/4 x 1 7/8 x 5/8 inches

For this vanity case, Lacloche Frères was inspired by Japanese woodcut prints of plum blossoms, an ancient motif in Asian art, inspiring poetry and visual works. The unusual combination of plum blossoms against ice captures the beauty of the improbable. Plum blossoms typically bloom against the last winter snows and signal the arrival of spring. Though they are a simple five-petal flower, their ability to bloom in harsh conditions gives them an otherworldly appeal and a reputation for resilience in the face of adversity.

65

Vanity Case by Van Cleef & Arpels, Paris, 1930, Manufactured by Strauss, Allard & Meyer

A vanity case in red enamel, with raised edge on the left and right sides, enhanced by diamond-set bands with thirty-six baguette-cut diamonds, push-piece set with rose-cut diamonds; interior with fitted mirror, powder compartment, and detachable lipstick holder; gold and platinum, with French assay marks

Signed Van Cleef & Arpels, Paris; 33336
Measurements: 7.1 x 4.8 x 1.2 cm, 2 13/16 x 1 7/8 x 1/2 inches

66

Vanity Case by Janesich, Paris, circa 1928, Manufactured by Strauss, Allard & Meyer

A vanity case in black enamel, accented by two bands of diamonds on the lid continuing on the sides, with collet-set diamond thumbpiece; interior with fitted mirror, powder compartment, and detachable lipstick holder; gold and platinum, with French assay marks

Signed Janesich, 16182, with maker's mark for Strauss, Allard & Meyer
Measurements: 8.0 x 5.7 x 1.8 cm, 3 3/16 x 2 1/4 x 1 1/16 inches

Beautiful in its simplicity, this case features the sparest design: two thin diamond lines on an expanse of black enamel, similar to the placement of belt straps on a leather suitcase, realized here with elegance.

ABSTRACTED MODERN

67

Vanity Case by Gold, Most & Fogel, New York, circa 1926

A vanity case in red and blue enamel, the corners accented by overlapping black enamel stripes, the central motif in the form of a cascading garland of flowers, leaves, and ribbons, set throughout with rose-cut diamonds, accented by sapphires, rubies, and emeralds, applied with black enamel, further enhanced by a clasp over the blue lid of rose-cut diamonds and calibré-cut emeralds, with ruby push-piece; interior with fitted mirror and two compartments; gold

Maker's mark for Gold, Most & Fogel, patent 1662028
Measurements: 7.7 x 5.3 x 1.5 cm, 3 1/16 x 2 1/8 x 9/16 inches

Not much is known about Gold, Most & Fogel. This elaborate vanity case is in the French style, taking elements of Art Deco and Garland Style design, but was made in Brooklyn. The patent filed by the company protects a special catch design that allows for easy one-handed opening.

68

Vanity Case by Tiffany & Co., Paris, circa 1925

A vanity case with black enamel top and lapis lazuli sides, the top decorated with a stepped pyramid design of blue enamel and gold border, partial gold frieze border, and a stylized potted flower, set with diamonds, emeralds, and rubies, the bottom applied with black enamel and step pyramid design of blue enamel and gold border; interior with fitted mirror, powder compartment, and removable rouge holder; gold and platinum, with French assay marks

Signed Tiffany à Paris
Measurements: 7.0 x 5.2 x 1.3 cm, 2 3/4 x 2 1/16 x 1/5 inches

69

Princess Andrée Aga Khan's Vanity Case and Cigarette Box by Cartier, Paris, circa 1925

A vanity case and cigarette box in black enamel, the central motif featuring a diamond-set monogram with the initials JAC, within a step-pyramid diamond frame, the ends accented by diamond-set plaques of similar step-pyramid design completed by diamond trim, with diamond-set thumbpiece; interior with fitted mirror, small powder compartment, match box, strike-a-light, and cigarette compartment; gold and platinum, with French assay marks

Signed Cartier Paris Londres New York, 0381
Measurements: 8.4 x 4.0 x 3.2 cm, 3 5/16 x 1 9/16 x 1 1/4 inches

A classic Art Deco cylindrical vanity case with the initials JAC for Joséphine Andrée Carron, Prince Sadruddin Aga Khan's mother, who was known as Princess Andrée Aga Khan when married to the Aga Khan III from 1929 to 1943.

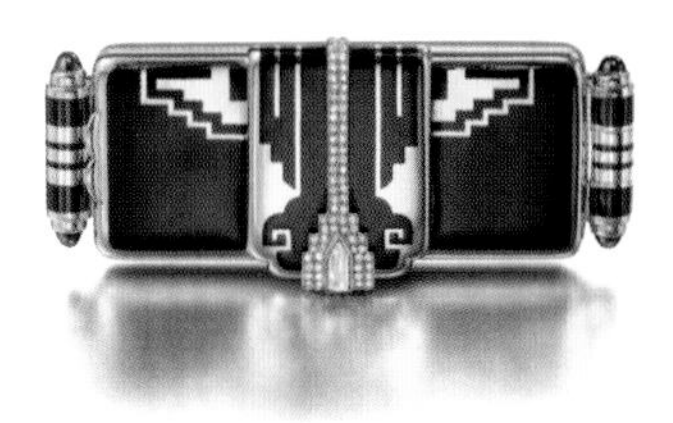

70

Compact Brooch by Cartier, Paris, 1929, Manufactured by Ploujavy

A miniature compact brooch, the front with a black enamel geometric and zigzag pattern, accented in the center by a diamond-set band terminated by a diamond plaque, the sides accented by gold bars applied with black enamel bands and set with cabochon sapphires; interior with fitted mirror and two compartments, surmounted by a small compartment; gold and platinum, with British importation marks

Signed Cartier, Made in France, 4880, JC for Jacques Cartier, with maker's mark for Ploujavy
Measurements: 6.2 x 2.7 x 1.0 cm, 2 7/16 x 1 1/16 x 3/8 inches

This is the only known brooch compact created by Cartier. This unusual form elevates the display qualities of the vanity case in the 1920s and transforms it into a wearable artwork, disguising the function. The same year, Cartier also created a commissioned compact on a watchband for Evalyn Walsh McLean, famed owner of the Hope Diamond.

On vanity boxes meant to rest on the tabletop, Cartier often hid the hinges, intending to create an uninterrupted surface for the eye and hand. On this box, however, the hinge on the right hand side is exploited for its decorative qualities and enhanced with both enamel and sapphires on the ends. The shape is mimicked on the left side, although that is mere decoration, to balance the composition. This beautiful vanity brooch demonstrates playfulness and exploration of form and function.

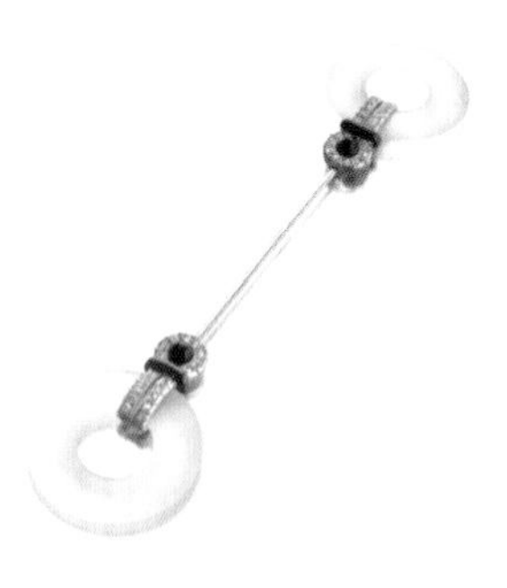

71

Jabot Brooch by Marzo, Paris, circa 1925

A brooch composed of two frosted rock crystal *bi*-disks connected to the center pin by diamond-set ties centering an onyx cabochon with a black enamel detail; mounted in white gold and platinum, with French assay marks

Signed Marzo Paris
Measurements: 10.7 x 2.5 x 0.4 cm, 4 1/4 x 1 x 1/4 inches

In the seventeenth century, upper-class men wore frilled neckpieces called jabots to cover the closure of their shirts. While the fashion for decorative neckpieces fell away after a century, the form of the long thin pin decorated on each end used to affix the fabric to the shirt endured. In the Art Deco period the jabot brooch became fashionable as a clever and flexible woman's accessory that could be used any number of ways on collars, scarves, or jauntily pinned to a hat. The charm of the jabot lies in the way the pin is hidden behind the clothing, while the two decorative ends seem to float. This pin by Marzo is classically Art Deco, combining strong geometric shapes influenced by the Chinese *bi*-disk (see 112) with a stark black-and-white color palette accentuating the strong design. The rock crystal seems to be held in place by two diamond straps, which in turn are pinned down by an enamel strap, and held in place by an onyx cabochon, while the true mechanism for attachment would be hidden.

72

Striped Agate Box, circa 1919

A box of cream and black agate carved from a single block, the triangular hinges and thumbpiece set with rose-cut diamonds; platinum

Measurements: 8.6 x 5.5 x 1.7 cm, 3 1/4 x 2 1/8 x 9/16 inches

This box is probably French; the move to the geometry of the 1920s is seen in the hinge and clasp details on this box, as compared to the delicate ribbon motif on the Ribbon Box [37]. The diamond details on this box are also functional, rather than purely decorative.

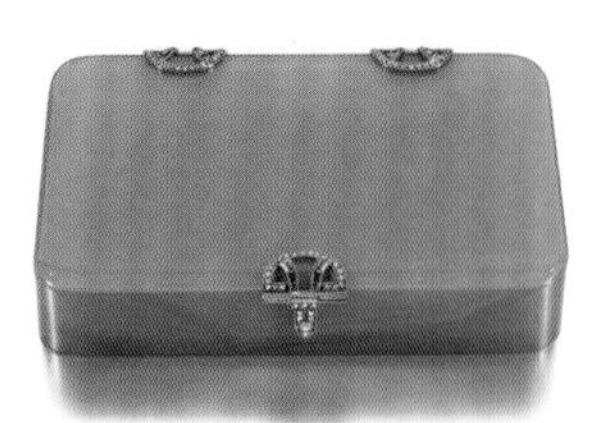

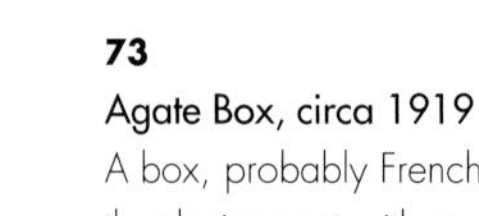

73

Agate Box, circa 1919

A box, probably French, carved from a single block of translucent cream-colored agate, the hinges and thumbpiece set with rose-cut diamonds and calibré-cut sapphires; platinum

Measurements: 8.7 x 6.1 x 1.8 cm, $3\frac{7}{16}$ x $2\frac{7}{16}$ x $1\frac{1}{16}$ inches

74

Cigarette Case and Mechanical Pencil by Cartier, Paris, circa 1928, Manufactured by Renault

A rectangular nephrite case, with a front compartment for cigarettes and a side compartment for matches with a striking surface under the lid, each accented by a red and blue enamel ropework pattern on gold, the front thumbpiece set with buff-top calibré-cut sapphire and ruby, the side set with one flat, engravable sapphire, with a detachable fluted gold pencil set at the top with a cabochon sapphire; gold, with French assay marks

Signed Cartier Paris Londres New York, Made in France, 03872, with maker's mark for Renault; pen signed Cartier-Paris
Measurements: 11.8 x 6.7 x 1.9 cm, $4\frac{11}{16}$ x $3\frac{7}{16}$ x $\frac{3}{4}$ inches

This case was carved from a solid block of nephrite and is one of the Russian-style items created by Cartier in the style of Fabergé. An earlier similar piece in the Cartier Collection features more literal gold ropework, but by the late 1920s the pattern had become abstracted into triangles.

75

Tree Pendant by Dusausoy, Paris, circa 1925

A plaque pendant depicting a malachite tree shading a cluster of rooftops set with rose-cut diamonds and segments of reeded coral, a rose-cut diamond fence in the foreground; mounted in platinum, with French assay marks

Signed Dusausoy, 27179
Measurements: 7.3 x 4.0 x 0.5 cm, $3\frac{7}{8}$ x $1\frac{5}{8}$ x $\frac{3}{16}$ inches

This Dusausoy pendant is an iconic example of Art Deco jewelry. The piece was featured in Henri Clouzot's article "Le Bijou moderne" from *L'Illustration*, December 3, 1927, amongst examples by Fouquet, Templier, Sandoz, and others. Clouzot wrote of "three categories in the jewelry industry. At the top, *la grande joaillerie*, which only uses the finest stones to create ornaments reserved for crowned heads and billionaires of the New World. At the other end of the range, *la bijouterie de fantaisie* (it would be better described as art jewelry), dedicated to the semi-precious stones. Between the two is the jewelry of the 'rue de la Paix,' which treats both the diamond with more freedom, and common stones with more sumptuousness."

The material treated most sumptuously in this pendant is the malachite used to create the tree. Where typical mosaicists would rely mainly on the color of the hardstone material in the creations, in an unusual move, the designer here used the swirls and patterning of the malachite to create the tree form. The diamonds are relegated to the pedestrian forms of the roof and fencing, showing that the artist cares more for the color and qualities of the material than the value. The color combination was chosen to be as strong as possible, with the contrasting colors of red and green, accompanied by black and white. Beautifully finished, even the edges have a cross-hatching pattern showing the immaculate attention to detail of a true master.

76

Compact by Cartier, Paris, circa 1929

A rectangular powder compact in black enamel, the opening and hinge accented by geometric motifs set with round and baguette diamonds; interior with fitted mirror and powder compartment with powder screen; yellow gold and platinum, with French assay marks

Signed Cartier Paris, Made in France, 01128, DR Cartier BTE 5606, with Cartier mark SCA
Measurements: 4.2 x 4.0 x 1.4 cm, $1\frac{5}{8}$ x $1\frac{9}{16}$ x $\frac{9}{16}$ inches

This compact is one of the black enamel and diamond pieces made by Cartier in the machine aesthetic. The diamond-set motifs imitate the jaws of a vise holding a block of material. Created by hand by master artisans, this compact is meant to evoke the impression of mechanical purity aspired to in the Machine Age through strong contrast of line, color, and material.

77

Vanity Case by Cartier, London, circa 1930

A vanity case in black enamel, the thumbpiece designed as a roll-down bar set with baguette and rose-cut diamonds; interior with fitted mirror and two covered compartments; silver, with British assay marks

Signed Cartier London, 4238
Measurements: 8.2 x 5.4 x 1.4 cm, $3\frac{1}{4}$ x $2\frac{1}{8}$ x $\frac{9}{16}$ inches

Designed in the machine aesthetic, this vanity case features a roll-down bar clasp, an unusual feature seen on a few boxes from this period. The smooth movement of the roll-bar is a nod to the interchangeable parts of the Machine Age, accented with diamonds.

78

Vanity Case by Cartier, London, circa 1936

A vanity case in black enamel, with a black enamel hinged strap that works as a clasp accented by a carved coral baton enhanced by diamonds; interior with fitted mirror, powder compact, and detachable lipstick holder; gold and platinum, with British hallmarks

Signed Cartier London, 5716, stamped J. C. for Jacques Cartier
Measurements: 6.7 x 4.9 x 2.9 cm, $2\frac{5}{8}$ x $1\frac{15}{16}$ x $1\frac{1}{8}$ inches

Designed in the machine aesthetic, this vanity case has an unusual closure, a hinged strap juxtaposing a bright coral cylinder against the sparkle of diamonds and smooth expanse of black enamel.

79

"Forget-Me-Not" Lipstick Case by Cartier, Paris, 1940

A lipstick case in black enamel with sliding cover, adjusted by a gold disk inscribed: *"ne m'oubliez pas"* (forget-me-not) centering a single collet-set diamond; silver

Signed Cartier, Paris, 565, Bte SGDG
Measurements: 6.0 x 2.1 x 2.1 cm, $2\frac{3}{8}$ x $\frac{7}{8}$ x $\frac{7}{8}$ inches

In 1934 Cartier created a black enamel lipstick case accented with a coral disk set with a diamond. Now in the collection of the Musée des Arts décoratifs, the container was designed to hold a Guerlain lipstick. Created in 1940, instead of coral, this lipstick case is set with a gold disk inscribed *"ne m'oubliez pas"* (forget-me-not). This saying was also the name of Guerlain's first lipstick. Created in 1870, ne m'oubliez pas was the first readily available commercial lipstick. At the time, lipstick was primarily worn by women of the stage and screen, but by the 1920s it was commonly accepted for evening wear, although *The New York Times* advised cautious application. By 1940 lipstick could be found in every handbag and brightly colored lips were fashionable day and night.

Jeweled Innovation:
Design and Manufacture in Art Deco Masterpieces

Sarah D. Coffin

80
Tree of Life Vanity Case by Cartier, Paris, circa 1930

Patron, Retailer, Maker, Manufacturer

As Paris resumed its role as artistic hub of the Western world after World War I, it reopened to the wealthy foreign visitors who had come before the war, and also to travelers and expats who were spurred by post-war modes of accessible travel—cars, trains, and ocean liners—and who frequented an ever-broadening social scene that included a new mix of foreigners who brought new tastes with them, leading to new fashions and accessories. These patrons, including women buying for themselves, headed to famous jewelry houses, such as Cartier, Van Cleef & Arpels, Boucheron, and Mauboussin, to expand their wardrobes to include jewelry and accessories for the newly fashionable sporting look, for jazz clubs, cigarette smoking, and cocktails, and with the greater acceptance of the use of makeup beyond the boudoir, for cosmetics. In eighteenth-century Paris, jewelers and *boîtiers* (box makers) had generally remained separate entities. But in the 1920s the *maisons de haute joaillerie*—fine jewelry houses—were quick to see the potential of new luxury accessories. Cigarette cases became the snuffboxes of the twentieth century aimed, like their predecessors, at both men and women. Added to them was a group of objects directed at women: vanities, compacts, and all-in-one *minaudières* provided portable luxury holders for makeup, so the bold new colors available could be applied while out of the house.

The tastes of these new customers were not the same as those of patrons of traditional *haute joaillerie*, and jewelry houses realized they would need to design objects that conveyed the modernist style even if the sources were traditional, such as drawing inspiration from the garden. The sources for the designs were as varied as the materials: from ancient world designs to modern botanicals, and from Japanese textiles (often with flowers) to Indian patterns, they were adapted into modern art. The houses helped the client create a new look through luxury accessories.

World's fairs, department stores, and other retail opportunities gave patrons direct access to purchasing in the 1920s. While top patrons requested the houses create jewelry designs for them, and sometimes suggested new designs for existing jewels, the houses, on the whole, were the ones designing the new boxes and sending their ideas, and the gems required, to the *boîtiers*. The houses then stocked the objects, so they were readily available to be seen and sold, tempting the jewelry clients into new accessories. Increasingly they also provided ready-made jewelry, but while the forms of the jewelry were generally based on historic precedent, such as brooches or necklaces, the closest vanity cases came to their precursors were to loose powder boxes or *nécessaires* of the eighteenth century, far from the world of the jeweler.

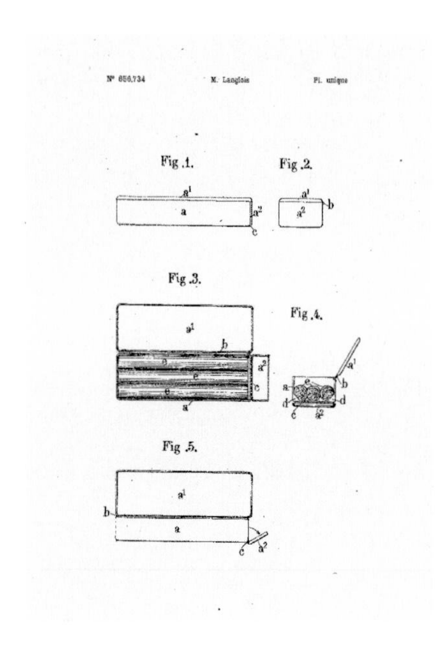

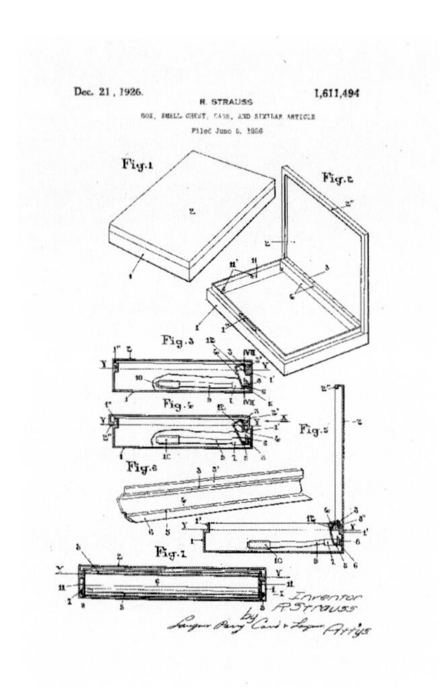

Patents for elements that ease opening and closing cigarette cases from Alfred Langlois, 1927 (top), and Strauss, Allard & Meyer, 1926.

The jewelry houses moved into the accessory market with these new forms. While they rarely started with a patron for the design, they did consider who the purchaser would be. Increasingly Indian maharajas and maharanis or Middle Eastern potentates were finding the cosmopolitan environment of Paris and the south of France to their liking. While they mixed with Western society, and some allowed themselves to be seen in places—like the casinos—not possible in India or Iran, they gravitated toward the Western objects that interpreted motifs from their own cultures. Thus the artistic heritage of these clients did inform the design process of some of these boxes. The Aga Khan and the Begum Aga Khan, Prince Sadruddin Aga Kahn's parents, had Villa Jane-Andrée at Cap d'Antibes where the house was full of the finest Islamic art, but they were also known as great collectors of the finest level of jewels from Cartier and Van Cleef & Arpels.

Role of the Maker

As well as their sophisticated and widely sourced design inspirations and highly accomplished craftsmanship, the boxes involved increasingly sophisticated mechanisms. The fine jewelry houses had a network of makers who regularly provided the skilled labor and basic structure for their designs. By the late 1920s and early 1930s demand for the accessories was so high that houses like Cartier and Van Cleef & Arpels were annexing the best of the *boîtiers*. Van Cleef & Arpels was Alfred Langlois's principal patron throughout the 1920s and signed an exclusive agreement with him in 1932. Before that, he filed his own patents [7], but with his exclusive agreement patents were granted to Van Cleef & Arpels [50]. In contrast was Strauss, Allard & Meyer, who remained a provider to multiple houses, notably Cartier, Van Cleef & Arpels, and others. This resulted in their patenting their own developments, including at least one in the United States in 1926. This patent details a closing device with no projecting part so that the box would be smooth and not catch, which was effected by a sliding panel hiding a spring blade device to raise the lid. This enabled Strauss, Allard & Meyer, despite remaining a French firm, to protect their inventions from feared copyists in the United States, as they supplied some boxes to Cartier for the New York store that opened in 1912. The similarity of the red enamel on a vanity case by Brooklyn-based Gold, Most & Fogel [67] to Strauss, Allard & Meyer's striking and distinctive red, used on a number of cases in this collection, suggests that the former firm may have hired a French emigré enamelist, possibly from Strauss, Allard & Meyer, and the American firm was certainly looking closely at the finest French production. Gold, Most & Fogel also filed a patent in 1926 for a device to allow one-handed opening, but not many examples of their work exist.

Alfred Langlois enjoyed an extensive career before joining Van Cleef & Arpels. He registered his maker's mark in 1902 and his innovative work included patents as early as 1908 for a cardholder, to ease the removal of calling cards. In 1909 he patented a small cigarette case and in 1927 he registered three patents for cigarette boxes, the second one "improved" and the third "new," which he registered in England and the United States, knowing that his work was being sold, and potentially imitated, by workshops in both countries. In 1929 a further patent was registered for another cigarette box, and also one for a *poudreuse* or powder box.[1]

Other subcontractors, such as those for Cartier, often were taken over by the firm or worked exclusively for them—such as Henri Lavabre [99], Henri Picq, Renault [21, 47], Bachaumont (the latter two being almost exclusively responsible for Arab-style patterns and abstracted geometric Chinese-inspired designs on boxes), and Ploujavy

[70]. Ploujavy's location was later listed at 9 rue d'Argenson,[2] the same address as the second workshop of Robert Linzeler, who had merged with Marchak in 1922 (their first workshop was on rue de la Cité). Linzeler also supplied Cartier from the rue d'Argenson address, showing the complexity of inter-related workshops often through co-location.

A box from Lacloche Frères made by Strauss, Allard & Meyer also demonstrates an interesting relationship with a contractor. The carving on the Floral Vanity Case [53] is a near exact match for a flower on a brooch by Lacloche, pictured in an article by Henri Clouzot in 1927 (p.138). The carver would likely have been hired by Lacloche and the flower supplied to Strauss, Allard & Meyer.

Chief among the makers contracted by various houses in this collection is Vladimir Makovsky (1884–1966), who was active in 1920s Paris. Little is known about Makovsky's life prior to his arrival in Paris from his native Russia, but he first appears there working with Marchak or Linzeler & Marchak [34] in the early 1920s producing plaques that were essentially small pieces of mother-of-pearl and hardstone inlaid or marquetried onto a ground of mother-of-pearl. Sometimes the mother-of-pearl work was incorporated into enamel surroundings. Chinese-made and, more commonly, Western-made mother-of-pearl-based inlays were highly prized by eighteenth-century snuffbox makers in Paris and Germany.

Makovsky may have found his way to Cartier through the doors of Alexander Marchak's firm, which became Linzeler & Marchak in 1922. Marchak's father, Joseph, founded a top-of-the-line jewelry firm referred to as the "Cartier of Kiev," and, like Makovsky, fled Russia during the revolution. A firm of that caliber, which won medals in Chicago in 1893 and Antwerp a year later, may have already been producing plaques or panels prior to the revolution as part of their oeuvre, and it is possible that Makovsky worked for them before emigrating. However, as Louis Cartier had already hired workmasters in Russia to compete with Fabergé, the firm may have established links to Makovsky before he emigrated.

Makovsky's plaques are sometimes signed, using either a VM monogram or an M in script. But he often did not sign his pictorial plaques, and it remains unclear as to whether this was due to contractual arrangements with different retailers, depended on whether he was the creator of the concept of the design or working from a house-provided design, or if he had a workshop and, when it provided some of the work, he did not sign it. As works of considerable quality remain unsigned, it appears that the first option is the most likely. As can be seen in many of the examples by Makovsky, the mother-of-pearl serves well to give a naturalistic effect to snowy scenes [34], and an ethereal cloud-like effect to the Asian-inspired boxes. Makovsky's subject matter had much in common with Russian fairy stories and illustrations, such as those of fellow Russian emigré Ivan Bilibin (1876–1942), also seen in lacquer and painted mother-of-pearl boxes popular in Russia. This type of decoration had great appeal in Paris, coinciding with the popularity of the Ballets Russes, which had been in Paris since 1909, employing some of the most avant-garde and colorful artists of the day, many of them Russian emigrés. The exoticism of the Ballets Russes extended to Schéhérazade and other non-Russian themes, giving the artists a chance to expand their repertoire to visions of Persia and eastern Asia.

Makovsky's work is related to a technique involving tinted mother-of-pearl set in lacquer, *lac burgauté*, that evolved in China and Japan, rising to great heights of popularity for export starting in the nineteenth century. It sometimes involved engraving and almost always dyeing mother-of-pearl. Frequently in tones of blue, green, and

Top: Alexander Makovsky, *Solikamsk*, Russia, 1910. This type of landscape painting influenced Vladimir Makovsky's mosaic work both in dreamlike quality and in subject matter. Bottom: Ivan Bilibin, illustration for *The Tale of the Golden Cockerel*, Russia, 1906. The richness of color, flattened perspective, and folklore topics used by Bilibin also appear in the work of Vladimir Makovsky.

Jacques Le Moyne de Morgues, "Papaver silvestris (poppy)," circa 1575. Artists have long looked to botanical prints for inspiration and many jewelers in the Art Deco era included such prints in their libraries.

Opposite:
81
Poppy Vanity Case by Janesich, Paris, circa 1928, Manufactured by Strauss, Allard & Meyer

purple, the dyed mother-of-pearl elements are set on a panel around which the lacquer is raised to the same level, after which the whole was lacquered many times over for a smooth surface, and to have the appearance of all being lacquer. The plaque in Lac Burgauté Garden Scene Vanity Case [89] shows the technique, which was imitated in the West as well as being imported from Asia [23]. In any comparison between Asian-executed decoration and Western-created chinoiserie, the composition and execution of the figures provides the key to discerning which items hail from the East. Cartier also imported many of the panels, as well as earlier examples of *lac burgauté* from Chinese and Japanese art objects, and lacquered wood, that could be reframed and integrated sometimes into box panels as well. Dealers who specialized in this technique supplied Cartier, but could also supply multiple firms. One such dealer, Yamanaka of Japan, had branches in New York, other American and European cities, as well as Japan.[3]

Bejeweled Garden

Historically, French garden design considered architectural structure as preeminent over, or at least as important as, any floral mixture, and this remained the dominant feature in early twentieth-century Paris. Parks were created as green spaces in the increasingly dense city. Green, the color of lawns, hedges, and parks, was the color most associated with nature in the city. In the seventeenth century, Louis XIV sought to integrate the patterns of hedge-planting with those of the interior design, where green dominated. In the nineteenth century, roses found their way into gardens in France, often as a collector's item, with owners showing off as many varieties as possible. Republican France had little interest in replicating the showplaces of the aristocracy, but the need for public green spaces within the layout of Haussmann's design for Paris meant that park design surged in turn-of-the-twentieth-century Paris. This was a time, with the advent of the elevator, when great blocks of flats were built and urban density grew.

With the interest in exoticism blooming, more color began to creep into Parisian life during the period leading up to World War I, but the arrival of the war put such exuberance on hold. No sooner was the war over than color started to bloom everywhere, and gardens were tended again, this time with more color. Jewelry turned to colored gemstones in a way never witnessed in Europe before.

Given the appeal of parks and architectural gardens in France, nothing suggested gardens as much as the color green, appearing in jewelry and the accessories of this era through emeralds, jadeite, nephrite, malachite, aventurine, enamel, and lacquer. The Poppy Vanity Case [81] uses an aventurine cladding over the gold on the body of the box, for a mottled bluey-green effect. Green is associated with spring and rebirth, and is closely associated with the feminine, perfect for vanity cases. Aventurine, a type of quartz in which mica and other mineral inclusions give a glittery effect, can be other colors depending on the mineral content, but green is the most common. The name derives from the stone's similarity to the Venetian aventurine glass, named from *a ventura*, Italian for "by chance," referring to the result of an accident in the eighteenth century, when a worker dropped some metal filings into molten glass giving the glittery effect that has remained popular in Venetian glass. The quartz was named later, and aventurine, sometimes called the "gambler's stone," is said to be a lucky crystal associated with wealth and prosperity, and winning in games of chance—making it a perfect stone choice to accompany the modern woman's trip to the roulette table at a nightclub.

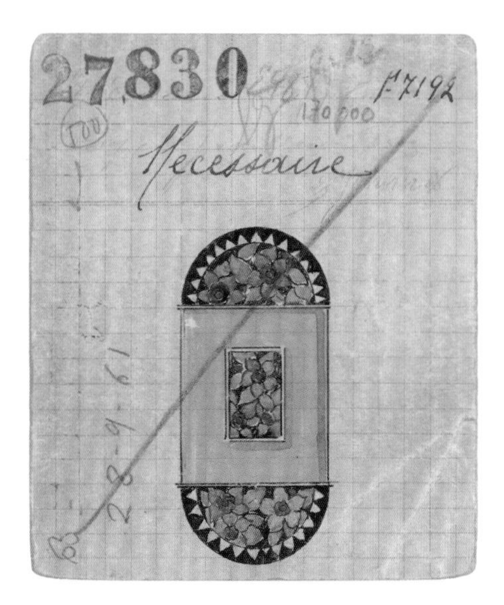

Original stock card, Van Cleef & Arpels, Paris, 1926.

While the glittering aventurine catches the light, the leaves on the pentagonal panel, a stone trompe l'oeil suggestion of a fold-over flap on a clutch, are made of jade. The so-called carving of jade, associated first with China, where it dates back thousands of years, is actually a mix of abrading through grinding with a granular mineral paste and using various cutting tools. Carved jade became associated with emperors and the upper levels of society by the eighteenth century when imperial patronage raised the artistic level. This patronage continued on until the end of the Qing dynasty in 1911, while artistic sources expanded. The quality of Chinese jade carving was much appreciated in the West from early trading days, and the stone was exported for use in snuffboxes, figurines, and other objects. After the jade supplies in China were significantly exhausted, much of what was carved there was imported from Burma (now Myanmar) before carving. With exposure to the West, the skilled craftsmen learned to use more up-to-date technologies in the twentieth century, including electric-powered cutting tools. For luxury goods, a desire for the top carvers' traditional styles and techniques mixed with more modern ones to produce some exquisite work as virtuosic elements that were incorporated into very European objects created by designers in the West.

The Poppy Vanity Case mixes greens with the strong red of coral for the poppies and deep purple of amethysts for the flower centers. All of this is highlighted within a zigzag diamond border, contained much the way boxwood hedges contain a geometrically patterned French garden. Red in the 1920s was a new bright color in the exotic fashion palette. Red coral appears both carved and as the inspiration for the specific red enamel created as a specialty of Strauss, Allard & Meyer. It is most likely that a piece of such coral would have been used to get a color match as they mixed colors to create the enamel examples (see 85, and 28). The poppies are evocative of China, where red was historically associated with royalty, suggesting a hint of the East, while the color also connects to the popular lipstick color of the 1920s, held within the vanity case.

The black at the ends and at the envelope edges of this box, like that of the background of the Tutti Frutti Tree of Life Vanity Case of 1925 [80], offers a reminder of the chicness of black, through a technique that was also enjoying great popularity in this era: the highly prized ability to get a good even single tone with a great shiny finish. The use of black that was not mourning attire was new to women's fashion and was a color meant for nightclubs and stepping out in Chanel's "little black dress." Black as a ground color for vanity and cigarette cases thus referenced contemporary fashion, but was also derived from a long-standing European love of Japanese lacquer.

While lacquer is often applied to wood, enamel is a glassy mixture that can be fused by high firing and applied to metal. In the case of these boxes, the metal was gold, a true luxury, as the black is opaque, not showing its undermetal, but the gold lends a higher shine and luminosity and is revealed when the boxes are opened. The evenness of the material defines the top masterworks of enamel, and it—and the gold to which it is applied—provides a sturdier case than lacquered wood.

Starting in the seventeenth century, when Japanese lacquer with raised gilding on a black ground was brought back to Europe with the East India companies, the combination of black and gold found its way onto French commodes and other objects as well, including small luxurious boxes. In between the eighteenth century and the twentieth the appeal of *lac burgauté* brought Asian lacquer, often under inlaid shell and stone work, to the world of small boxes. As with lacquer work, the care of polishing repeatedly in layers to create an even shiny surface is the sign of a top-level

82
Amber and Snakeskin Vanity Case by Van Cleef & Arpels, Paris, 1926, Manufactured by Strauss, Allard & Meyer

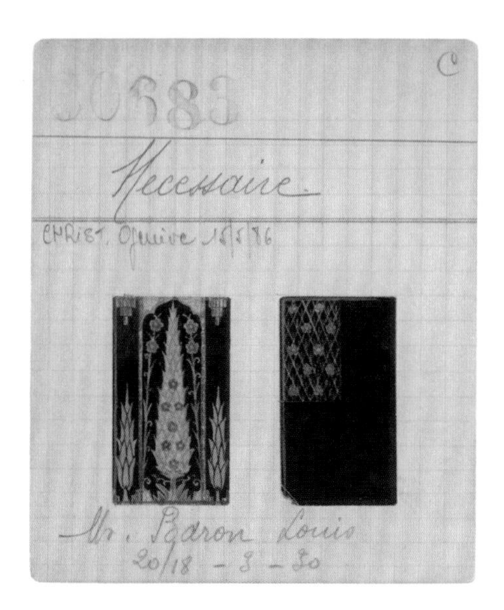

Original stock card and retail book drawing, Van Cleef & Arpels, Paris, 1928.

enamelist. In enamel work, first a clear undercoat is applied—a frit or fondant, which literally means melting—then subsequent layers build up, are fired, polished, and refired. This means that for the Poppy Box, after the gold panels that form the base for the enamel were created, the box would then be assembled with the overlay of green aventurine, the specialist panel with carved hardstones, and finally the diamond work would be set into the enameled banding.

The use of amber to cover the snakeskin in the middle of a vanity case *nécessaire* [82] is an innovative approach to pattern that also suggests the exoticism of the Art Deco period. Snakeskin was not often used due to its fragility, although the pattern was seen in art, as in Edgar Brandt's cobra lamp. Here, the snakeskin pattern is colored and protected by the amber on top of it. The idea of putting pattern under translucent enamel was popular in late eighteenth- and early nineteenth-century French and Swiss snuffboxes, and had been revived by Fabergé, Cartier, and others early in the twentieth century. However, with those examples, engine-turned metal was under the enamel; here natural materials take over. It is likely that Van Cleef & Arpels had specially sourced the snakeskin and amber, and also had the carved stonework from their own supplies, while Strauss, Allard & Meyer created the box and mounted the plaques onto the top to finish the production. The snakeskin's natural patterning suggests a pool of water surrounded by a floating garden, which involved at least four steps and sets of hands to create.

Also set against black, the Tree of Life Vanity Case in the Tutti Frutti style [80] conveys the essence of this exoticism both in the carved emeralds and rubies that make up the potted tree, and also in the shape, like that of a cypress, a motif also seen in the vanity case by Van Cleef & Arpels manufactured by Alfred Langlois [83]. In the first, the carved and cut emeralds, rubies, diamonds, and citrines are set into platinum mounts and the whole is affixed to a black-enameled gold lid. The clasp, which is also the pot that holds the tree, snaps up so that it is level with the tree when the case is opened, but on the side when closed. The contrast of the engraved Indian stones with the Western baguette- and emerald-cut diamonds and citrines shows the diversity of design sources employed for this very Western object. The symbolism of both is also related to Mughal iconography in designating a Garden of Paradise with its use of cypress trees. In fact, the word "paradise" comes from the Avestan (Indo-Iranian) word for an enclosed park, *pairida za*. The arrangement in three parts is like that of a prayer rug or cloth seen in both India and Persia, with stylized formal design elements. While undoubtedly there is a specific source for the design, especially for this case by Langlois [83], it was almost certainly something from a published collection or in a museum, rather than in the collection of the purchaser. Thus this latter case could have appealed not only to a Western client with a taste for the exotic, but also to both Indian and Iranian ones as well.

83
Cypress Tree Vanity Case by Van Cleef & Arpels, Paris, 1928, Manufactured by Alfred Langlois

Roses formed a major element of the nineteenth-century garden. They appear in geometric stylizations in the textile work of Paul Poiret with Paul Iribe, Jeanne Lanvin, and others, inspiring motifs that appeared on accessories such as the compact and lipstick baton in red lacquer by Lacloche Frères, Paris [85], and a vanity case [84], both manufactured by Strauss, Allard & Meyer. This shade of red, which seems to have found an extraordinary frequency in the works of Strauss, Allard & Meyer, was probably inspired by red coral, a material frequently used in Chinese and chinoiserie designs [10, 28, 34, 63, 65, 84, 85, 87, 89]. The front of the rose compact has a carved amber lid set with coral carved with rose motifs studded with diamonds. In contrast, the vanity case has the roses made of diamond-studded panels set in platinum on a black enamel ground, all of which is mounted on the red enamel to simulate a piece of cloth wrapped around the edges.

Georges Lepape, plate for *Les choses de Paul Poiret*, 1911, featuring a dress with a *rose d'Iribe*, a stylized flower that was often copied.

84
Rose Vanity Case by Lacloche Frères, Paris, circa 1925,
Manufactured by Strauss, Allard & Meyer

85
Rose Compact and Lipstick Baton by Lacloche Frères, Paris, circa 1928, Manufactured by Strauss, Allard & Meyer

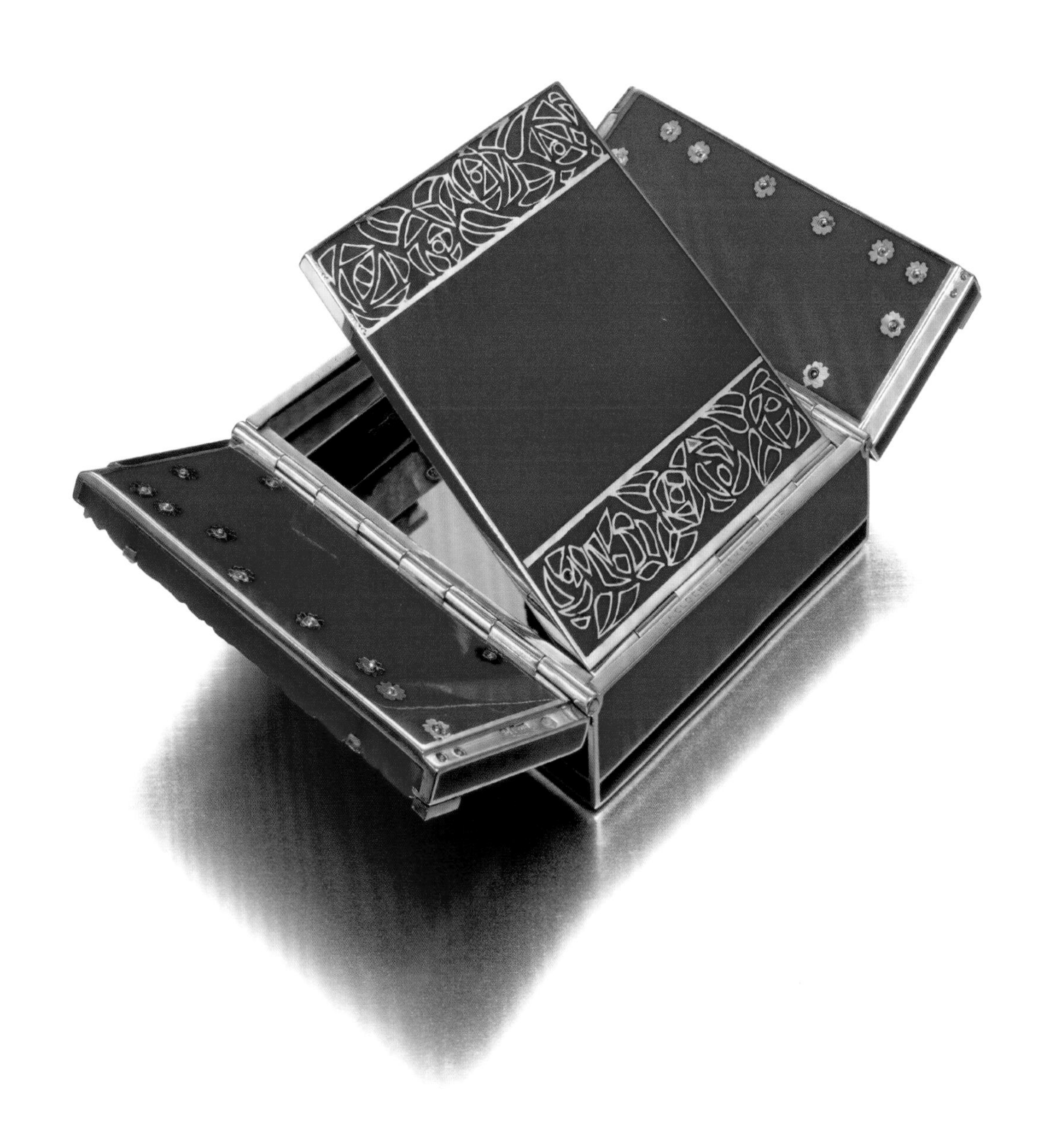

86
Princess Andrée Aga Khan's Mughal Emerald Vanity Case by Cartier, Paris, circa 1929

Cartier Paris

87
Floral Sash Vanity Case by Strauss, Allard & Meyer, Paris, circa 1925

88
Chrysanthemum Vanity Case by Lacloche Frères, Paris, circa 1928, Manufactured by Strauss, Allard & Meyer

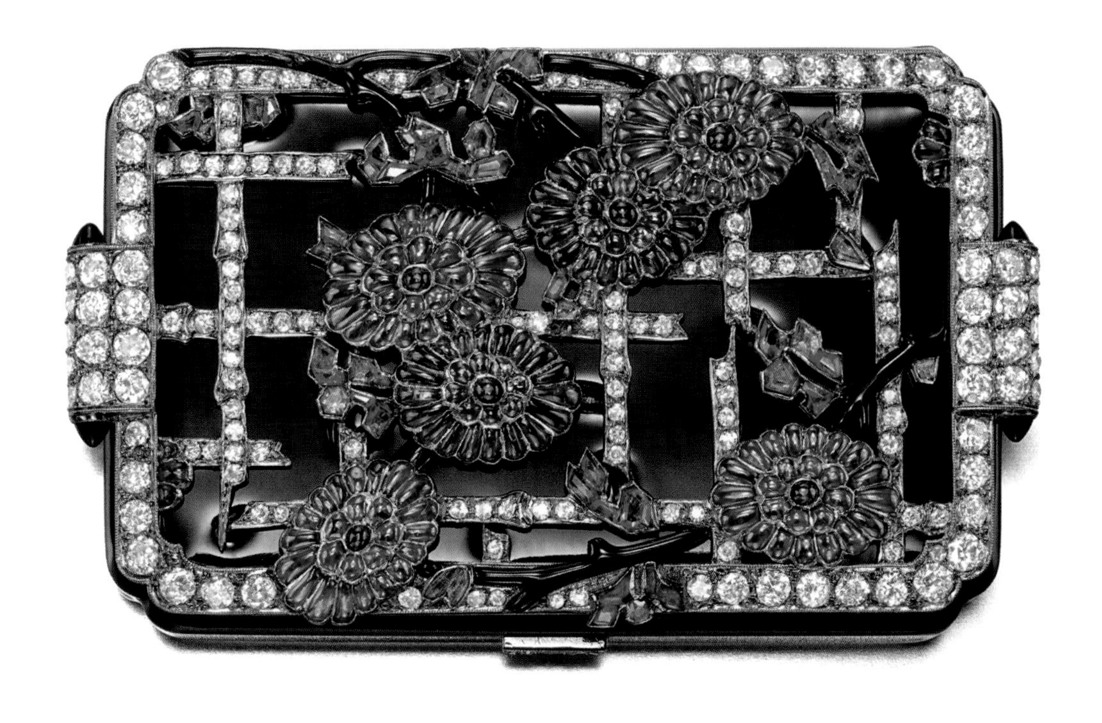

74125

Princess Andrée Aga Khan wearing a Cartier Mughal emerald necklace and emerald boule tiara that would have coordinated with one of her Cartier cigarette cases.

Kikugawa Eizan, *Woman under Wisteria Trellis*, Japan, circa 1825. Japanese woodcuts influenced the patterns on many of the boxes in the collection, particularly the florals. The bamboo trellis here is reflected in the chrysanthemum box [88].

These two boxes, with other examples in the collection [88, 64], were made for Lacloche Frères, a retail firm that sometimes supplied other retailers, and also subcontracted with Strauss, Allard & Meyer among other distinguished manufacturers to produce a broad variety of compacts, vanity and cigarette cases in the 1920s. Opening a branch in London in 1912, the firm was in a position to buy the contents of Fabergé's London store during World War I and more assets when the Soviets took power. The firm was in the interesting position of being both retailer and supplier, demonstrating the interconnectedness of the industry.

The ultimate garden ornament is a carved Mughal emerald, in the form of a flowerhead used in the chic Cartier vanity case [86] owned by Princess Andrée Aga Khan, Prince Sadruddin Aga Khan's mother. Mughal emeralds, originally from Colombia, were imported to India starting in the seventeenth century, where they were then carved to suit Mughal tastes, often inspired by foliate forms. When Jacques Cartier went to India, he received orders from maharajas and often acquired stones such as this from them and others to make into their jewelry or to recycle into new objects. The box is a formal arrangement of lines, which, when opened by the two diamond wings on the side, leaves the emerald attached to the compartment below.

Chrysanthemums and other flowers are featured on an envelope vanity case [87]. Strauss, Allard & Meyer mixed their signature red, with blue floral enamel, likely based on a textile design. Stylized chrysanthemums form the crest of the emperor of Japan and the imperial family, suggesting that the paring down of a natural form was inspired by Japanese motifs and techniques that included *uroshi* lacquerwork. The enamel flowers with visible gold between them would have required careful hand application. The artists probably used a stencil and wax to ensure that the narrow dividing lines between the areas of color did not disappear during firing. The combination of the chevron lines in the red enamel borders looks much like a sash, held together with a diamond and cabochon sapphire-mounted clasp.

Another vanity case [88] also features the motif of chrysanthemums, but this time in a way that does not just speak to *japonisme*. It also may represent the collaboration of two firms for different parts of the box. Lacloche, for whom the box was made, may have supplied from its jewelers the flowers on the exterior. The use of various sizes of buff cut gems to create the effect of flowers in three dimensions, perhaps even in a breeze, suggests a Western aesthetic applied to a traditional Japanese use of chrysanthemums on a trellis. Inside the box, created by Strauss, Allard & Meyer, are stylized flowerheads in black enamel on white gold that are almost identical in their form to those enamelled in blue on the exterior of the Floral Sash Vanity Case [87], by the same firm. They are much closer to actual Japanese design in their two-dimensionality. It seems likely that Strauss, Allard & Meyer completed the box, and may have had it sent back to Lacloche to add this specific mount on top, with its more European taste stonework depicting a *japonesque* theme.

89
Lac Burgauté Garden Scene Vanity Case by Janesich, Paris, circa 1929, Manufactured by Strauss, Allard & Meyer

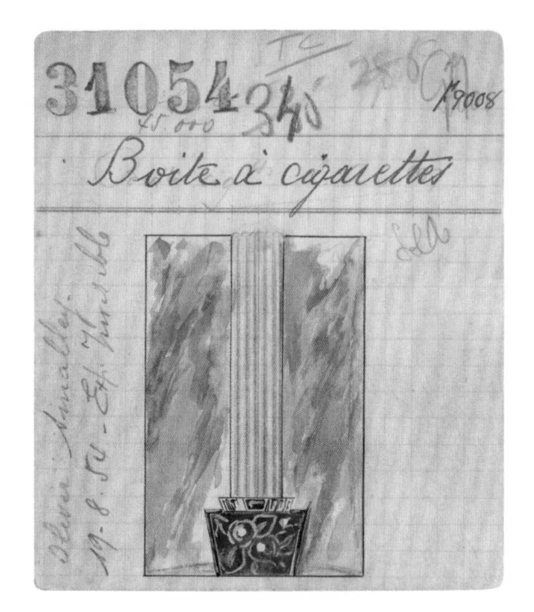

Lapis Lazuli Blues

In contrast to the pieces inspired by figurative garden design are the distinctly geometric boxes emphasizing color and texture. The boxes featuring lapis lazuli in the collection demonstrate the power and popularity of this material as a strong source of color in Art Deco design. Two boxes made by Van Cleef & Arpels in 1928 [90, 91] both have the dynamic linearity of a plane taking off on a runway. The year these pieces were made was a time of technological advances in travel. In 1927, Charles Lindbergh had landed in Paris on the first non-stop transatlantic flight. These pieces exhibit the sense of streamlined speed against lapis, the color of sky. In the first example, though, the ground is jadeite, overlaid with a rock crystal "airstream," with a lapis thumbpiece evoking a plane. This is recorded in the Van Cleef & Arpels stock book as having the baguette diamond portions by Rubel and the box—with the sculpted lapis, black enamel, and diamond elements—made by Strauss, Allard & Meyer. Rubel, who did a variety of jewelry work for Van Cleef & Arpels, also features as the supplier of the baguettes for the second box, and Strauss, Allard & Meyer appear both for the box and for the lapis, crystal, and jade elements as well as the metalwork. It is interesting that these are numbered consecutively, which means they were likely made concurrently. According to archival records, the same client purchased both boxes, which were eventually reunited in this collection.

Original stock card and retail book drawing, Van Cleef & Arpels, Paris, 1928.

90
Box by Van Cleef & Arpels, Paris, 1928, Manufactured by Strauss, Allard & Meyer

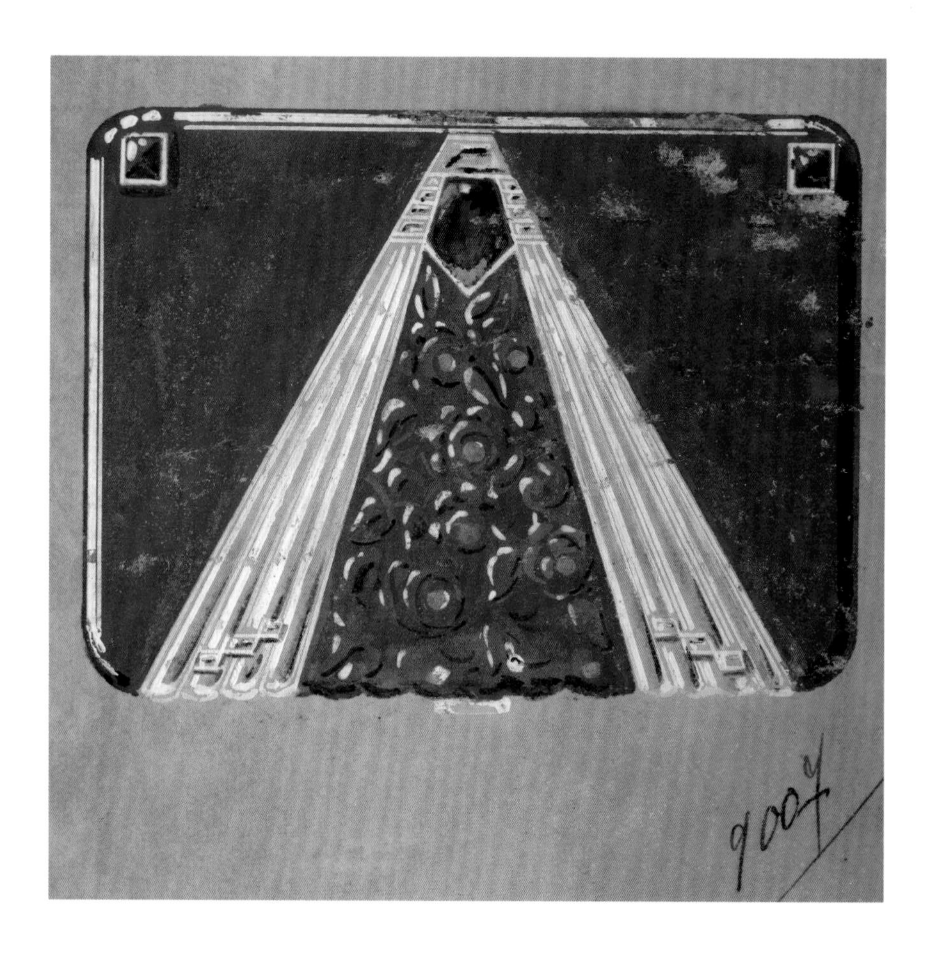

Original stock card and retail book drawing,
Van Cleef & Arpels, Paris, 1928.

91
Box by Van Cleef & Arpels, Paris, 1928, Manufactured by Strauss, Allard & Meyer

JANESICH · Nº 12635

The firm of Janesich, founded in Trieste in 1835, had established a Parisian branch by the end of the nineteenth century. They were especially known for supplying their aristocratic clientele with cigarette and powder cases in the 1920s. They, too, often looked to Strauss, Allard & Meyer to create boxes for them, and all the Janesich boxes in this collection are stamped by both. Two in the collection [92, 93] feature lapis lazuli. One is mounted with a monogram of rose-cut diamonds set in a platinum circle. The borders are of yellow-enameled ends and thumbpiece, also set with diamonds. The whole of the lapis is curved at the edge, a great technical feat. While rich in color, lapis is soft and fragile enough that mounting it with rounded edges that are less likely to chip or using panels with borders of enamel and metalwork makes a more practical design. The other box features a chamfered edge with diamond-studded mounts for the thumbpiece and the hinge that create a stunning contrast. Clearly Strauss, Allard & Meyer, who produced these boxes for Janesich, were as advanced with lapis as with their signature red enamel and coral.

93
Vanity Case by Janesich, Paris, circa 1928, Manufactured by Strauss, Allard & Meyer

Opposite:
92
Vanity Case by Janesich, Paris, circa 1928, Manufactured by Strauss, Allard & Meyer

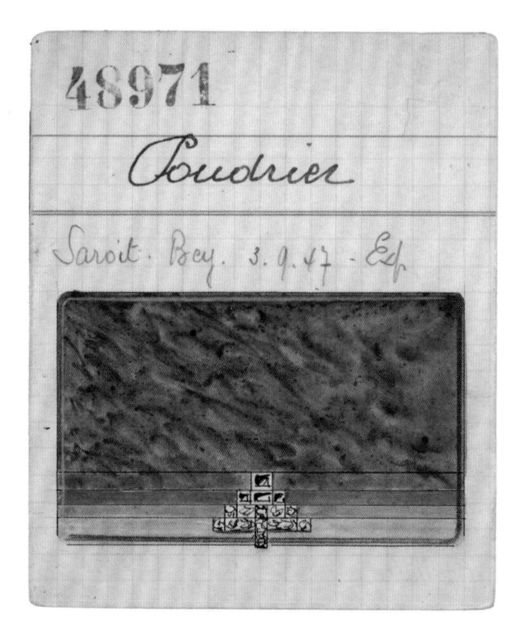

Original stock card, Van Cleef & Arpels, Paris, 1938.

A decade later, in 1938, Strauss, Allard & Meyer produced a case for Van Cleef & Arpels [94] that exhibits their enthusiasm for the deep blue of lapis, but this time executed in enamel. The art of enameling has a number of different techniques, but they all involve the repeated application of a vitreous material applied as a dried frit to the metal surface, in this case, gold, that then is fired, sanded, polished and the process repeated in careful even applications to achieve a rich color and highly shiny surface. The distinctions come if the enamel is placed in compartments (*cloisons*) surrounded by metal borders. While cloisonné enamel was historically used for elaborate floral designs, it is employed to strong effect here separating the shades of blue from a simulated lapis, to a pale color. The skill of the enamelist is also seen in the replication of lapis veining seen in the darkest blue area.

The floral vanity case [95] manufactured for Van Cleef & Arpels by Alfred Langlois in 1930 features a spring-action hidden clock and a pencil. These functions represent an early type of *minaudière,* a term Van Cleef & Arpels patented in 1932 for an all-in-one set: vanity, cigarette, lighter, dance-card holder, pencil, watch, and comb. Creations of the 1930s were bigger and could double as a small purse when carried with a velvet holder with straps. The addition of the hidden watch was increasingly popular with women who did not want to be dependent on men to know the time, nor to be seen checking what the hour was. The pop-up mechanism, which operates in a somewhat similar fashion to the calling-card holder that Langlois patented years before, allowed for a discreet look while reapplying lipstick. While the *minaudière,* according to Van Cleef & Arpels, was invented in response to Florence Gould's arrival in the shop with her lipstick, cigarettes, and lighter all stuffed into a Band-Aid box and thereby suggesting to Louis Arpels the need for an elegant solution, he clearly had products that combined many of these functions already.

This box has a rare combination of marks that refer to a specific moment in Van Cleef & Arpels's history. After exhibiting in the 1924 Grand Central Palace Exhibition in New York, the firm wanted to open a New York shop to gain proximity to their American clients. They found a location and opened in 1929, coinciding with the Wall Street crash. By spring of 1930 it was clear that the Depression meant it was not the right time to expand and they closed their doors in New York until their return to the World's Fair in 1939, after which they stayed and opened a New York store. During the brief time of their preparation for and opening of the New York store in 1929–30, they marked a few pieces with "NY" for sale there, including this box. But it must have been sent back to Paris when the New York shop closed, and thus has a Paris stock card and number too.

The case combines the lavish use of real lapis, but secured from edge chipping by a platinum surround holding baguette-cut diamond triangles and stylized hexagonal-cut lapis flowerheads, with red and green enamel leaves. The design is clean, geometric Art Deco of a kind that would have appealed to American buyers, with a touch of the exotic, evoking Moorish tranquil pools, with surrounding tiles creating stone patterns, such as those in the Alhambra in Granada, Spain.

94
Vanity Case by Van Cleef & Arpels, Paris, 1938,
Manufactured by Strauss, Allard & Meyer

Original stock card, Van Cleef & Arpels, Paris, 1930.

95
Floral Vanity Case, Watch, and Pencil by Van Cleef & Arpels, Paris, 1930, Manufactured by Alfred Langlois

VAN CLEEF & ARPELS

Four boxes by Cartier form an encyclopedia of lapis lazuli mosaics [96, 97, 98, 99]. The Scale Pattern Box combines gold, turquoise, and lapis in an inlay and marquetry arrangement to create a pattern with banded ends [96]. A group of boxes and vanities in this combination is recorded from 1928–30 in Cartier's Paris archive, including a cigarette case with scale pattern dating to December 1928.[4] The color and combination of turquoise and lapis as materials speak directly to the Egyptian revival, a fashion that emerged after the opening of King Tutankhamun's tomb in 1922–25 and the ensuing publication and display of the treasures in it. The scale pattern, which suggests a fish, was used in ancient Egypt, as well as other cultures near the sea, and evokes the colors of the Mediterranean, which was so fashionable in the 1920s. The scales are created by cutting the stone almost like glass millefiori canes or wood marquetry to get the same shape and coloration of the stone to set by inlaying with gold triangles between.

A cigarette case and lipstick baton set [97] also uses gold, turquoise, and lapis lazuli. In this case, the turquoise on the box is set like a mosaic of square tesserae surrounded by solid bands of lapis set like cloisonné enamel around it and around the lipstick holder, whose ends are a mosaic of concentric triangles with gold mounts. This too suggests the colors of the Mediterranean and Egyptian antiquities.

The third, a cigarette case [98], uses an inlay of marquetry lapis, probably originally all one piece that was cut in sections to enable a slightly convex surface for the box, and to support the pressure of applying the central medallion with a Chinese carved jade, all the while suggesting veining in the lapis. The edges are green enamel, to protect the lapis and offset the jade, while the corners are of gadroon-carved mother-of-pearl. The combination suggests a Chinese inspiration, with the use of mother-of-pearl for the gadroon corners, which is Eastern in materials and, like the Machine Age aesthetic of a car radiator grille, Western in spirit.

The last, a vanity case by Cartier [99], is very Chinese in spirit, materials, and design, though modern in function. The coral and carved jade contrast with the lapis and with a scrolling cloud shape outlined in diamonds. The sea-like element of the lapis is created with the natural figure of the stones set in a mosaic of cut pieces. The box is marked by Lavabre, a firm that worked exclusively for Cartier from 1906–21 and created pieces for them through the 1930s. Nadelhoffer describes the relationship as "whenever enameled gemstone objects needed additional work, Cartier turned to the workshop of Henri Lavabre in the rue Tiquetonne, where between fifteen and twenty expert craftsmen were employed for up to twelve hours a day."[5]

A page of Cartier Egyptian jewelry in *The Illustrated London News*, January 26, 1924. The company adapted real Egyptian faience antiquities to modern taste and also employed the blue and green color combination on original pieces.

THE "TUTANKHAMEN" INFLUENCE IN MODERN JEWELLERY.

REPRODUCED BY COURTESY OF CARTIER, LTD., 175, NEW BOND STREET, W.1.

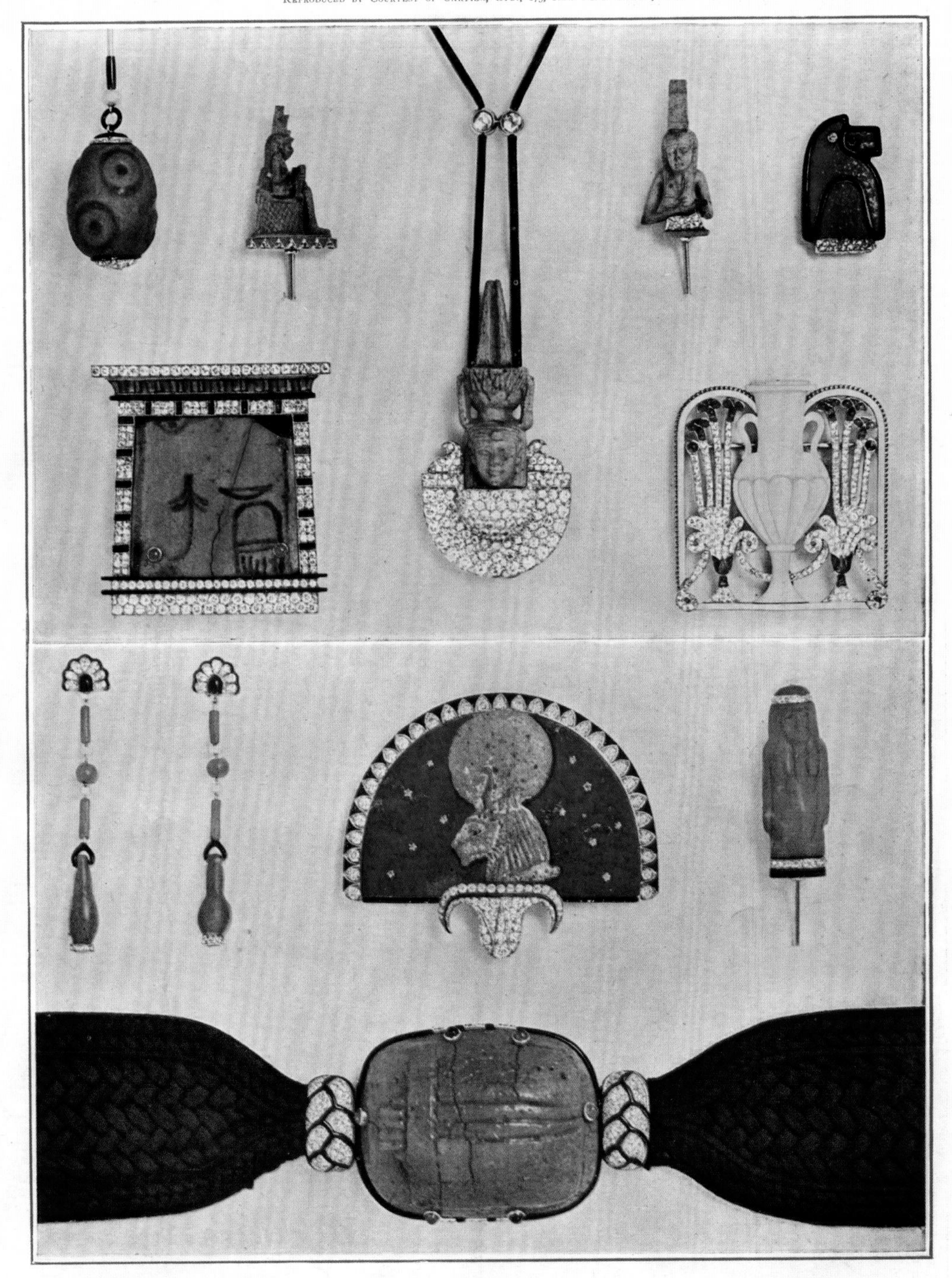

EGYPTIAN TRINKETS FROM 1500 TO 3000 YEARS OLD ADAPTED AS MODERN JEWELLERY: BROOCHES, PENDANTS, EARRINGS, AND HAT-PINS SET WITH REAL ANTIQUES, AND A TUTANKHAMEN REPLICA.

Women interested in Egyptology, who desire to be in the Tutankhamen fashion, can now wear real ancient gems in modern settings as personal ornaments. We illustrate here some typical examples, by courtesy of Cartier, the well-known Bond Street jewellers. Taken in order from left to right, beginning at the top, the objects are described as follows:—(1) A bead of glazed faience of the Twenty-second Dynasty (about 900 B.C.). Its deep colour shows its age. (2) A figure of Isis and child in glazed faience (Twenty-sixth Dynasty, 600 B.C.) set as a hat-pin. (3) A faience head of Isis (600 B.C.) set as a pendant. (4) A faience bust of Isis (600 B.C.) set as a hat-pin. (5) A glazed faience head of Hapi, the monkey-god of the Nile (Twenty-second Dynasty, 900 B.C.) set as a hat-pin. (6) A miniature temple in glazed faience (900 B.C.) set as a brooch. (7) This is the only object on the page which is not an actual Egyptian antique. It is a miniature replica of the most beautiful alabaster vase found in Tutankhamen's Tomb. (8) Ear-rings of lotus seeds and glazed faience tubes (Eighteenth Dynasty, 1500 B.C.) set with diamonds and onyx. (9) A sacred ram in glazed faience (600 B.C.) set as a brooch. (10) A figure of Ta-urt, protecting goddess of women, in sardonyx (Thirteenth Dynasty) set as a hat-pin. (11) A scarab (Twenty-first Dynasty, 1000 B.C.) set in coloured stones as a clasp for a twisted silk belt.

96
Scale Pattern Box by Cartier, Paris, circa 1928

97
Cigarette Case and Lipstick Baton by Cartier, Paris, circa 1929

98
Leaf Motif Cigarette Case by Cartier, Paris, circa 1930

99
Vanity Case by Cartier, Paris, circa 1927, Manufactured by Henri Lavabre

The Cartier watchmaking workshop on rue Lafayette in Paris under Maurice Couet, circa 1927. Cartier Paris Archives

Art of Time

Art Deco clocks and watches added to the opportunity for the combination of masterful execution of movements and casework as new developments in clock making, especially the "mystery clock," and watches for women became fashionable. By 1853, Cartier sold pocket watches, although they were bought from watchmakers.[6] In the 1920s and 1930s they continued to outsource the creation of mechanisms and housings for clocks and watches although Cartier made exclusive arrangements with Maurice Couet (1885–1963). From a family of clockmakers, Couet had worked in the workshop of Prévost, one of the primary suppliers of movements to Cartier during the early years of the twentieth century. After 1911, Couet set up a workshop to produce table clocks exclusively for Cartier in the rue Saint Martin, where he also created their mystery clocks.[7] When he moved his workshop for Cartier in 1919, Couet was further able to add to his workshop lapidaries and enamelists, both full-time and as contractors, of the caliber necessary to produce the casework comparable in quality to his clockworks. This enabled Cartier to use this workshop for more than clocks—including objects such as vanity and cigarette cases.[8] The division of labor and the design responsibility for the cases of the extraordinary clocks made by Couet are unclear. What is clear is the beauty of the unusual pieces that came from the collaboration between his workshop and Louis Cartier.

In the 1920s Couet sometimes worked with the Cartier subsidiary the European Watch and Clock Company in collaboration with Edmond Jaeger, of the Swiss Jaeger-LeCoultre family watchmaking company. They supplied movements, where Couet supplied some of the casework in collaboration with specialists. Although much of the execution of watch and clock movements was done in a special unit at the Jaeger-LeCoultre workshops in Switzerland, Couet remained in Paris, and his name appears both on its own and in association with the European Watch and Clock Company, on clocks of the top level for Cartier. The European Watch and Clock Company movements are also seen on top-level clocks and watches without Couet's name. While Cartier's branches in London and New York had simpler clocks made in their own workshops, from 1919, Cartier had the European Watch and Clock Company handle the export of the more elaborate clocks, which were made in Paris.

The multi-workshop approach worked for other houses, such as Van Cleef & Arpels, but it was only much later that Van Cleef & Arpels worked out exclusive arrangements with clock and watchmakers, preferring to establish special—but not exclusive—arrangements with Vacheron Constantin or Verger Frères, who supplied fine works to other houses too. It is thus not surprising to find that all but three of the clocks and watches in this collection are from Cartier. Of these three, one is the Cloud Clock circa 1925 by Verger Frères, with a movement by Vacheron Constantin [104], another a watch and vanity case circa 1928 by Janesich that has a chrysanthemum floral design [116] much like that in Strauss, Allard & Meyer's envelope vanity case [87]. The third is the Van Cleef & Arpels *minaudière*-like box [95].

Couet presented his first mystery clock to Cartier around 1912. He and others had created previous illusory clocks but Couet's mathematical abilities, combined with a refined clock-making ability, enabled him to create a new system. It was based on the concept of rotating disks attached to the hands. Rather than the hands rotating, he created a multi-layered sandwich of crystal disks into which each hand is fixed that connected to gears in the frame of the case, with the movement often housed in the base. In the 1920s, Couet continued to develop several versions of the mystery clock for Cartier, including fourteen with Chinese elements and six with the "Portique" structure based on a Shinto shrine gate. Every part was handmade and, in 1925, would have involved six or seven specialists. Besides the watchmaker, there was a designer, the *orfèvre-boîtier*, the enameler, the lapidary, the stone setter, and the polisher.[9]

The Imperial Guardian Lion mystery clock [100] has two citrine layers with serpent-like dragon hands appearing to swim in the golden sea surrounded by rose-cut diamond-studded Arabic numerals in Chinese calligraphic style set on a carved coral stem. The base is an elaborate sculpture of carved green nephrite, coral pearls, and enamel that display what was a mix of older works—in this case nineteenth-century Chinese carved animals—with Cartier's own elements made by the house-contracted masters, all combined magnificently in their larger creations.[10] Cartier and Couet produced fourteen animalier-figural mystery clocks between 1922 and 1931; they were the most expensive decorative objects produced by Cartier, certainly at this period, and possibly ever. This was the tenth such clock and was made in 1929.[11]

The later aquamarine and coral mystery clock [101] stands in stark contrast to the Guardian Lion. While the production path for this clock would have been similar, it displays a pared-down form, rich in materials. Here the rock crystal or citrine layers usually used for the mystery portion are replaced with what appears to be an enormous aquamarine, which is, in fact two layers of aquamarine. The strong and reductive case, with gadrooned coral and lapis, shows a spare and more minimalist look.

The casemakers were often the same as those whose stonework and enameling graced the cigarette boxes and vanity cases in the collection. In fact Verger Frères, who made the mechanical picture frame with plaque by Makovsky [102], had a panoply of artisans—from gold, platinum, and silversmiths, enamelers, lapidaries, and stone cutters, to watchmakers, casemakers, designers, and renderers—in their employ, although they were unique in this. While originally in partnership with Vacheron Constantin, with whom they remained linked until 1938, they produced pieces for Cartier, Lacloche, Van Cleef & Arpels, and Tiffany, among others, supplying both casework and movements. They were the only firm, other than Cartier, that produced mystery clocks, which they did for Van Cleef & Arpels, Ostertag, and for retailers in the United States.[12] With their connection to Makovsky, evident from the picture frame in this collection retailed by the New York firm of Charlton & Co., they may have also introduced Makovsky's work to the American retailers whom they supplied.

Imperial guardian lions in the Forbidden City, Peking (Beijing), China, 1901.

The Imperial Guardian Lion mystery clock, featured in a photograph of Cartier items by Anton Bruehl, titled "Gifts with a Princely Gesture," *Vogue*, December 8, 1930.

100
Imperial Guardian Lion Mystery Clock by Maurice Couet for Cartier, Paris, 1929

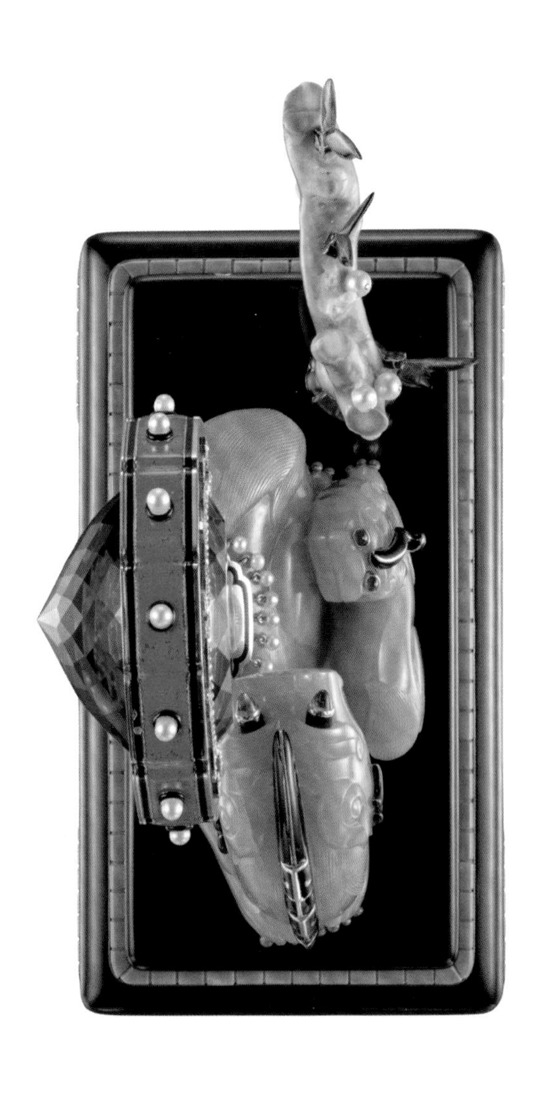

101
Aquamarine Mystery Clock by Maurice Couet for Cartier, Paris, 1931

102

Mechanical Photograph Frame by Verger Frères for Charlton & Co., Paris, 1927, with Mosaic by Vladimir Makovsky

With a significant history of watchmaking, the area of clock and watch housings was a natural for Cartier as part of their luxury market. Van Cleef & Arpels and others started to sell watches, especially those worn as jewelry, although these firms did not have anyone in-house or on an exclusive contract to produce their timepieces until much later. Generally they used Swiss clock and watchmakers such as Vacheron Constantin, whose mechanism graces a fine retrograde movement cloud clock by Verger with a Vacheron Constantin movement but no retailer signature [104]. The term "retrograde" refers to the way time was marked on a semicircular disk across which the hour hand moved and was then brought back to the starting position by a spring mechanism, causing the hand to be known as a retrograde hand.[13]

Bejeweled timepieces, from large mystery table clocks to small standing watch-form clocks, enabled these firms, led by Cartier with its long-standing interest in luxury clocks, to find new patrons to expand the breadth of their high-quality productions. Smaller desktop clocks used rock crystal, not only for the watch-holding form, but also for easel stands. Examples of these include the Cartier and Couet Putti Clock [108], which has a calendar centered by a rock crystal panel engraved with putti, much in the aesthetic of Austrian and Swedish glass shown in the 1925 Exposition internationale des Arts décoratifs et industriels modernes, the same year as this clock was made. The clock shows a jeweler's skills in the delicate band of diamonds that separate the face from the frame. Another, of similar square shape, incorporates a *lac burgauté* panel, no doubt from the same suppliers as the boxes with panels in this technique [107]. Two others with rounded tops, also by Cartier, are a stellar mystery clock [106] and a topiary desk clock of circa 1927 [110], with carved sapphire trees in jade pots by Cartier. Another Cartier comet mystery desk clock, with onyx surround, shares a radiating aesthetic of engine-turning with Fabergé and late eighteenth-century enameling [105]. The interest

A portrait of the Qianlong Emperor in his study, China, circa 1850. Many beautiful objects are displayed around the room, including a table screen on the left, the inspiration for the form of this clock.

103
Screen Clock by Cartier, Paris, 1925

104
Cloud Retrograde Clock by Verger Frères, Paris, 1927,
Movement by Vacheron Constantin

in comets, constellations, and other celestial visions enhanced Couet's clocks throughout his life, but the first inventions in this mode, "planet" or "comet" clocks, began on commission from Cartier in 1912. The first of these clocks had two superimposed dials that created the illusion of a diamond star gliding across sky blue enamel. Later versions used hands for the full "mystery" effect (see 106). The square, round, and arched frames seen in the desk clocks [106, 108, 110] were sometimes used as photograph frames for the illustrious.

Two pocket watches tell of color and exoticism. One is a solid coral case, carved out to fit the clock face of a Cartier pocket watch [109]. The other, also by Cartier circa 1924, is in gold and enamel with the face of the clock appearing as the face of an Egyptian with blue and gold headdress showing the influence of the excavation of King Tutankhamun's tomb, discovered in 1922 and opened between early 1923 and early 1925 [111]. Both the chamber decoration, published in 1923, and the actual tomb with the burial mask, published in 1925, set off a large group of jewelry influenced by what was found. In this case, the differences of coloration and subtle distinctions in the arrangement of the neckpiece depiction suggest that the enameler worked from a black-and-white image—and possibly a printed sketch—rather than from first-hand observation of a close-up color photograph. The pocket watch itself combines the technology of modern life with ancient motifs, rather than the more direct quotations sometimes found in jewelry, such as scarabs, reminding us, with jewelry houses retailing watches, of the connection of watch decoration with jewelry.

The increasing independence of women in the 1920s coincided with the popularity of women's watches. Pendant necklace-form watches (see 114, 113, 112, 115, and vanity cases with hidden watches [116, 95]) represented ways in which women could own watches that they could see discreetly and still appear to be wearing jewelry. Similarly, vanity cases with watches offered an unobtrusive way of checking the time, while reapplying lipstick. The newly fashionable women's timepieces combined with table and desk clocks to expand the accessories markets of the houses of *haute joaillerie* by using much of the same talent to design and make the casework and surrounding works of art in a combination of skillful design-sourcing, multi-sourced specialist craftsmanship, and creative use of new forms.

105
Comet Semi-Mystery Clock by Maurice Couet for Cartier, Paris, circa 1912

106
Comet Semi-Mystery Clock by Maurice Couet for Cartier,
Paris, circa 1918

107
Lac Burgauté Desk Clock by Maurice Couet for Cartier, Paris, circa 1925

108
Putti Desk Clock with Calendar by Maurice Couet for Cartier, Paris, circa 1920

109
Pocket Watch by Cartier, Paris, circa 1925

110
Borne Desk Clock by Maurice Couet for Cartier, Paris, circa 1927

111
Egyptian-Revival Tutankhamun Pocket Watch by Cartier, Paris, circa 1924

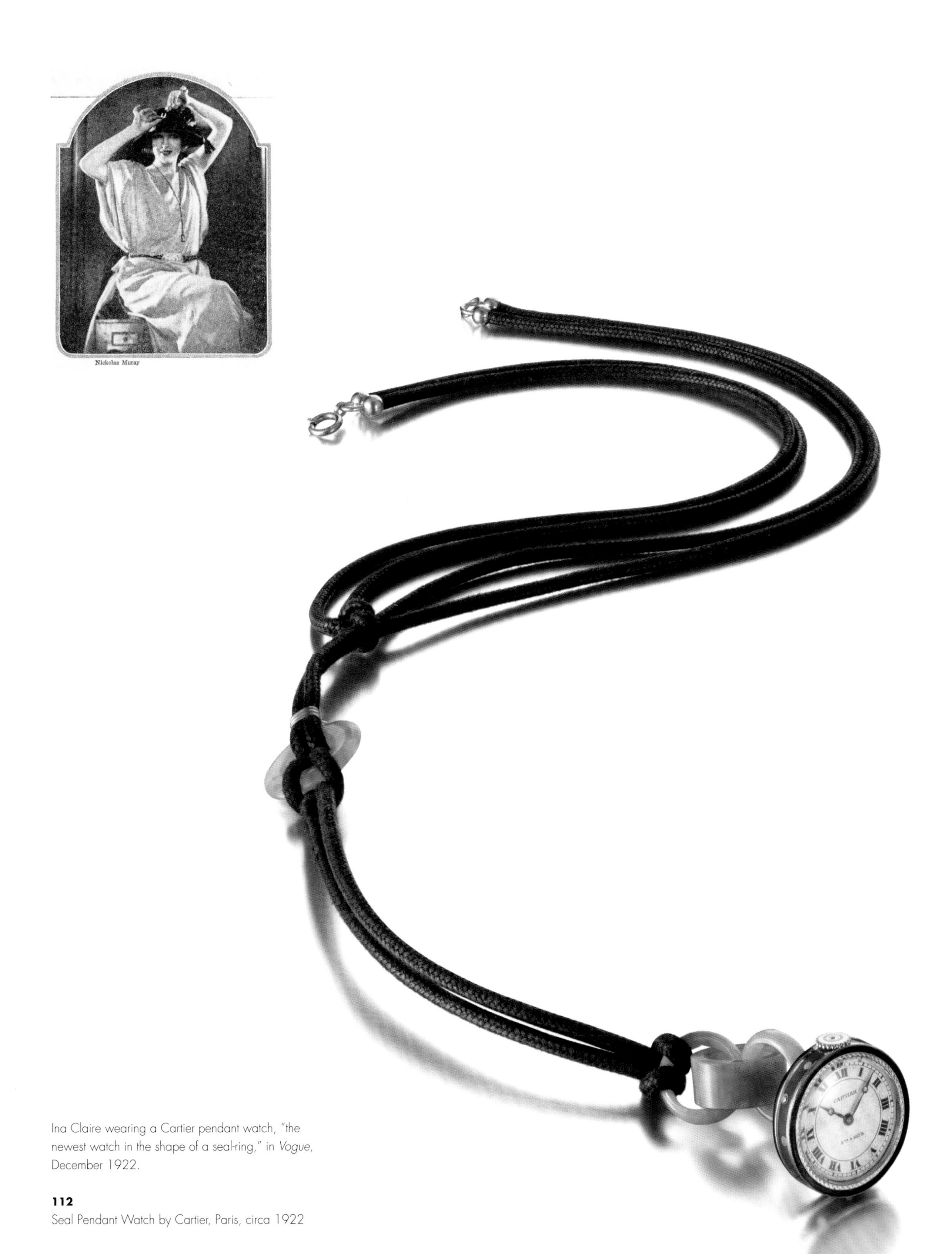

Ina Claire wearing a Cartier pendant watch, "the newest watch in the shape of a seal-ring," in *Vogue*, December 1922.

112
Seal Pendant Watch by Cartier, Paris, circa 1922

113
Acorn Pendant Watch by Cartier, Paris, circa 1925

114
Acorn Pendant Watch by Cartier, circa 1925

115
Tree of Life Pendant Watch by Cartier, Paris, circa 1925

Catalogue Texts

Sarah Davis

BEJEWELED GARDEN

80

Tree of Life Vanity Case by Cartier, Paris, circa 1930

A vanity case composed of an onyx top and a hardstone base, decorated with a stylized tree composed of carved emeralds, two carved ruby birds, and cabochon ruby berries, the diamond-set trunk modeled with citrines, with diamond-set leaves at the base, the tree trunk continues over a rounded edge to the clasp, modeled as a carved emerald pot with sapphire accents and gold outline and mechanism, the hinges set with diamonds, citrines, cabochon rubies, cabochon emeralds, and prong-set emeralds; interior with fitted mirror, lipstick holder, and powder compartment; gold and platinum, with French assay marks

Signed Cartier Paris
Measurements: 13.0 x 8.25 x 3.0 cm, 5 x 3 ¼ x 1 inches

The sacred tree, often called the Tree of Life or the Tree of Knowledge, is one of the oldest decorative motifs in the world, appearing in most cultures and religions as a verdant tree (see 83). In the Ottoman and Persian cultures it was traditionally represented by a tall attenuated cypress, similar to the form on this Cartier box created from engraved emeralds from India. Cartier also interpreted the ripe fruits that sometimes appear with the sacred tree as ruby cabochons. Two carved ruby birds also appear on the tree, a traditional representation of the human soul that gathers on the tree and takes flight upon death. The tree of life in the seasonal cycles represents life and death, as well as the desire for immortality and knowledge. Cartier has acknowledged the importance of the changes in the tree with a diamond scattering of fallen leaves and flowers.

Carved gemstones began appearing in Cartier jewelry after 1911, when Jacques Cartier began traveling to India to meet with the maharajas and bring back precious carved material. (While the stones were purchased from and carved in India, the rough stones were likely Colombian.) The stones led to the famous creations of the 1920s and 1930s incorporating combinations of carved rubies, emeralds, and sapphires into bracelets, brooches, clips, and necklaces. At the time, they were known as leaf-work pieces, but in the 1970s the appearance of these jewels at auction astonished viewers and led them to be called "Tutti Frutti." Created of carved Indian emeralds and rubies on a diamond stem, this vanity case follows in the same leaf-work tradition. A handful of other cases exist with small, carved emerald trees, but this is the largest and most elaborate. In fact the large size and hardstone material make it unlikely that this would ever have been carried, but rather left in pride of place upon a desk or vanity table.

81

Poppy Vanity Case by Janesich, Paris, circa 1928, Manufactured by Strauss, Allard & Meyer

A vanity case composed of aventurine with black enamel sides, the central motif featuring coral poppies with amethyst and diamond centers, jadeite leaves and sapphire bubbles, edged with a geometric border of diamonds and black enamel, with a diamond-set clasp; interior with two compartments for powder and rouge, a central detachable lipstick holder, and a fitted mirror; yellow gold and platinum, with British hallmarks

Signed Janesich, numbered 13421, maker's mark for Strauss, Allard & Meyer
Measurements: 8.4 x 5.6 x 1.6 cm, 3 ⅜ x 2 ¼ x ¾ inches

The central motif on this vanity case takes the form of a banner hanging from a bar with curved ends reminiscent of Asian architectural elements. The diamond and black enamel triangles edging the flag modernize the design. The foliate flag center is carved in relief, contrasting with the smooth field of aventurine. An unusual material, aventurine is a form of quartz known for aventurescence, an optical effect that is essentially glitter formed by deposits in the stone. While botanicals had long informed jewelry design, after World War I, poppies were special for their association with remembrance.

82

Amber and Snakeskin Vanity Case by Van Cleef & Arpels, Paris, 1926, Manufactured by Strauss, Allard & Meyer

A vanity case with an amber-covered snakeskin panel centering a rectangle of anemone flowers in amethyst with lapis lazuli and cabochon ruby centers and jadeite leaves, the rectangle outlined with diamonds, the rounded black enamel terminals similarly decorated with hardstone flowers and outlined with triangular diamond trim, the reverse in black enamel, with a diamond-set button clasp; interior with fitted mirror and powder compartment; gold and platinum, with French assay marks

Stamped Van Cleef & Arpels, 27830
Measurements: 9.5 x 4.5 x 1.5 cm, 3¾ x 1¾ x 11/16

This unusual case features an amber panel covering a snakeskin ground. This inspired combination uses the amber as a lens to view the natural patterning. This pairing is then juxtaposed against vari-colored hardstone flowers within geometric forms of a rectangle and half circles outlined in diamond lines and triangles. Seemingly disparate elements come together in this case to create a richly unified example of the ingenuity, geometry, and color utilized in the Art Deco period.

83

Cypress Tree Vanity Case by Van Cleef & Arpels, Paris, 1928, Manufactured by Alfred Langlois

A vanity case decorated with three stylized gold cypress trees, the center tree applied with cream-colored enamel accented by turquoise enamel flowers and grass, partially framed by ornate cream-colored enamel foliate sections, all within a black enamel ground, enhanced by bands of baguette diamonds, the reverse applied with a modified black enamel lozenge motif accented by small turquoise enamel flowers, the sides set with onyx panels; interior with fitted mirror, two powder compartments and a lipstick tube; gold and platinum, with French assay marks and British importation marks

Signed Van Cleef & Arpels, numbered 30683, with maker's mark for Alfred Langlois
Measurements: 8.7 x 5.0 x 1.1 cm, 3⅜ x 2 x 7/16 inches

This vanity case uses layered triangles of cream enamel and gold combined with whimsical curls to create an exotic and dream-like garden scene combining Art Deco geometry and playful color with a form and subject taken from Persian prayer cloths. The architectural framing at the top and bottom of the center section represents a mihrab, the prayer niche placed in a mosque to indicate the direction of prayer. The use of cypress trees indicates that this is a view into the Gardens of Paradise. The baguette diamonds are a clear statement of the Art Deco, incorporating rectangular and triangular shapes to bring a clear geometry to the foliate motif, however the separation of the scene into three parts is another clear reference to prayer cloths. The form certainly caught Prince Sadruddin's eye as a beautiful interpretation of a Muslim prayer object, and this was one of his earliest box purchases.

The original design drawing from Langlois shows a whiplash curve reminiscent of the Art Nouveau in the vines behind the central tree. This was changed to a more symmetrical treatment in keeping with strong Art Deco geometry. The reverse of the case is decorated with a repeating floral and geometric pattern inspired by repeating Persian decorative motifs. This piece is a rare and superb example of exotic and nature-based Art Deco pieces that Van Cleef & Arpels produced and is one of the most important examples of the period.

84

Rose Vanity Case by Lacloche Frères, Paris, circa 1925, Manufactured by Strauss, Allard & Meyer

A vanity case in red enamel, the front decorated on the left and right side with ribbon-like bands of diamond-set roses on a field of black enamel framed by rose-cut diamonds, with pearl thumbpiece; interior with fitted mirror, two compartments, and a detachable lipstick tube; gold and platinum, with French assay and British hallmarks

Signed Lacloche Frères, 6782, with maker's marks for Strauss, Allard & Meyer
Measurements: 9.2 x 5.3 x 1.1 cm, 3⅝ x 2 1/16 x 7/16 inches

While roses have been a popular motif in jewelry for centuries, the abstracted geometric rose that appears on this vanity case comes from the design influence of couturier Paul Poiret. The rose was ubiquitous on Poiret's fabrics, even appearing on the label sewn into his clothes. In 1908 he published *Les robes de Paul Poiret,* with drawings by Paul Iribe featuring roses composed of just a few curving lines; in subsequent years Erté and Georges Lepape included roses in their drawings for Poiret. In France, the modified rose became known as the *rose d'Iribe,* since he designed the earliest roses used by Poiret. Examples of Poiret's rose fabric appeared in *Vogue* in 1913 and 1914. Each design was progressively more abstracted and geometric, like the roses on this box a decade later.

85

Rose Compact and Lipstick Baton by Lacloche Frères, Paris, circa 1928, Manufactured by Strauss, Allard & Meyer

A rectangular compact of red and black enamel, the front composed of a carved amber lid inlaid with carved coral sections of rose design, studded with diamonds, intersected by two bands of diamonds, flanked by black enamel stripes and diamond accents, with sugarloaf cabochon coral thumbpiece framed by diamonds; interior opens to reveal a red lacquer surface with bands of stylized roses and the sides with gold flowerheads set with diamond centers, beneath fitted with a mirror and compartment; with matching lipstick baton with detachable lipstick holder, set at each end with a pearl; both in gold and platinum, with French assay marks and British importation marks

Signed Lacloche Frères, Paris; numbered 73080 and 8319, with maker's marks for Strauss, Allard & Meyer
Vanity Case: 4.9 x 3.8 x 1.5 cm, 1 15/16 x 1 1/2 x 5/8 inches
Lipstick Baton: 6.7 x 1.8 x 1.8 cm, 2 5/8 x 3/4 x 3/4 inches

This case exhibits a rose motif nearly identical to the one employed on the Rose Vanity Case [84], another case manufactured by Strauss, Allard & Meyer for Lacloche Frères. While the roses on 84 were created from diamonds, on this set they appear carved from coral and on the interior, as gold lines in red enamel.

86

Princess Andrée Aga Khan's Mughal Emerald Vanity Case by Cartier, Paris, circa 1929

A vanity case with alternating black enamel and polished gold stripes, with black enamel sides, the central motif set with a carved cabochon emerald of floral design, accented by diamonds and a black enamel border, flanked by curved diamond-set tabs to open the case, when opened the carved Mughal emerald remains attached to the interior; interior with fitted mirror and two compartments; gold and platinum, with French assay marks

Signed Cartier Paris, Made in France, 00799, with Cartier mark SCA
Measurements: 7.0 x 5.3 x 1.5 cm, 2 3/4 x 2 1/8 x 9/16 inches

Starting in 1909, Jacques Cartier traveled to India to take orders from the maharajas and to purchase beautiful antique engraved stones that were later incorporated into many of Cartier's most important Art Deco designs. The Mughal emeralds used by Cartier in their creations during the 1920s were originally from Colombia, imported into India beginning in the late seventeenth century, where they were carved with floral motifs derived from seventeenth-century Indian architecture. This sleek case features an unusual design that is centered on highlighting one such carved emerald.

Lines of gold and black enamel draw the eye to the emerald, carved with a floral form. The diamond tabs at the sides are used to open the case, which reveals the emerald is not affixed to the top of the case, but to the lipstick compartment below and forms an unusual clasp. The stone is bezel set in a black enamel surround accented with diamonds in a palmette-form, all of which draws attention to the central stone.

This is one of two boxes in the collection that belonged to Prince Sadruddin's mother, Joséphine Andrée Carron, Princess Andrée Aga Khan, who also owned a spectacular carved Mughal emerald necklace designed by Charles Jacqueau in the same period. A handful of such magnificent necklaces incorporating carved Mughal emeralds were created for some of the wealthiest and most knowledgeable connoisseurs of art in the 1920s, including J. P. Morgan and Baron Eugène de Rothschild, demonstrating the jewels' desirability.

87

Floral Sash Vanity Case by Strauss, Allard & Meyer, Paris, circa 1925

A vanity case of envelope design accented in the center by a blue enamel floral motif sided by bands of red enamel, accented with three cabochon sapphires at the front and sides, the reverse with a blue enamel center; interior with fitted mirror and makeup compartment, set at the side with a removable lipstick holder; gold, with French assay marks

Maker's mark for Strauss, Allard & Meyer, 7875
Measurements: 7.1 x 5.2 x 1.3 cm, 2 13/16 x 2 1/16 x 1/2 inches

The central panel of this vanity case mimics a typical Japanese textile design in pattern and color for a woman's obi, a sash for traditional dress. Floral pattern variants are often seen on a kimono's obi brocade, many with the deep red and blue seen on this case. Strauss, Allard & Meyer created a box with the same envelope form and removable lipstick for Van Cleef & Arpels. Now in the collection of the Cooper Hewitt, Smithsonian Design Museum, it features a pattern of blue enamel rays.

88

Chrysanthemum Vanity Case by Lacloche Frères, Paris, circa 1928, Manufactured by Strauss, Allard & Meyer

A vanity case depicting a stylized nature scene of chrysanthemums composed of buff-top calibré-cut ruby, amethyst, and sapphire blooms with onyx centers and stems and emerald leaves on a diamond-set trellis, outlined in diamonds with diamond-set handles, on a field of black enamel, the reverse and interior of the case in white gold decorated with black enamel chrysanthemums, diamond-set push-button clasp; interior with fitted mirror, lipstick holder, and two powder compartments; white gold, with French assay marks and British importation marks

Signed Lacloche Frères, Paris, 74125 and 8622, with maker's mark for Strauss, Allard & Meyer
Measurements: 7.6 x 4.1 x 1.3 cm, 2 15⁄16 x 1¾ x ⅝ inches

The floral scene on this vanity case is a typical Asian motif of flowers on a trellis, found most often in Japanese textiles, woodcuts, and ceramics. This particular case has an unusual level of detail. Each stone of the chrysanthemums was specially cut to create the petal shape needed. The flowers are not shown as simple symmetrical flowers, but instead they are displayed in a more naturalistic way as slightly turned in various directions, requiring complicated stone cutting to create the proper perspective. Instead of being a straight grid, the trellis is depicted with broken ends, and with bulging sections, evoking the shape of bamboo. The scene depicted is not a perfect creation, but rather an element in a garden that has weathered over time. The interior and back feature a floral vine motif in black enamel against highly polished metal. It is rare to find such exquisite detail on the interior of a case.

89

Lac Burgauté Garden Scene Vanity Case by Janesich, Paris, circa 1929, Manufactured by Strauss, Allard & Meyer

A vanity case, the front with a *lac burgauté* panel, framed by a diamond border, the sides and back applied with red enamel, with pearl thumbpiece; interior with fitted mirror, powder compartment, and detachable lipstick holder; gold and platinum, with French assay marks

Signed Janesich, 6295, with maker's mark for Strauss, Allard & Meyer
Measurements: 8.5 x 5.5 x 1.2 cm, 3⅜ x 2⅛ x ½ inches

The elaborate *lac burgauté* panel was likely imported from Japan and then inlaid into this vanity case. The name *lac burgauté* refers to the materials used: *lac* is lacquer (also spelled *laque* and *lacque*) and *burgau* is abalone, the source of the blue-green shell. While the name refers specifically to abalone, tinted mother-of-pearl was often used interchangeably (see also 23 and 22). This particular scene with trees and foliate plants accented by rushing water and a pagoda house in the background is inspired by Chinese landscape painting and scholars' gardens created for reflection during the Ming dynasty.

LAPIS LAZULI BLUES

90

Box by Van Cleef & Arpels, Paris, 1928, Manufactured by Strauss, Allard & Meyer

A jadeite box centering a frosted striated rock crystal column terminating at an arrow motif of three carved lapis lazuli roses with diamond centers outlined in black onyx and accented with baguette diamonds, the arrow turns over the edge of the box, terminating at the diamond-set button clasp, the side is further accented with two collet-set diamonds; white and yellow gold, with French assay marks

Signed Van Cleef & Arpels, Paris, 31054, with maker's mark for Strauss, Allard & Meyer
Measurements: 7.5 x 5.1 x 1.6 cm, 3 x 2 x ¾ inches

This box (with 91) is one of a pair of hardstone boxes created by Strauss, Allard & Meyer for Van Cleef & Arpels utilizing similar materials and motifs, including rays of fluted frosted rock crystal, identical patterns of carved lapis lazuli flowers set with diamond centers, and strong use of triangle patterns accented with diamonds. Both boxes also similarly feature designs that turn over the front edge of the box. These inventive boxes make strong use of the Art Deco interest in geometry and bold colors, drawing on a blue-green palette.

Created together, these boxes entered the Van Cleef & Arpels inventory consecutively on the same day, February 29, 1928. Both boxes were purchased by the same client, an Oliver Smalley (details of his life are unknown). Eventually, the boxes were separated and Prince Sadruddin Aga Khan acquired first this jade box and, several years later, purchased the lapis lazuli box, reuniting this incomparable pair. Individually, they are beautiful and iconic of the best of Art Deco design, but surviving as a pair they give additional insight into the design work of Strauss, Allard & Meyer and how various design motifs were incorporated into a unified whole.

91

Box by Van Cleef & Arpels, Paris, 1928, Manufactured by Strauss, Allard & Meyer

A lapis lazuli box with rounded corners, centering a triangular panel of carved lapis lazuli flowers with diamond centers, sided by triangular fluted frosted rock crystal segments accented with lozenge-shape calibré-cut diamonds, the triangle accented at the tip by a cabochon jadeite pentagon and calibré-cut diamonds, two sugarloaf jadeites at the corners, diamond-set button clasp; white gold, with French assay marks

Signed Van Cleef & Arpels, Paris, 31057, with maker's mark for Strauss, Allard & Meyer
Measurements: 6.0 x 7.6 x 1.6 cm, 2⅜ x 3 x ⅝ inches

See 90 for discussion of both boxes.

92

Vanity Case by Janesich, Paris, circa 1928, Manufactured by Strauss, Allard & Meyer

An octagonal vanity case with trapeze- and baguette-cut diamonds arranged in a geometric motif, the button clasp set with two baguette-cut diamonds; interior with fitted mirror, lipstick holder, and powder compartment; gold and platinum, with French assay marks and British importation marks

Signed Janesich, no. 12635, with maker's mark for Strauss, Allard & Meyer
Measurements: 7.4 x 4.6 x 1.8 cm, 2 15/16 x 1⅞ x ⅝ inches

The simplicity of this vanity case is tempered by the use of unusual trapeze-cut diamonds arranged with baguette cuts in an architectural form, mirrored by another.

93

Vanity Case by Janesich, Paris, circa 1928, Manufactured by Strauss, Allard & Meyer

A vanity case composed of lapis lazuli with yellow enamel sides, decorated on the front with a diamond-set monogram with the letters "CS" within an ornate frame, bordered by a diamond trim, the four corners enhanced by ornate diamond-set accents, with a yellow enamel thumbpiece accented by a diamond-set openwork plaque; interior with fitted mirror, powder compartment, and removable rouge holder; gold and platinum, with French assay marks

Signed Janesich, 7212, 6707, with maker's mark for Strauss, Allard & Meyer
Measurements: 8.4 x 5.4 x 1.6 cm, 3 5/16 x 2⅛ x ⅝ inches

Prince Sadruddin and Princess Catherine were drawn to this case for the coincidental diamond monogram "CS" on the top. The initials are enclosed in a modified *ruyi* pattern, an auspicious symbol meaning "as your heart desires." The box is composed of a bright blue lapis lazuli body with flecks and streaks of pyrite. The vivid yellow enamel details pick up the metallic yellow of the inclusions. The striking color combination of bright yellow enamel and lapis also recalls Chinese blue and yellow porcelain. While modern porcelain developed in China during the Han dynasty (206 BCE–220 CE), yellow glaze was discovered in the Hongzhi period of the Ming dynasty (1488–1505). At this time, blue and white was the most popular color combination, the yellow glaze was also paired with the blue and quickly became popular and iconic. During the Qing period (1644–1912), the glazes became brighter, developing into colors known as "lemon yellow" and "sky-clearing blue," closest to the shades on this box.

94

Vanity Case by Van Cleef & Arpels, Paris, 1938, Manufactured by Strauss, Allard & Meyer

A vanity case with marble-like blue enamel, the front accented by four graduated steps of darker to lighter blue enamel, accented with a geometric diamond plaque and thumbpiece set with French-cut and baguette diamonds; interior with fitted mirror and compartments for powder and rouge; gold and platinum, with French assay marks and British importation marks

Signed Van Cleef & Arpels, Paris, no. 48971, with maker's mark for Strauss, Allard & Meyer
Measurements: 8.1 x 4.9 x 1.2 cm, 3 3/16 x 1 15/16 x ½ inches

Ahmed Saroit Bey was the Egyptian Ambassador to France from 1946–1950, at which time he purchased this box. The unusual enamel work in this piece seems inspired by lapis lazuli, but in a subtle design move the colors used to create the faux stone are shown in four blue stripes at the front of the box. By breaking out these colors, the designers are announcing the faux nature of the stone and calling attention to their skill with enamel.

95

Floral Vanity Case, Watch, and Pencil by Van Cleef & Arpels, Paris, 1930, Manufactured by Alfred Langlois

A vanity case with a central lapis lazuli panel terminating in baguette diamond triangles, surrounded by geometric stylized lapis lazuli flowers with diamond centers and red and green enamel leaves on a baguette and round diamond vine, with a diamond-set button clasp; interior with fitted mirror, powder compartment, and ivory writing tablet, a hidden spring lock releases a rectangular watch on one side and a pencil on the other; in gold and osmior (18-karat gold and platinum) with French assay marks

Signed Van Cleef & Arpels, 33860, NY43114, stamped AL for Alfred Langlois
Measurements: 8.5 x 4.5 x 1.2 cm, 3 3/8 x 1 3/4 x 1/2 inches
Movement: No. 5057, baguette-style movement, 5 bridges, 17 jewels

Striving to be both functional and beautiful, this case features a myriad of useful tools including a powder compartment, a writing tablet and pencil, and a watch, all carefully concealed in a stunning package. The polychrome enamel, lapis, and diamond face is both figurative and geometric, pushing the abstraction of flowers to the extreme with hexagons and squares in a rich palette. The composition and central lapis lazuli panel evokes a lush garden around a calm pool.

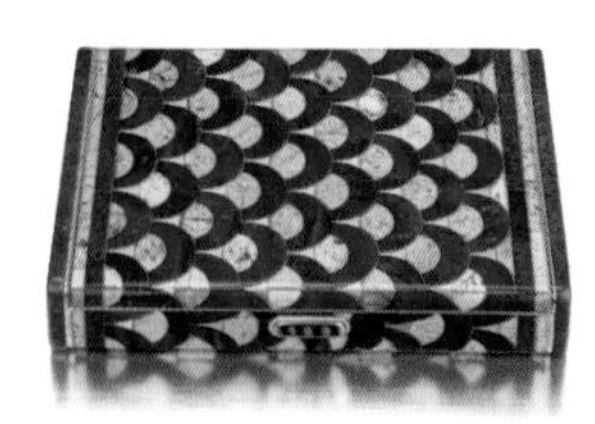

96

Scale Pattern Box by Cartier, Paris, circa 1928

A box inlaid with turquoise and lapis lazuli with gold accents in a stylized scale pattern on four sides with a band of lapis lazuli and turquoise at each end, the ends with lapis lazuli panels, the clasp button set with four sapphires; interior with fitted mirror; gold, with French assay marks

Signed Cartier Paris Londres New-York, Made in France, 03143
Measurements: 8.4 x 5.8 x 1.5 cm, 3 5/16 x 2 5/16 x 5/8 inches

This box is part of a series of boxes with geometric patterns created in turquoise, lapis lazuli, and gold (see 97 for discussion of color). There are two examples in the Cartier Collection, one with a zigzag pattern and the other featuring squares inside circles. This third box features a scale pattern, an ancient form seen across many cultures from Ancient Egypt to China to Pompeii. The design is so-called for the way the pattern is arranged likes the overlapping scales on a fish, invoking the importance of the sea to these cultures. All three boxes exhibit the pure geometry and bright colors iconic of the Art Deco, while still demonstrating how much inspiration Cartier drew from the designs and patterns of ancient cultures.

97

Cigarette Case and Lipstick Baton by Cartier, Paris, circa 1929

A rectangular case featuring a central motif composed of square turquoise segments set diagonally, flanked by bands of lapis lazuli, the front and back sides continuing the turquoise and lapis lazuli bands, the ends set with lapis lazuli, with diamond and sapphire thumbpiece; interior inscribed "Allard (?) Reuss, 33 rue Barbet de Jouy, July – 7 – 29"; with matching lipstick baton with detachable fluted lipstick holder; both gold, with French assay marks

Box signed Cartier-Paris, Made in France, 0335
Lipstick baton signed Cartier Paris, 0204
Box: 8.2 x 5.4 x 1.5 cm, 3 1/4 x 2 1/8 x 9/16 inches
Lipstick Baton: 5.7 x 1.5 x 1.5 cm, 2 1/4 x 9/16 x 9/16 inches

After the discovery of Tutankhamun's tomb in 1922 and the resulting craze for all things Egyptian, Cartier began incorporating Egyptian antiquities into their designs; often the pieces were faience in blue and green colors very similar to turquoise and lapis lazuli. This led to the combination of turquoise, lapis lazuli, and gold often used by Cartier in many of their Egyptian-inspired jewels and employed here in this cigarette case and lipstick tube (see also 96).

98

Leaf Motif Cigarette Case by Cartier, Paris, circa 1930

A cigarette case decorated with lapis lazuli marquetry with a green enameled reed border, the lid applied with a carved jade segment of scrolling foliate motif, the sides of lapis lazuli with blue enamel stripes, the corners of mother-of-pearl and round diamonds; gold and platinum, with French assay marks and British importation marks

Signed Cartier Paris Londres New York, Made in France, 4083, 128036, 8175, HSA724
Measurements: 8.3 x 6.0 x 1.7 cm, 3⅜ x 2⅜ x ⅝ inches

This box displays the popular blue and green color combination found in many Cartier Art Deco jewels. Of Chinese inspiration, the central motif is the interlacing floral design (see 17 and 15). The deep blue of the lapis lazuli is treated in an unusual way, as a random pattern of cracked segments. This design is likely drawn from the crackle glazes first popularized in twelfth-century China with imperial porcelain known as Ru ware that was much copied in the following eras.

While the main motif draws inspiration from the classical Asian sources Cartier looked to throughout the Art Deco period, the corners of this piece depict a touch of the Machine Age aesthetic popular in the late 1920s and early 1930s. The diamonds that wrap around the green enamel border are evocative of nuts and bolts, while the reeded mother-of-pearl segments bring to mind a conveyer belt or other mechanical device.

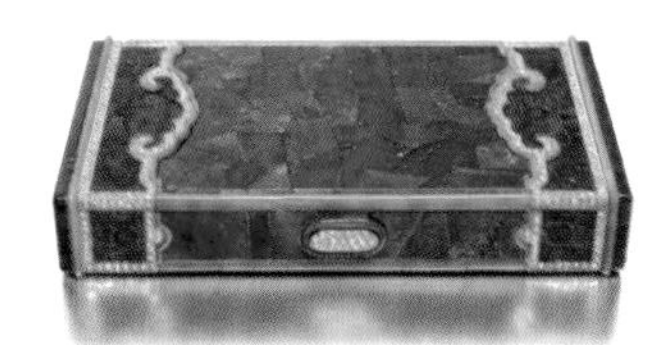

99

Vanity Case by Cartier, Paris, circa 1927, Manufactured by Henri Lavabre

A vanity case with lapis lazuli marquetry (see 98) on the central panel, the edges decorated with carved jade panels with carved *ruyi* (see 93) outlined by round diamond and coral borders of scrolling cloud shapes, the pattern continues around to the reverse, coral rims applied to the edges, the short ends set with lapis lazuli panels, the diamond-set button clasp encircled by red lacquer; interior with fitted mirror, two powder compartments with powder puffs, and lipstick holder; gold and platinum, with French assay marks

Signed Cartier Paris Londres New York, Made in France
Measurements: 9.9 x 5.2 x 1.7 cm, 3⅞ x 2 1⁄16 x ⅝ inches

While Cartier often combined jade and lapis in their Art Deco creations, this box has the addition of the intense orange coral rims. Used by Cartier only on a few select jewels from this period (including Ganna Walska's famous chimera bangle), the color combination is strong and shocking, creating a piece that makes an intense visual impression.

ART OF TIME

100

Imperial Guardian Lion Mystery Clock by Maurice Couet for Cartier, Paris, 1929

A clock designed as a carved nephrite Chinese imperial guardian lion and a young lion, the carved lion embellished with black enamel and gold mane and red enamel claws, with eyes of cabochon emeralds for the large lion and cabochon rubies for the young lion, supporting a circular clock with carved citrine face, rose-cut diamond-set hands in the shape of a dragon, and black enameled chapter ring with rose-cut diamond Arabic numerals stylized as Chinese calligraphy, the red enamel border studded with pearls, all atop a carved coral ball resting on a pearl-fringed enamel saddle blanket atop the guardian lion, beside a carved coral branch with carved stone leaves and pearls, supported by a base of black-enameled gold accented with calibré-cut corals; platinum and gold

Signed Cartier, 2639, 3809, 47, with maker's mark for Maurice Couet
Measurements: 17.0 x 9.3 x 16.2 cm, 6 11⁄16 x 3 11⁄16 x 6⅜ inches
Movement: European Watch & Clock Co., 4646, 3 adjustments, 13 jewels

In 1925 the *Gazette du bon ton* referred to Cartier's mystery clocks as "marvels of the clockmaker's art, unreal and seemingly woven from moonbeams." The mystery was in the way the hands moved around the dial of the clock without any apparent connection to the movement. This illusion was not the result of magic but of a fortuitous collaboration between Louis Cartier and Maurice Couet, a clockmaker of inventive genius, who sandwiched the hands between two crystal disks set underneath large stone faces; the toothed edges of the disks connected to a mechanism below.

This clock belongs to a remarkable group of fourteen animalier or figural clocks that were produced by Cartier and the Couet workshop between 1922 and 1931. According to Hans Nadelhoffer, this clock was made in 1929. Central to the design of this clock is the unusual carved jade figure, referred

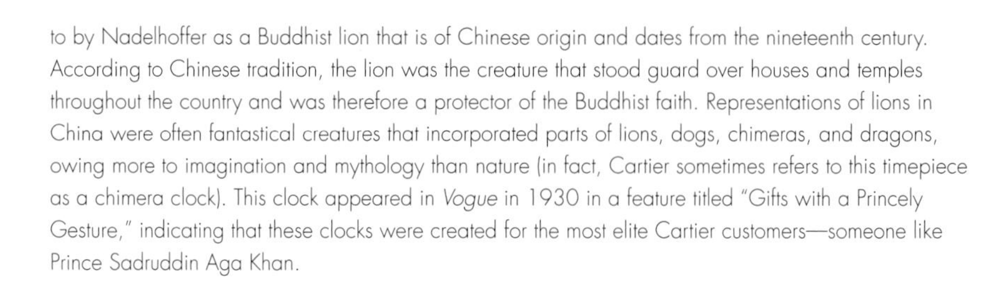

to by Nadelhoffer as a Buddhist lion that is of Chinese origin and dates from the nineteenth century. According to Chinese tradition, the lion was the creature that stood guard over houses and temples throughout the country and was therefore a protector of the Buddhist faith. Representations of lions in China were often fantastical creatures that incorporated parts of lions, dogs, chimeras, and dragons, owing more to imagination and mythology than nature (in fact, Cartier sometimes refers to this timepiece as a chimera clock). This clock appeared in *Vogue* in 1930 in a feature titled "Gifts with a Princely Gesture," indicating that these clocks were created for the most elite Cartier customers—someone like Prince Sadruddin Aga Khan.

101

Aquamarine Mystery Clock by Maurice Couet for Cartier, Paris, 1931

A clock with a square Santa Maria aquamarine dial enclosing platinum hands, within a platinum chapter ring with coral Roman numerals and coral sides, supported on an aquamarine pedestal mounted in gold, on a rectangular platinum base, the front and reverse panels decorated with fluted coral and sides with fluted lapis lazuli; with French assay marks

Signed Cartier Paris London New-York, 2930, 2913
Measurements: 7.0 x 5.6 x 3.1 cm, 3¾ x 2 3/16 x 1 3/16 inches

Of all the types of mystery clocks created by Maurice Couet for Cartier, the most surprising and enchanting are also the smallest. Based on Asian screens, the clocks feature dials that appear to be gigantic gemstones, hundreds of carats, suspending hour and minute hands in the center. While most mystery clock dials were rock crystal, a handful of these were made with citrine dials, including most of the small screen clocks, and only one mystery clock, this one, was ever made with an aquamarine.

This clock follows the screen form of the wide and flat clock connected to a brick-shaped base with a narrow connection, but there end the design similarities to the other gemstone mystery clocks that seem staid in comparison to the bold blue and orange color scheme employed here. The materials and colors are found in some of Cartier's Egyptian revival pieces at this time [111], but here the form of the clock is stripped down to a geometric minimum, relying strongly on contrasting colors and textures. This clock is a superb construction singular both in materials and design.

102

Mechanical Photograph Frame by Verger Frères for Charlton & Co., Paris, 1927, with Mosaic by Vladimir Makovsky

A photograph frame that presents an elaborate garden mosaic depicting a moonstone urn in the foreground, mother-of-pearl clouds and abalone foliage, gold trees, and a hardstone garden path and a building with arched windows in the midground, and a garden path continuing to the background, bordered by black enamel with rose-cut diamond-set corners, the sides decorated with mosaic geometric patterns, held within a pair of black onyx brackets on a carved agate plinth, the brackets set with four jade cabochons within gold collets, the lower jades are push-pieces that reveal the photograph frame by flipping the box and opening black enamel and gold doors

Signed Charlton & Co., France, with maker's mark for Verger Frères, 9703, mosaic signed M by Vladimir Makovsky
Measurements: 10.5 x 10.2 x 3.5 cm, 3¼ x 2¼ x ½ inches

In the early twentieth century, fine jewelers offered photograph frames mainly in the style of Fabergé with colored guilloché enamel and diamond details. By the Art Deco period, the best makers were less interested in photograph frames and produced only a few minor pieces. Created by Verger Frères for the Paris office of the American jeweler Charlton & Co., this fantastic frame stands apart as a singular piece, with more in common with the finest Art Deco clocks than with frames. Known for their fine clocks and jewelry, Verger Frères made important pieces for all of the great jewelry houses, including Van Cleef & Arpels, Cartier, Ostertag, Tiffany, and Boucheron.

Vladimir Makovsky created the mosaic of a verdant landscape at the center of this piece. While the larger panels Makovsky designed for jewelers were often used as clock faces, this panel was given central placement and not obscured with clock hands. Makovsky shows his study of fine art in this work and, within the two-dimensional mosaic medium, he strived to create the classic foreground, middle ground, and background while also employing perspective in the receding garden path, an unusual feature in his work and an impressive feat in this difficult medium. Makovsky was probably influenced by the work of Alexandre Benois, a fellow Russian expatriate in Paris who was a painter and critic known for his groundbreaking sets and costumes for the Ballets Russes. Benois spent a lot of time painting the gardens at Versailles, and much of his work employs the classical arrangement with a magical and scenic feel, like the mosaic Makovsky designed on this piece.

Verger Frères set this exquisite mosaic on an agate plinth with onyx brackets, the type of base used for the intricate clocks they produced in this period. This base is very similar to an agate and enamel base used on a clock the company produced for Tiffany & Co. around the same time. The inventive mechanism that reveals the photograph is unsigned, but was likely produced by special order from one of the clockmakers they worked with. When the two jade buttons are pressed, the mosaic box flips over and the enamel and gold doors open. The presentation is both theatrical and enchanting. When Prince Sadruddin Aga Khan purchased the frame, it contained a picture of Charles Lindbergh, the aviator who made his famous flight from New York to Paris the same year this clock was created, 1927.

103

Screen Clock by Cartier, Paris, 1925

A clock with a mother-of-pearl dial in a star pattern with diamond-set Roman numerals and hands outlined in black enamel trim, the hour hand in the form of a fan, the clock face with fluted coral borders and outlined in onyx, mounted on onyx arches set in gold, on an onyx and gold base; with French assay marks

Engraved on the front *Fait par Cartier à Paris*
Measurements: 9.2 x 6.9 x 12.8 cm, 3⅝ x 2¾ x 5 1/16 inches
Movement: Longines 3766972, 19 jewels, 8 day

The *écran pendule* or screen clock was one of the iconic Cartier designs of the Art Deco period. Identifiable by the use of a rectangular clock accented with coral or hardstone batons above and below, arched legs connecting to the base, and onyx or black enamel and gold, this style appeared in 1922 and was made into the 1930s. Some later variations were created as mystery clocks. The form is based on the Chinese table screens used by scholars in the Ming and Qing dynasties (1368–1911). Interested in the arts, painting, and music, as well as law, literature, and theory, these scholars surrounded themselves with beautiful and luxurious contemplative objects, made to give the eye something beautiful to assist the meditative mind. A scholar's studio would be filled with beautiful paintings, calligraphy tools, furniture, musical instruments, and objects for preparing and serving tea and wine. The table screen could be placed by a window or on a desk, originally to shield the scholar and his ink and paper from the breeze or the sun, but beside this practical function the screens were beautiful works of art. The screen form lent itself to adaptation into a clock that is also both beautiful and functional. Further referencing the Asian influence is the stylized *ruyi* fan used for the hour hand and repeated around the gold feet of the arches (see 93 for *ruyi*). Where the Chinese table screens were often delicate, this clock reflects the bolder Machine Age aesthetic that came out of the technological advances of the time, as can be seen in the pipe-like form of the arches with gold and enamel brackets and fittings.

104

Cloud Retrograde Clock by Verger Frères, Paris, 1927, Movement by Vacheron Constantin

A clock composed of a semicircular rock crystal dial carved in the center with a cluster of stylized clouds and sun rays accented with rose-cut diamonds, the chapter ring adorned with diamond-set Arabic numerals, upon a black onyx base held by eight carved melon-shaped frosted rock crystal feet with diamond-set arrow surmounts

Signed Verger France
Measurements: 16.5 x 5.5 x 11 cm, 6½ x 2⅛ x 4⅜ inches
Movement: Vacheron Constantin, 404463, 8 adjustments, 17 jewels, 8-day clock

The Verger Frères partnership with Vacheron Constantin produced several fantastic retrograde Art Deco clocks of various design. One of the most fanciful timekeeping mechanisms was the retrograde movement perfected in the nineteenth century. This clock is a superb example: instead of the traditional circular form, this clock uses a semicircle to display the time. Through an ingenious mechanism, the hour hand rotates for twelve hours before a spring brings it back to the initial twelve, while the longer minute hand operates similarly over a sixty-minute interval.

This clock is striking for the unusual half-circle form and the bold black-and-white design, using frosted rock crystal and diamonds against polished onyx. The dynamic central motif depicts a swirling storm cloud with rays of light breaking through, with glinting diamond accents. Verger Frères would have created this clock for one of their many fine retailers, such as Ostertag, Van Cleef & Arpels, Cartier, Tiffany, or Boucheron.

105

Comet Semi-Mystery Clock by Maurice Couet for Cartier, Paris, circa 1912

A clock with a circular black onyx frame centering a guilloché enamel dial patterned to resemble rays of light, the hands represented by rose-cut diamond-set stars, the chapter ring featuring chased gold Roman numerals and rosettes on a white champlevé enamel ground, the bezel set with rose-cut diamonds set in platinum, with a folding gold strut

Signed Cartier, strut engraved 547
Measurements: 7.8 x 7.8 x 2.8 cm, 3 1/16 x 3 1/16 x 1 1/8 inches
Movement: 8 days, 19 jewels, Longines, gilded brass

While clockmaker Maurice Couet is known for creating the astonishing large-sized mystery clocks, his first commission was working closely with Louis Cartier on a series of enchanting small celestial clocks depicting the movement of comets or planets. Created as early as 1912, these pieces would later come to be known as "semi-mystery" for their sophisticated mechanism. While the faces are not fully transparent, like the larger mystery clocks, there are no gears or obvious attachments revealing the movement of the stars marking the hours and minutes. (See also 106.)

106

Comet Semi-Mystery Clock by Maurice Couet for Cartier, Paris, circa 1918

A clock of a circular rock crystal frame centering sky blue guilloché enamel in a ray pattern, the hands represented by rose-cut diamond-set stars, the chapter ring of white champlevé enamel featuring Roman numerals alternating with rosettes, the bezel set with rose-cut diamonds mounted in platinum, with folding rock crystal strut back

Signed Cartier, 4168
Measurements: 8.6 x 8.6 x 3.0 cm, 3 3/8 x 3 3/8 x 1 1/4
Movement: 8 days, brass, 15 jewels, lever escapement, Breguet steel spring

This comet mystery clock fits in both with the celestial series of clocks (see 105) and the rock crystal clocks [107].

107

Lac Burgauté Desk Clock by Maurice Couet for Cartier, Paris, circa 1925

A clock with a square panel of rock crystal with beveled edges framing a circular dial inset with a Chinese lacquer panel, within a shaped gold bezel of deep blue enamel with orange translucent enamel Roman numerals, rose-cut diamond and ruby arrow hands, each corner inset with a cabochon ruby in a gold bezel, with a folding rock crystal strut

Signed Cartier, 1802, 957
Measurements: 7.6 x 7.4 x 3.0 cm, 3 x 2 7/8 x 1 3/16 inches
Movement: European Watch & Clock Co., 8-day desk clock, 15 jewels, 3 adjustments, lever escapement

The Maurice Couet workshop began creating small rock crystal clocks balanced against a folding strut around 1912. Louis Cartier was fascinated with rock crystal, and in the early part of the century it had been used frosted and elaborately carved in jewelry. Appearing in square, round, or arch shape, the clocks were the first place the material was used in a streamlined and modern way that would later be reflected in Cartier's Art Deco jewelry. While the design of jewelry and objects underwent enormous changes from 1912 through 1930, remarkably, the design of this clock series changed very little. The rock crystal here surrounds a *lac burgauté* panel (see 89) depicting a scene of women weaving silk from spools to cloth.

108

Putti Desk Clock with Calendar by Maurice Couet for Cartier, Paris, circa 1920

A clock with a square panel of rock crystal with beveled edges framing a circular glass dial depicting two frolicking putti within a chapter ring of gold Roman numerals and rosettes on a white champlevé enamel ground, rose-cut diamond scroll hands, encircled by a second similarly decorated ring with an additional set of numerals and a diamond-set pointer indicating the day, four rose-cut diamond rosettes at the corners, diamonds mounted in platinum, with a folding rock crystal strut

Signed Cartier, 4288
Measurements: 9.2 x 9.2 x 3.0 cm, 3⅝ x 3⅝ x 1³⁄₁₆ inches
Movement: 8 days, brass, 4 bridges, 15 jewels

A handful of Cartier rock crystal strut clocks were made with engraved glass panels depicting putti engaged in playful pursuits. The two cherubic figures on this clock are resting on clouds and holding a garland of roses. Both the roses and the putti are symbolic of romantic love (see also 39 and 38). Putti, usually depicted as nude chubby male babies, sometimes winged, are closely associated with the Renaissance and Baroque periods in art, but have rarely fallen out of style. The romantic nature of the carved center relates closely to the decoration common in the Belle Époque, but the simplified palette of frosted glass and rock crystal centering a geometric composition modernizes the use of the putti.

Maurice Couet was a master clockmaker who liked to challenge himself with unusual design elements. This rare clock includes a second numbered circle outside the chapter ring and a long third hand indicating the day of the month. Couet would have conceived this design, then ordered a movement capable of powering three hands. The design is elegantly handled and the calendar ring beautifully incorporated into the overall design. This is the only known Art Deco Cartier clock with a calendar ring.

109

Pocket Watch by Cartier, Paris, circa 1925

A watch in a circular case carved from a single block of coral, inset with a square-shaped watch dial with Arabic numerals and blued steel hands, with a black enamel border

Signed Cartier, France, on the dial, no. 08081 on crown
Measurements: 3.2 x 3.0 x 1.4 cm, 1¼ x 1³⁄₁₆ x ½ inches
Movement: Swiss by A. Schild ébauche, Grenchen, 16 rubies, nickel lever

This unusual pocket watch takes its inspiration from the form of a coral stopper to an antique Chinese snuff bottle. Popular in the Qing dynasty (1644–1912), snuff bottles were objects of status and beauty carried by nearly everyone as a replacement for tobacco. Carried in the pocket, snuff bottles were made of a variety of materials such as porcelain, jade, ivory, wood, coral, and amber, and they often featured rounded coral stoppers.

With Cartier's interest in antiquity and China, the designers were familiar with beautiful examples of snuff bottles. In 1904, the firm produced a rounded smelling salts bottle for J. P. Morgan that was based on the design of a snuff bottle. Mrs. William K. Vanderbilt owned a 1925 snuff bottle that was converted to a perfume flacon. As a twist on the place of a snuff bottle in the pocket, removed for use and admiration, Cartier adopted the form for this pocket watch, similarly removed for function and display.

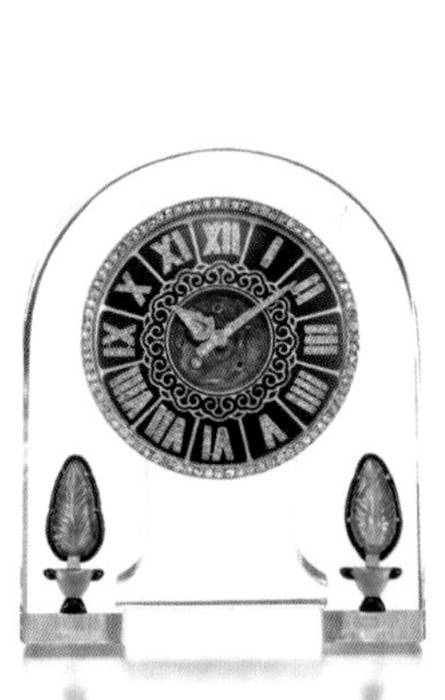

110

Borne Desk Clock by Maurice Couet for Cartier, Paris, circa 1927

A clock composed of an arched rock crystal panel with circular dial centered by a carved jade medallion embellished with cabochon sapphires and a diamond, within a gold and black enameled chapter ring with rose-cut diamond-set Roman numerals and diamond and sapphire hands, encircled by a rose-cut diamond bezel mounted in platinum, further decorated with a pair of topiary motifs formed of carved sapphire leaves, jade, and black enamel, with a folding rock crystal strut

Signed Cartier, Made in France, 2376, 1346
Measurements: 9.5 x 7.9 x 3.5 cm, 3¾ x 3⅛ x 1⅜ inches
Movement: 8-day, European Watch & Clock Co., Swiss made, 15 jewels, 2 adjustments

Called a *borne* (boundary marker or milestone) for the shape of the rock crystal, this model features two potted cypress trees composed of carved sapphires, jade, and black enamel that are artistically similar to the double cypress tree motif found on panther boxes as early as 1917 (see 5). The foliate-form carved sapphires align this clock with important jewelry and objects incorporating carved Indian stones (see 80 and 115). The blue-green color combination and the cloud-like motif on the chapter ring are additional exotic touches.

111

Egyptian-Revival Tutankhamun Pocket Watch by Cartier, Paris, circa 1924

A pocket watch depicting the burial mask of Tutankhamun in polychrome enamel against a ground of red guilloché enamel, with a circular engine-turned dial with Roman numerals on the outer chapter ring for a 12-hour clock and Arabic numerals on the inner ring for a 24-hour clock, with blued steel hands; gold, with French assay marks

Signed Cartier Paris
Measurements: 6.2 x 2.4 x 0.8 cm, 2 7/16 x 1 3/4 x 5/16
Movement: 18 jewels, 8 adjustments

The discovery of Tutankhamun's tomb in 1922 heightened the renewed interest in Egyptian art that was already present during the Art Deco. In the years it took to excavate and finally open the sarcophagus in 1925, when the gold burial mask depicted on this pocket watch was found, Cartier had mastered creating exquisite pieces mixing the bold modern aesthetic of the 1920s with Egyptian inspiration.

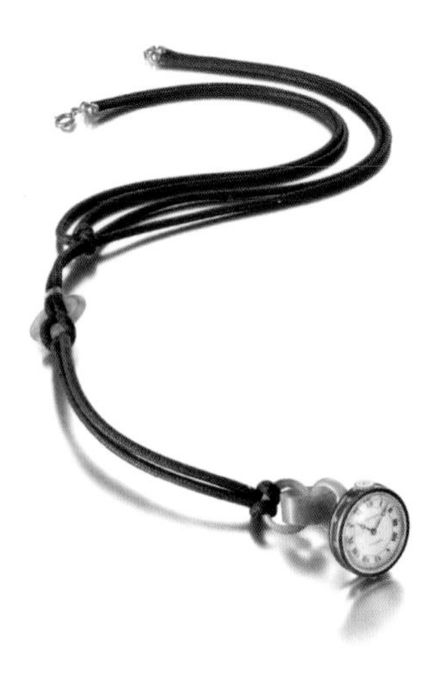

112

Seal Pendant Watch by Cartier, Paris, circa 1922

A watch in the shape of a seal with a circular dial with black enamel Roman numerals held within a gold case decorated with red and black enamel with gold details, supported on three interlocking jade rings on a black silk cord, the cord with a jade *bi*-disk; gold, with French assay marks

Signed Cartier, BTE SGDG
Pendant: 4.4 x 2.4 x 2.4 cm, 1 3/4 x 15/16 x 15/16 inches; necklace length: 58 cm, 22 7/8 inches
Movement: European Watch & Clock Co., 15 jewels, 5 bridges, 3 adjustments, Swiss, 1713059

Seals have been used for thousands of years, since the ancient civilizations of Mesopotamia and Egypt. Meant to be pressed into wax or clay as a signature, and often worn as jewelry denoting rank and power, seals evolved over the years to be increasingly elaborate and beautiful. With the advent of widespread literacy, the need for seals all but disappeared, and Cartier repurposed the form of a signet ring here for a watch, touching on a long-established tradition, and giving the new small machine the place traditionally reserved for a person's most powerful totem.

The design of the pendant watch is completed with three interlocking links carved from a single piece of jade and suspended from a silk cord completed with a *bi*-disk, a traditional Chinese symbol of the sun. A similar model to this necklace was shown in *Vogue* in 1922.

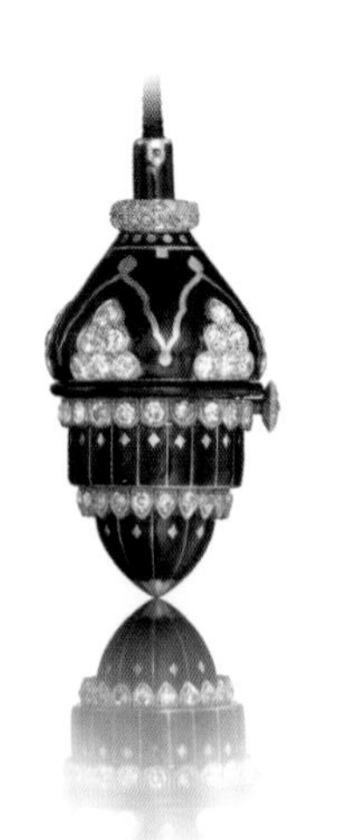

113

Acorn Pendant Watch by Cartier, Paris, circa 1925

A concealed watch in the form of an acorn in black enamel with gold detail and single-cut and rose-cut diamonds, the top opens to reveal a circular dial with white enameled chapter ring, black enameled Arabic numerals and blued steel hands, suspended from a black silk cord with a black enamel and diamond cylindrical slide and clasp; gold and platinum, with French assay marks

Signed Cartier Paris
Pendant: 4.0 x 2.0 x 2.1 cm, 1 5/8 x 13/16 x 7/8 inches; necklace length: 47 cm, 18 1/2 inches
Movement: European Watch & Clock Co., 76302, 18 jewels, all adjustment

At the turn of the twentieth century, pocket watches were the most popular watch form, as they had been since the sixteenth century. Cartier played with creating some pendant watches attached to brooches and even one on a pearl necklace, but the watches still very much adhered to the circular watch form and felt large for jewelry. With the advent of wristwatches by the end of the first decade and into the teens, the technology of clock mechanism advanced and reduced in size, allowing the exceptional designers at Cartier to experiment with the watch form, concealing it within jeweled creations.

Cartier began creating pendant watches in 1921 and *Vogue* proclaimed them all the rage. For the first time, instead of being used by women to mark time in the household, watches were created to accessorize the height of fashionable evening wear. By 1925, the pendant watch was considered more fashionable than the wristwatch. This watch, in the form of an acorn, features gold and diamond detailing, echoing the form of a Persian mihrab, or prayer niche [83]. Special attention was paid to the platinum stone settings, with some round and others pointed to create the illusion of a pear-shaped stone. The consideration of design in this watch is even extended to the diamond-set clasp, which would have been exposed by the newly fashionable bobbed hair. The extreme length of this pendant was designed to flatter the long fitted evening gowns of the era, and for the insouciant gesture of checking the time. (See also 114.)

114

Acorn Pendant Watch by Cartier, circa 1925

A concealed watch in the form of an acorn (see 113) with a round diamond-set cap surmounted by a jade boule with black enamel detail, the sides in fluted onyx and diamond, the gold dial in white enamel with black enamel Arabic numerals, with a diamond-set winding button, suspended from a black silk cord with a diamond and black enamel bead; platinum and gold

Numbered 3043, 1944, 16874, not signed but purchased directly from Cartier
Pendant: 3.5 x 1.9 x 2 cm, 1⅜ x 13/16 x ¾ inches; necklace length: 49.5 cm, 19 inches
Movement: Swiss, 18 jewels, all adjustment, no. 3917

115

Tree of Life Pendant Watch by Cartier, Paris, circa 1925

A necklace suspending a pendant, centering a carved emerald tree outlined in sapphire, sprouting from a square planter of round and baguette diamonds on an onyx and diamond base, surrounded by carved emerald bushes with red enamel detail on a red and black enamel ground, the edges set with diamond, emerald, and onyx, the bottom of the pendant with a watch of hexagonal dial with an engine-turned face and Roman numerals within a red enamel bezel edged with black enamel, with blued steel hands; the pendant suspended with a diamond-set loop from a necklace of onyx beads spaced with rose-cut diamond and onyx-set cylinders and carved emerald beads accented with red enamel and diamond beads; platinum, with French assay marks

Signed Cartier, Paris, 1664
Pendant: 3.7 x 2.5 x 2.5 cm, 1½ x 1 x 1 inches; necklace length: 68.5 cm, 27 inches
Movement: European Watch & Clock Co., 15439, 23965, 8 adjustments, Swiss, 6 bridges

This lavish pendant depicts a verdant and ordered garden centering an engraved leaf-shaped emerald from India representing a sacred tree, often called the Tree of Life or the Tree of Knowledge (see 80). While Cartier excelled in creating mythological worlds within their jewelry, it is unusual to see such a fully formed landscape on a small piece also concealing a watch. While the pendant watch had become popular by the mid-twenties (see 113), this is one of the most elaborate, making use of carved gemstones, diamond accents, and a striking color combination carried through from the pendant to the necklace.

116

Watch and Vanity Case by Janesich, Paris, circa 1928

A vanity case with black and pink enamel stripes, the central stripe of cream enamel with pink enamel and gold floral design, set with a watch at one end outlined in round diamonds, the long edges of the case similarly set with round diamonds and accented with baguette diamonds, the sides set with ribbed frosted rock crystal segments and amethyst segments linked by baguette diamonds, the button clasp set with round diamonds; interior with fitted mirror, powder compartment, and lipstick holder; gold, with French assay marks and British importation marks

Signed Janesich, no. 13096, 8268
Measurements: 8.3 x 4.8 x 1.3 cm, 3¼ x 1 15/16 x ⅕ inches
Watch: Swiss by Movado, 15 jewels, 4 adjustments

This vanity case features an unusually bold color scheme, even for the Art Deco period, combining not only color, but varied textures and materials. The bright pink enamel makes a strong statement against the black enamel, frosted rock crystal, faceted amethyst, and the central cream panel. The central piece, decorated with meandering floral vines, references Asian sources (see also 11), but the flowers have been so abstracted that they appear more like cogs in a machine, or the interior of a watch. This case is one of two in the collection to feature watches (see also 95). There were occasional attempts in the Art Deco period to incorporate watches into vanity and cigarette cases as an added function. The disparate elements in this piece are pulled together by masterful use of the gold striping, round diamond borders, and baguette diamonds.

Afterword
The Origin of the Collection

Sarah Davis

This magnificent collection of Art Deco objects contains some of the greatest examples of twentieth-century design in any medium. Including 116 pieces by makers such as Cartier, Van Cleef & Arpels, Boucheron, Lacloche Frères, and others, the collection is a cross-section of the best elements of Art Deco design, from Asian influenced, to foliate motifs, to geometric patterns. In addition to being the greatest single collection of boxes and clocks from this era, the items were personal gifts from Prince Sadruddin to his wife, Catherine, from 1972 to 2003, representing the sweetness of their more than thirty-year marriage and their famed reputation for collecting important art.

Born in Paris, France, Prince Sadruddin Aga Khan was the son of Sir Sultan Mahomed Shah Aga Khan and Princess Andrée Aga Khan. Through his father, Prince Sadruddin was a direct descendent of the Prophet Muhammad. He served a lifelong career of public service, spending nearly forty years at the United Nations, including twelve years as the United Nations High Commissioner for Refugees from 1966 to 1978. Passionate about art and culture, he was the founding publisher of *The Paris Review*. He was also interested in environmental issues and established the Bellerive Foundation (now part of the Aga Khan Foundation) in the late 1970s. After his death in 2003 at the age of 70, he was eulogized by United Nations Secretary General Kofi Annan, who said, "He combined respect for humankind with concern for our environment. He worked on behalf of the poor and dispossessed while celebrating humanity through culture and art." Annan concluded his tribute by praising Prince Sadruddin as "a role model to many of us . . . his example will continue to inspire new world citizens for several generations to come."

In addition to his humanitarian work, Prince Sadruddin was one of the great art collectors of the twentieth century. His extensive collection of Islamic art was unequaled. Over the years, parts of his collection were exhibited in New York, London, and Zurich, including a touring show, *Princes, Poets and Paladins*, which was organized by the British Museum in 1998. The full collection is housed at the new Aga Khan Museum in Toronto, established by Prince Sadruddin's nephew, the present Aga Khan. High-profile auctions have also been held of his collections of African art, Gustav Klimt works, and gold boxes.

116
Watch and Vanity Case by Janesich, Paris, circa 1928

As the son of the imam, from a royal house going back to the Fatimid caliphs of Egypt, Prince Sadruddin was exposed to the finest of art, jewelry, music, and culture, and this fostered a great appreciation and understanding for the arts. One of Cartier's most famous tiaras, the Halo, was created in 1934 for Prince Sadruddin's mother, the Begum Andrée Aga Khan, and is now part of the Cartier Collection. Several pictures exist of her bedecked in fine Cartier jewelry and two of the boxes in this collection came from her.

A 1991 interview with Prince Sadruddin in *The UNESCO Courier* gives some insight into the influence his upbringing had on his life: "I think people are primarily influenced by their family environment. Because of my origins I belong both to the East and the West. Iran is the cradle of our family, but we have never lived there. I was born in Paris, and my mother was French. Through my father, who had a strong influence on me, I came into contact with Islam when I was very young. We travelled widely in the Islamic countries and often visited Egypt."

The contrast and harmony of East and West is a constant theme in the collection. Eastern culture is the inspiration for most of the motifs, yet they were completed by the finest artists and jewelers of the Western world to meet the evolving needs of the modern woman asserting her exotic style and independence. Produced for only a short time, from 1910 to 1938, the vanity cases, cigarette boxes, watches, and clocks in this collection are a record of the excitement of the era. The world was changing and opening up and these pieces, the finest creations of the top jewelers and artisans, reflected that momentum with their bright colors, bold shapes, and stylized exotic references.

The Aga Khan and Andrée Carron on the day of their civil wedding in France, 1929. A few days later there was a religious ceremony in Bombay (Mumbai), India.

Prince Sadruddin Aga Khan with his parents in 1935.

A family portrait including the Begum (Sadruddin's step-mother); Amyn (Ali Khan's younger son); Sadruddin; Ali Khan (Sadruddin's half-brother); Karim (Ali Khan's elder son, who became Aga Khan IV); and seated, Aga Khan III and Rita Hayworth, wife of Ali Khan.

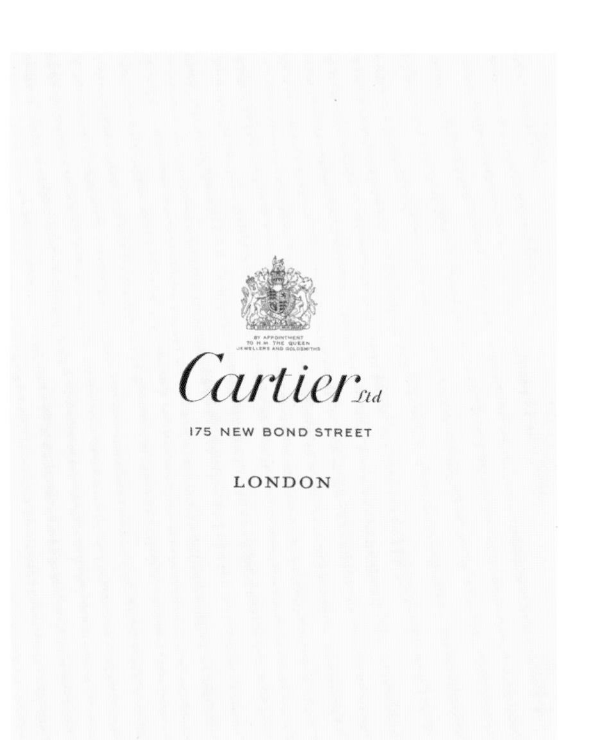
Cartier Ltd

175 NEW BOND STREET

LONDON

A sales letter and folio of images Cartier sent Prince Sadruddin Aga Khan for the Cigarette and Vanity Case [58]. The prince has handwritten notes to his assistant, "I'll take it for £850. Let's try, if not we will increase offer. SAK." He comes back again, "Don't let it go!! SAK." Cartier accepted the offer and the prince had the box by the end of the month, July 1968. This is part of the archive kept on the entire collection.

BY APPOINTMENT
TO H.M. THE QUEEN
JEWELLERS AND GOLDSMITHS

CARTIER S.A. – 13 RUE DE LA PAIX
PARIS

Cartier Ltd

175 - 176 NEW BOND STREET
20 ALBEMARLE STREET
LONDON W.1.

CARTIER INC – 653 FIFTH AVENUE
NEW YORK

DWP/JD.

TELEGRAMS PRECIOUS LONDON W1
TELEPHONES 01-493 6962 (5 LINES)

9th July, 1968.

Prince Sadruddin Aga Khan,
Château de Bellerive,
Collonge - Bellerive,
Canton de Geneva,
Switzerland.

I'll take it for £850. let's try if not we will increase offer
SAK

Sir,

I write to ask if you expect to be in London shortly, as I have a particularly fine vanity case that I would like you to see.

This case is made in 18 carat gold and black enamel with a diamond and jade ornamentation and is priced at £950.0.0.

As you will see from the photograph, the centre compartment holds cigarettes and at either end are smaller compartments for the rouge or powder.

Don't let it go!!
SAK

I cannot be quite certain as to the date of manufacture of this, but I think it was made in the 1920's and is an unusually fine specimen.

If you are in London in the near future, perhaps you would be kind enough to spare a few moments to see this piece.

12/7

Assuring you at all times of my careful attention,
I have the honour to remain, Sir,
Your obedient servant,

pp CARTIER Ltd.
D. W. Poulton

encl.

DIRECTORS: J. J. CARTIER (FRENCH) · C. NATER (SWISS) · D. A. FRASER · E. BELLENGER (FRENCH) · MADAME CLAUDEL (FRENCH)

Notes

East and West: Oriental Exoticism in the Decorative Arts

1 "Rustam pursues Akvan, the onager-div," from the *Shahnama* of Shah Tahmasp, fol. 294r, attributable to Muzaffar 'Ali, Tabriz, Iran, circa 1530–1535. Aga Khan Museum, Toronto, accession number AKM162 (https://www.agakhanmuseum.org/collection/artifact/rostam-pursues-akvan-onager-div). See Sheila R. Canby, *Princes, Poets and Paladins: Islamic and Indian Paintings from the Collection of Prince and Princess Sadruddin Aga Khan* (London: British Museum, 1998), no. 27, p. 51.

The *Shahnama* (Book of Kings; also *Shahnameh*) by Firdausi (circa 940–1020; also Ferdowsi, Firdawsi) is the major epic of Persian literature. A particularly fine illuminated manuscript was produced for the Safavid shah Tahmasp I between about 1522 and 1535, and given to the Ottoman sultan Selim II circa 1568. The manuscript's 380 folios include 258 illustrations, with work by the major Iranian artists of the period. An epitome of sixteenth-century Iranian painting, the manuscript was broken up in the 1970s, with the largest portions now at the Metropolitan Museum of Art in New York and in the Islamic Republic of Iran.

2 "A noble hunt," attributable to Muhammad 'Ali, Mughal India, circa 1610 (borders circa 1640). See Canby, *Princes, Poets and Paladins*, no. 102, p. 138.

3 "Firdausi and the three court poets of Ghazna," from the *Shahnama* of Shah Tahmasp, fol. 7r, attributable to Aqa Mirak, Tabriz, Iran, circa 1532. AKM156 (https://www.agakhanmuseum.org/collection/artifact/firdausi-and-three-court-poets-ghazna-folio-shahnameh-book-kings-shah-tahmasp-i). See Canby, *Princes, Poets and Paladins*, no. 24, p. 47. The young man on the right of the picture may be Shah Tahmasp himself.

"Haftvad and the worm," from the *Shahnama* of Shah Tahmasp, fol. 521v, ascribed to Dust Muhammad, Tabriz, Iran, 1540. AKM164 (https://www.agakhanmuseum.org/collection/artifact/story-haftvad-and-worm-folio-shahnameh-shah-tahmasp). See Canby, *Princes, Poets and Paladins*, no. 29, pp. 52–53.

4 See, for example, "Ibrahim Mirza's garden party," from the *Divan* by Sultan Ibrahim Mirza, MS 33, fols. 86b–87a, signed by 'Abdullah Shirazi (also known as 'Abdullah al-Muzahhib), Qazvin, Iran, 1582. AKM282 (fol. 86b is shown at the museum website: https://www.agakhanmuseum.org/collection/artifact/manuscript-diwan-sultan-ibrahim-mirza). See Canby, *Princes, Poets and Paladins*, no. 38, p. 63.

5 "The munificence of Ja'far al-Baramaki toward 'Abd al-Malek" from *Akbar-i Barmakiyan* (Traditions of the Barmecids), created for Emperor Akbar, Mughal India, circa 1595. See Canby, *Princes, Poets and Paladins*, no. 87, p. 119–20.

Two pages from the *Akhlaq-i Nasiri* (The Nasirean Ethics) by Nasir al-Din Tusi, MS 39, fols. 71 and 95, created for Emperor Akbar, Mughal India, circa 1590–95. Fol. 95 ascribed to Sajnu (or Sahu). AKM288 (the museum website shows another folio [149v]: https://www.agakhanmuseum.org/collection/artifact/school-courtyard-boys-reading-and-writing). See Canby, *Princes, Poets and Paladins*, nos. 92 and 93, pp. 124–26.

6 "Gushtasp slays a dragon on Mount Saqila," from the *Shahnama* of Shah Tahmasp, fol. 402r, attributable to Mirza 'Ali, Tabriz, Iran, circa 1530–35. See Canby, *Princes, Poets and Paladins*, no. 28, p. 52.

7 "The court of Gayumars," from the *Shahnama* of Shah Tahmasp, by Sultan Muhammad, Tabriz, Iran, circa 1522. AKM165 (https://www.agakhanmuseum.org/collection/artifact/court-gayumars-folio-shahnameh-book-kings-shah-tahmasp). This work was considered one of the masterpieces of its day and is still regarded as one of the most important works of Iranian painting.

Feminine Elegance: Jeweled Accessories for the Modern Woman

1 For a general history of smoking in the twentieth century, especially as it relates to the use of smoking accessories, see Martin Barnes Lorber and Rebecca McNamara, *A Token of Elegance: Cigarette Holders in Vogue* (Milan: Officina Libraria, 2015). A comprehensive study of smoking in Great Britain can be found in Penny Tinkler, *Smoke Signals: Women, Smoking and Visual Culture in Britain* (Oxford and New York: Berg, 2006). The history of American production and consumption of tobacco is explored in Allan M. Brandt, *The Cigarette Century: The Rise, Fall, and Deadly Persistence of the Product That Defined America* (New York: Basic Books, 2007).

2 The first major studies linking smoking to cancer were published in the early 1950s, leading to the landmark study by the Surgeon General in 1964 that officially defined the position of the U.S. government that smoking was a direct, primary cause of lung cancer.

3 Brandt, *Cigarette Century*, 27–29; Lorber and McNamara, *Token of Elegance*, 28–30.

4 James Buchanan "Buck" Duke (1856–1925) is widely considered the modern American tobacco industry's founding father. While many others developed successful companies, it was Duke who largely supplied the world with cigarettes by 1900. Ironically, he is said to have detested cigarettes, being a cigar smoker himself. His genius came in recognizing the potential for sales, and he created a company so large (American Tobacco Trust) that it became a target of the Sherman Anti-trust Act in 1911 and was forced into a legendary break-up of firms, including among others Lorillard, Liggett & Myers (L&M), and R. J. Reynolds. See Chris Harrald and Fletcher Watkins, *The Cigarette Book: The History and Culture of Smoking* (New York: Skyhorse Publishing, 2010), 81–82.

5 Lorber and McNamara, *Token of Elegance*, 29–30.

6 Ibid., 34–35.

7 Ibid., 35.

8 Holly Edwards, *Noble Dreams, Wicked Pleasures: Orientalism in America, 1870–1930* (Princeton, NJ: Princeton University Press; Williamstown, MA: Sterling and Francine Clark Institute, 2000), 204, as quoted in Lorber and McNamara, *Token of Elegance*, 35.

9 Charles Venable, *Silver in America* (Dallas, TX: Dallas Museum of Art, 1995), 193. Emmanuel Ducamp and Wilfried Zeisler, "Russia: Fabergé and His Competitors," in Harrison et al., *Artistic Luxury: Fabergé, Tiffany, Lalique* (New Haven and London: Yale University Press, 2008), 196–97.

10 The House of Fabergé was one of the most prolific makers of smoking accessories, particularly cigarette cases, from 1900 to the Russian Revolution of 1917. The Musée des Arts décoratifs in Paris contains one of the most important collections of cigarette cases by Fabergé. See also John Traina, *The Fabergé Case* (New York: Harry N. Abrams, 1998), 43–49.
11 Ducamp and Zeisler, "Russia" in Harrison et al., *Artistic Luxury*, 201–2.
12 Stephen Harrison, "Artistic Luxury in the Belle Époque," in *Artistic Luxury*, 70.
13 Lorber and McNamara, *Token of Elegance*, 39.
14 Ibid., 39–40.
15 Ibid., 40.
16 Tinkler, *Smoke Signals*, 60.
17 Ibid., 52–53.
18 Edith Wharton and Ogden Codman Jr., *The Decoration of Houses* (New York: Scribner, 1902), 151.
19 Brandt, *Cigarette Century*, 57.
20 Ibid., 67.
21 Trade Catalogue, *Smoker's Articles*, H. T. Cushman Mfg. Co., Bennington, Vermont, 1923.
22 Harrald and Watkins, *Cigarette Book*, 98–99.
23 Tinkler, *Smoke Signals*, 44.
24 Ibid., 54–57.
25 Virginia Nicholson, *Among the Bohemians, Experiments in Living, 1900–1939* (New York: William Morrow, 2004), 152–55.
26 Margaret Young-Sanchez et al., *Cartier in the 20th Century* (Denver, CO: Denver Art Museum; New York: Vendome Press, 2015), 135–49.
27 For more information on the fair, and the decorative arts that were shown there, see Stephen Harrison, "Modernity Revealed: The World's Fairs of 1900 to 1925," in Jason T. Busch and Catherine L. Futter, *Inventing the Modern World, Decorative Arts at the World's Fairs, 1851–1939* (New York: Skira Rizzoli, 2012), 194–205.
28 Ibid., 196.
29 As quoted in Graydon Carter, ed., *Bohemians, Bootleggers, Flappers, and Swells: The Best of Early Vanity Fair* (New York: Penguin Press, 2014), 222.
30 Ibid., 223.
31 Katharine Morrison McClinton, *Art Deco: A Guide for Collectors* (New York: Clarkson N. Potter, 1972), 10.
32 Harrison, *Artistic Luxury*, 2–3.
33 Young-Sanchez, *Cartier*, 23–24.
34 Stefano Papi, "Icons of Style," in Young-Sanchez, *Cartier*, 226–27.
35 *Les Robes de Paul Poiret racontée par Paul Iribe* (Paris: 1908).
36 Evelyne Possémé, "Art Deco Jewelry," in *Art Deco 1925* (Lisbon: Calouste Gulbenkian Foundation, 2009), 86.
37 Traina, *The Fabergé Case*, 59.
38 Kirk Varnedoe, *Vienna 1900: Art, Architecture & Design* (New York: The Museum of Modern Art, 1986), 82–83.
39 Ibid., 80.
40 Ibid., 83.
41 Ibid., 81.
42 Ibid., 90.
43 Ibid., 94.
44 Nancy Troy, *Modernism and the Decorative Arts in France: Art Nouveau to Le Corbusier* (New Haven and London: Yale University Press, 1991), 118.
45 Young-Sanchez, *Cartier*, 75.
46 Ibid., 75–76.
47 McClinton, *Art Deco*, 7.
48 Ibid., 7–8.
49 Possémé, *Art Deco 1925*, 87–88.
50 Henri Clouzot, "*Le Bijou moderne*," *L'Illustration* (Paris), December 3, 1927.
51 For a comprehensive discussion of modernism in all aspects of design during this era, see Richard Guy Wilson et al., *The Machine Age: 1918–1941* (New York: Harry N. Abrams, 1986).
52 J. Gallotti, "L'Exposition de joaillerie et d'orfèvrerie du Musée Galliera," *Art et Décoration* 56 (1929), 33–50, as cited and discussed in Possémé, "Art Deco Jewelry."

Jeweled Innovation: Design and Manufacture in Art Deco Masterpieces

1 I am indebted to Catherine Cariou of Van Cleef & Arpels for this updated documentation of Langlois's work.
2 "SA Ploujavy, 9 rue d'Argenson, Paris, 8e," listed in *Archives nationales: La France et la Belgique sous l'occupation allemande 1940–1944* (Paris: Centre historique des archives nationales, 2002), 221; sous-série AJ40, 733 : - 1709.
3 Judy Rudoe, *Cartier 1900–1939* (London: British Museum Press, 1997), 190.
4 Rudoe, *Cartier 1900–1939*, 215, no. 138.
5 Hans Nadelhoffer, *Cartier* (San Francisco: Chronicle Books, 2007), 101.
6 Ibid., 263.
7 Ibid., 266.
8 Ibid., 271, 275.
9 See ibid., 276, for the clearest explanation of the process.
10 Ibid., 282.
11 Ibid.
12 See ibid., fn 2, in which Nadelhoffer says that Georges Verger (1884–1945) was a jewelry and clock designer who designed clocks with movements by Vacheron Constantin, for whom his father (Ferdinand) already held the agency. He also indicates that the American firms to whom Verger provided works were Black, Starr & Frost, Caldwell, and Tiffany. To this list must be added Charlton in New York due to the Mechanical Photograph Frame [102], 339.
13 Nadelhoffer, *Cartier*, 266.

Bibliography

Barracca, Jader, et al. *Le Temps de Cartier.* Milan: Edition Publi Prom, 1989.

Brandt, Allan M. *The Cigarette Century: The Rise, Fall, and Deadly Persistence of the Product That Defined America.* New York: Basic Books, 2007.

Busch, Jason T., and Catherine L. Futter. *Inventing the Modern World: Decorative Arts at the World's Fairs, 1851–1939.* New York: Skira Rizzoli, 2012.

Canby, Sheila R. *Princes, Poets & Paladins: Islamic and Indian Paintings from the Collection of Prince and Princess Sadruddin Aga Khan.* London: British Museum, 1998.

Carter, Graydon, ed. *Bohemians, Bootleggers, Flappers, and Swells: The Best of Early Vanity Fair.* New York: Penguin, 2014.

Chaille, François. *The Cartier Collection: Jewelry.* Paris: Flammarion, 2004.

Chaille, François, and Franco Cologni. *The Cartier Collection: Precious Objects.* Paris: Flammarion, 2012.

———. *The Cartier Collection: Timepieces.* Paris: Flammarion, 2006.

Clouzot, Henri. "Le Bijou moderne," *L'Illustration* (Paris), December 3, 1927.

Coffin, Sarah D. *Set in Style: The Jewelry of Van Cleef & Arpels.* New York: Smithsonian Cooper-Hewitt, 2011.

Couvreur-Schiffer, Liesel, et al. *Van Cleef & Arpels.* Exhibition catalogue, Musée de la Mode et du Costume. Paris: Paris Musées, 1992.

Dias, João Carvalho, et al. *Art Deco 1925.* Lisbon: Calouste Gulbenkian Foundation, 2009.

Edwards, Holly. *Noble Dreams, Wicked Pleasures: Orientalism in America, 1870–1930.* Princeton, NJ: Princeton University Press; Williamstown, MA: Sterling and Francine Clark Institute, 2000.

Forster, Jack. *Cartier, Time Art: Mechanics of Passion.* Milan: Skira, 2011.

Gabet, Olivier, et al. *Japonismes.* Paris: Flammarion, 2014.

Geoffroy-Schneiter, Bérénice, et al. *Cartier Panthère.* New York: Assouline, 2015.

Harrald, Chris, and Fletcher Watkins. *The Cigarette Book: The History and Culture of Smoking.* New York: Skyhorse Publishing, 2010.

Harrison, Stephen, et al. *Artistic Luxury: Fabergé, Tiffany, Lalique.* New Haven and London: Yale University Press, 2008.

Humbert, Jean-Marcel. *Egyptomania: Egypt in Western Art 1730–1930.* Paris: Réunion des Musées Nationaux, 1994.

Iribe, Paul. *Les Robes de Paul Poiret, racontées par Paul Iribe.* Paris: Paul Poiret, 1908.

Jodidio, Philip. *Pattern and Light: The Aga Khan Museum.* New York: Skira Rizzoli, 2014.

Legrand-Rossi, Sylvie, et al. *Touches d'exotisme: XIVe–XXe siècles.* Exhibition catalogue, Musée de la Mode et du Textile. Paris: Union Centrale des Arts Décoratifs, 1998.

Lorber, Martin Barnes, and Rebecca McNamara. *A Token of Elegance: Cigarette Holders in Vogue.* Milan: Officina Libraria, 2015.

McClinton, Katharine Morrison. *Art Deco: A Guide for Collectors.* New York: Clarkson N. Potter, 1972.

Nadelhoffer, Hans. *Cartier: Jewelers Extraordinary.* London: Thames & Hudson; New York: Harry N. Abrams, 1984. Reprinted as *Cartier.* London: Thames & Hudson; San Francisco: Chronicle Books, 2007.

Nicholson, Virginia. *Among the Bohemians: Experiments in Living, 1900–1939.* New York: William Morrow, 2004.

Niklès van Osselt, Estelle, et al. *Asia Imagined: In the Baur and Cartier Collections.* Milan: 5 Continents Editions, 2015.

Possémé, Evelyne. *Van Cleef & Arpels: The Art of High Jewelry.* Paris: Les Arts Décoratifs, 2012.

Rudoe, Judy. *Cartier 1900–1939.* New York: Metropolitan Museum of Art, 1997.

Salome, Laurent, and Laure Dalon. *Cartier: Style and History:* Paris: Réunion des Musées Nationaux, 2013.

Takashina, Shuji, et al. *Japonisme et Mode.* Exhibition catalogue, Palais Galliera. Paris: Paris Musées, 1996.

Traina, John. *The Fabergé Case.* New York: Harry N. Abrams, 1998.

Troy, Nancy. *Modernism and the Decorative Arts in France: Art Nouveau to Le Corbusier.* New Haven and London: Yale University Press, 1991.

Varnedoe, Kirk. *Vienna 1900: Art, Architecture & Design.* New York: Museum of Modern Art, 1986.

Venable, Charles. *Silver in America.* Dallas: Dallas Museum of Art, 1995.

Wilson, Richard Guy, et al. *The Machine Age: 1918–1941.* New York: Harry N. Abrams, 1986.

Young-Sanchez, Margaret, et al. *Cartier in the 20th Century.* New York: Vendome Press, 2014.

Index

Bold entries indicate a photograph of an item. Italic entries indicate text in the catalogue descriptions. Where the letter "c" follows, it refers to caption text and the associated image.

In the entries for jewelry houses and makers, individual item numbers are given in brackets, bold for photographs and italic for catalogue entries; where there are more than four items, textual references are given first *en bloc*, followed by photographs, followed by catalogue entries.

Published to accompany the exhibition
Jeweled Splendors of the Art Deco Era: The Prince and Princess Sadruddin Aga Khan Collection
at the Cooper Hewitt, Smithsonian Design Museum, New York, April 7–August 20, 2017

First published in the United States of America in 2017
by Thames & Hudson Inc., New York
500 Fifth Avenue, New York, NY 10110
thamesandhudsonusa.com

First published in the United Kingdom in 2017
by Thames & Hudson Ltd,
181A High Holborn, London WC1V 7QX
www.thamesandhudson.com

Library of Congress Control Number
2016943975

British Library Cataloguing-in-Publication Data:
A catalogue record of this book is available from the British Library.

ISBN: 978-0-500-51947-9

Editor: Sarah Davis
Photographer: Doug Rosa
Designer: Judith Hudson
Photo Retouching: Matthew Dempsey of Mocean Digital
French to English translator for "East and West: Oriental Exoticism in the Decorative Arts": Anthony Roberts

Printed and bound in China

Illustrations
Pages 2–3: Cigarette Case and Match Box [45]
Pages 4–5: Vanity Case [15]
Page 6: Cloud Retrograde Clock [104]
Page 256: Mechanical Pencil [40]

Photo credits
11: Cartier Paris Archives © Cartier; 12: Photograph by Elliott & Fry, © National Portrait Gallery, London; 13: © Illustrated London News/Mary Evans Picture Library; 16: Van Cleef & Arpels Archive; 20: Musee des Arts décoratifs. Photos Les Arts décoratifs, Paris/Jean Tholance; 24 left: Aga Khan Museum, AKM160; 24 right: Boucheron Archive, Paris; 26 top: Marc Ryckaert/ Naamsvermelding vereist; 26 bottom: Cartier Paris Archives © Cartier; 28 top: Newark Museum Gift of Dr. Louis C. West, 1967 67.417; 28 bottom: Cartier Paris Archives © Cartier; 30: Cartier Paris Archives © Cartier; 37: Aga Khan Museum, AKM319; 60: The Metropolitan Museum of Art. Ex coll.: C. C. Wang Family, Gift of Douglas Dillon, 1980.426.2; 70: The Metropolitan Museum of Art. Rogers Fund, 1922; 72: Musee des Arts Asiatiques-Guimet, Paris, France; 90: Mary Evans Picture Library/Alamy Stock Photo; 92 both: Eduardo Garcia Benito/Vogue © Conde Nast; 93: Museum of Fine Arts, Boston; 95: Bequest of William K. Vanderbilt, 1920. The Metropolitan Museum of Art; 109, 110, 128: Van Cleef & Arpels Archive; 162: Collection of the Victoria & Albert Museum; 164, 166, 167: Van Cleef & Arpels Archive; 180, top: Mary Evans Picture Library; 180, bottom: Mead Art Museum, Amherst College, MA, USA/Gift of William Green/Bridgeman Images; 182, 184, 188, 190: Van Cleef & Arpels Archive; 193: © Illustrated London News/Mary Evans Picture Library; 200: Cartier Paris Archives © Cartier; 201 top: Library of Congress Prints and Photographs Division; 201 bottom: Anton Bruehl/ Vogue © Conde Nast; 221: Nickolas Murray/Vogue © Conde Nast; 244: Getty Images; 245: Getty Images. Photographed by Dimitri Kassel for *Life* magazine

The editor would like to thank the following people:

Jamie Camplin at Thames & Hudson for championing the project, as well as Neil Mann for his expert copyediting and editorial support, Beth Tondreau at BTDnyc for planning, and Judith Hudson for superb book design. The archivists who helped research these pieces: Claudine Sablier, Département du Patrimoine, Boucheron; Michel Aliaga, Head of Cartier Heritage Documentation; Catherine Cariou, Directrice du Patrimoine, Van Cleef & Arpels; and Amy McHugh, Assistant Coordinator of Research, and Annamarie Sandecki, Archivist, Tiffany & Co. For her expertise in Asian art, Ling-Yi Chien. Also, Ulysses Dietz, Chief Curator and Curator of Decorative Arts, Newark Museum, and Janet Zapata, jewelry historian.